First World War
and Army of Occupation
War Diary
France, Belgium and Germany

50 DIVISION
Headquarters, Branches and Services
Commander Royal Engineers
27 May 1916 - 31 May 1919

WO95/2816/2

The Naval & Military Press Ltd
www.nmarchive.com
Published in association with The National Archives

Published by

The Naval & Military Press Ltd

Unit 10 Ridgewood Industrial Park,

Uckfield, East Sussex,

TN22 5QE England

Tel: +44 (0) 1825 749494

www.naval-military-press.com

www.nmarchive.com

This diary has been reprinted in facsimile from the original. Any imperfections are inevitably reproduced and the quality may fall short of modern type and cartographic standards.

© **Crown Copyright**
Images reproduced by permission of The National Archives, London, England, 2015.

Contents

Document type	Place/Title	Date From	Date To
Heading	War Diary Of C.R.E. 50th Div From 1/6/16 To 30/6/16		
War Diary	Westoutre	01/06/1916	30/06/1916
Heading	War Diary C.R.E. 50th Division. July 1916 Volume No. 15		
War Diary	Westoutre	01/07/1916	31/07/1916
Heading	War Diary Of C.R.E. 50th Division Volume XVII From 1st To 31st August 1916		
War Diary	Westoutre	01/08/1916	07/08/1916
War Diary	Fletre	08/08/1916	10/08/1916
War Diary	Bernaville	11/08/1916	14/08/1916
War Diary	Vignacourt	15/08/1916	15/08/1916
War Diary	Montigny	16/08/1916	31/08/1916
Heading	C.R.E. 50th. Divisional Engineers September 1916		
Heading	War Diary Of C.R.E. 50th (Northumbrian) Divisional September 1916 Volume No. XVIII		
War Diary	Montigny	01/09/1916	08/09/1916
War Diary	Mellingcourt Albert Road	09/09/1916	14/09/1916
War Diary	A.D.H.Q. Railway Copse	15/09/1916	19/09/1916
War Diary	Railway Copse	20/09/1916	28/09/1916
War Diary	A.D.H.Q. Railway Copse	29/09/1916	30/09/1916
Miscellaneous	Summary Of Camp Of 7th Inf R.E.	27/09/1917	27/09/1917
Miscellaneous	C.R.E. 50th Division		
Miscellaneous	C.R.E. 50th Div.	27/09/1917	27/09/1917
Miscellaneous	Brief Summary Of Work Done By 7th Bn. Durham Lt Inf.	27/09/1917	27/09/1917
Heading	War Diary Of C.R.E. 50th (Northumbrian) Division R.E. Volume XIX October 1916		
War Diary	A.D.H.Q. Railway Copse	01/10/1916	05/10/1916
War Diary	Fricourt	06/10/1916	11/10/1916
War Diary	Fricourt Circus	12/10/1916	20/10/1916
War Diary	Fricourt	21/10/1916	24/10/1916
War Diary	Fricourt Farm	25/10/1916	31/10/1916
Heading	War Diary Of C.R.E. 50th (Northumbrian) Divisional R.E. Volume No. XX November 1916		
War Diary	Fricourt Farm	01/11/1916	19/11/1916
War Diary	Albert 12 Rue De Bapaume	20/11/1916	21/11/1916
War Diary	Fricourt Farm	22/11/1916	30/11/1916
Heading	War Diary Of C.R.E. 50th Divisional R.E. Volume XXI December 1916		
War Diary	Fricourt Farm	01/12/1916	24/12/1916
Heading	War Diary Of C.R.E. 50th (Northumbrian) Divisional R.E. Volume No. XXII January 1917		
War Diary	Fricourt Farm	01/01/1917	28/01/1917
War Diary	Ribemont	29/01/1917	31/01/1917
Heading	War Diary Of C.R.E. 50th Division Volume XXIII February 1917		
War Diary	Ribemont	01/02/1917	12/02/1917
War Diary	La Baraquette (R29.c.8.5 Sheet 62D)	13/02/1917	23/02/1917
War Diary	P C Gabrielle Ref 20d Central (Sheet 62c)	24/02/1917	26/02/1917
War Diary	P C Gabrielle	27/02/1917	28/02/1917

Type	Description	From	To
Heading	War Diary Of C.R.E. 50th (Northumbrian) Divn. R.E. Volume XXIV March 1917		
War Diary	P C Gobrielle (M 20d Central Sheet 62c)	01/04/1917	05/04/1917
War Diary	P C Gobrielle	06/04/1917	09/04/1917
War Diary	Mericourt S/Somme	10/04/1917	17/04/1917
War Diary	Mericourt Sur Somme	18/04/1917	30/04/1917
War Diary	Moulliens Au Bois	30/04/1917	30/04/1917
Heading	War Diary Of C.R.E. 50th (Northumbrian) Divisional Royal Engineers. Volume No. XXV April 1917		
War Diary	Mollins Au Bois	01/04/1917	04/04/1917
War Diary	Ramecourt	05/04/1917	08/04/1917
War Diary	Le Cauroy	09/04/1917	10/04/1917
War Diary	Bernaville	11/04/1917	11/04/1917
War Diary	Arras	12/04/1917	22/04/1917
War Diary	Advanced Div H.Q.	23/04/1917	25/04/1917
War Diary	Couterelle	26/04/1917	30/04/1917
Miscellaneous	Report on part taken by R.E. and Pioneers in Operation near Wancourt between April 14th and 26th, 1917	29/11/1917	29/11/1917
Map			
Heading	War Diary Of C.R.E. 50th (Northumbrian) Division Volume No. XXVI May 1917		
War Diary	Couturelle	01/05/1917	02/05/1917
War Diary	Neuville Vitasse	03/05/1917	04/05/1917
War Diary	Couturelle	05/05/1917	18/05/1917
War Diary	Beaumetz Les Loges	19/05/1917	22/05/1917
War Diary	Beaumetz Lez Loges and Couin	23/05/1917	23/05/1917
War Diary	Couin	24/05/1917	31/05/1917
Heading	War Diary Of C.R.E. 50th (Northumbrian) Divisional Royal Engineers. Volume XXVII June 1917		
War Diary	Couin	01/06/1917	17/06/1917
War Diary	Boisleux-Au-Mont S.17.a.8.4	18/06/1917	23/06/1917
War Diary	Boisleux-Au-Mont	24/06/1917	30/06/1917
Heading	War Diary Of C.R.E. 50th (Northumbrian) Divisional Royal Engineers Volume XXVIII July 1917		
War Diary	Boisleux-Au-Mont S.17.a.8.4	01/07/1917	07/07/1917
War Diary	Boisleux-Au-Mont	08/07/1917	31/07/1917
Heading	War Diary Of C.R.E. 50th (Northumbrian) Divisional Royal Engineers Volume XXIX August 1917		
War Diary	Nr. Boisleux Au-Mont	01/08/1917	11/08/1917
War Diary	Boisleux Au Mont	12/08/1917	31/08/1917
Heading	War Diary Of C.R.E. 50th (Northumbrian) Divisional Royal Engineers Volume XXX September 1917		
War Diary	Boisleux-Au-Mont	01/09/1917	30/09/1917
Miscellaneous	On His Majesty's Service.		
Heading	War Diary Of C.R.E. 50th Divisional Royal Engineers Volume XXXI October 1917		
War Diary	Boisleux St Marc	01/10/1917	05/10/1917
War Diary	Achiet Le Petit	06/10/1917	16/10/1917
War Diary	Lederzeele	17/10/1917	19/10/1917
War Diary	Proven	20/10/1917	23/10/1917
War Diary	Flverdinghe	24/10/1917	31/10/1917
Miscellaneous			
Miscellaneous	Summary Of Work Done By R.E. Field Companies And Pioneers Of 50th Division		
Miscellaneous	Stories Issued From Henin Dump During Period		
Map			

Heading	War Diary Of C.R.E. 50th Divisional Royal Engineers Volume XXXII November 1917		
War Diary	Elverdinghe	01/11/1917	09/11/1917
War Diary	Eperlecques	10/11/1917	30/11/1917
Miscellaneous	C.R.E. 50th Division	12/11/1917	12/11/1917
Miscellaneous	List Of Stores Issued From Boesinghe R.E. Dump Up To 8/11/17		
Map			
Heading	War Diary Of C.R.E. 50th (Northumbrian) Divisional R.E. Volume No. XXXIII December 1917		
War Diary	Eperlecques	01/12/1917	09/12/1917
War Diary	Ypres	10/12/1917	31/12/1917
Miscellaneous	C.R.E. 149th Infantry Brigade.	17/12/1917	17/12/1917
Heading	War Diary Of C.R.E. 50th (Northumbrian) Divisional R.E. Volume XXXIV January 1918		
War Diary	Ypres	01/01/1918	21/01/1918
War Diary	Wizernes	22/01/1918	29/01/1918
War Diary	Ypres	30/01/1918	31/01/1918
Miscellaneous	Summary Of Work Done By Field Companies and Pioneers Of 50th Division	07/01/1918	07/01/1918
Miscellaneous	General		
Miscellaneous	Duckboard Tracks		
Miscellaneous	Reconstruction On Divisional Headquarters (Menin Gate)		
Miscellaneous	Summary Of Work Done By Field Companies and Pioneers Of 50th Division.	07/01/1918	07/01/1918
Miscellaneous	General		
Miscellaneous	Duckboard Tracks		
Miscellaneous	Reconstruction Of Divisional Headquarters (Menin Gate)		
Miscellaneous	Material Issued At Transit Dump		
Map			
Heading	War Diary Of C.R.E. 50th (Northumbrian) Divisional R.E. Volume XXXV February 1918		
War Diary	Ypres	01/02/1918	23/02/1918
War Diary	Wizernes	23/02/1918	23/02/1918
Heading	C.R.E. 50th Division. March 1918		
Heading	War Diary Of C.R.E. 50th (Northumbrian) Divisional R.E. Volume No. 36 March 1918		
War Diary	Wizernes	01/03/1918	08/03/1918
War Diary	Moreuil	09/03/1918	10/03/1918
War Diary	Harbonnieres	11/03/1918	20/03/1918
War Diary	Beaumetz	21/03/1918	21/03/1918
War Diary	Beaumetz To Le Mesnil	22/03/1918	22/03/1918
War Diary	Le Mesnil To Forincaucourt	23/03/1918	23/03/1918
War Diary	Friancourt	24/03/1918	25/03/1918
War Diary	Forencourt To Harbonment To Marcellane	26/03/1918	28/03/1918
War Diary	Sourdon To Boves	29/03/1918	29/03/1918
War Diary	Boves To Sains En Amenois	30/03/1918	30/03/1918
War Diary	Douriez	31/03/1918	31/03/1918
Heading	C.R.E. 50th (Northumbrian) Division April 1918		
Heading	War Diary Of C.R.E. 50th (Northumbrian) Division For Month Of April 1918		
War Diary	Douriez	01/04/1918	03/04/1918
War Diary	Robecq	04/04/1918	07/04/1918
War Diary	Robecq To Merville	08/04/1918	08/04/1918

War Diary	Merville	09/04/1918	10/04/1918
War Diary	Merville To La Tournant Near Lo Motte	11/04/1918	11/04/1918
War Diary	La Motte	12/04/1918	13/04/1918
War Diary	Thiennes	14/04/1918	15/04/1918
War Diary	Roquetoire	16/04/1918	19/04/1918
War Diary	Aire	20/04/1918	26/04/1918
War Diary	Arcis Le Ponsart	27/04/1918	30/04/1918
Heading	War Diary Of C.R.E. 50th (Northumbrian) Division R.E. Volume XXXVIII May 1918		
War Diary	Arcis-En-Ponsart	01/05/1918	04/05/1918
War Diary	Beaurieux	05/05/1918	28/05/1918
War Diary	Lhery	29/05/1918	30/05/1918
War Diary	Lebreauil	31/05/1918	31/05/1918
Heading	War Diary Of Headquarters 50th (Northumbrian) Divisional Royal Engineers. Volume XXXIX June 1918		
War Diary	Vert La Chapelle	01/06/1918	08/06/1918
War Diary	Mondement	09/06/1918	16/06/1918
War Diary	L'Ermite	17/06/1918	30/06/1918
Heading	War Diary Of Headquarters 50th (Northumbrian) Divisional Royal Engineers Volume XL. July 1918		
War Diary	L'Hermite	01/07/1918	01/07/1918
War Diary	St Loup Connantray	02/07/1918	04/07/1918
War Diary	Huppy	05/07/1918	23/07/1918
War Diary	Martin Eglise	24/07/1918	31/07/1918
Heading	War Diary Of Headquarters 50th Divisional Royal Engineers Volume XLI August 1918		
War Diary	Martin Eglise	01/08/1918	09/08/1918
War Diary	Near Dieppe	10/08/1918	31/08/1918
Heading	War Diary Of 50th (Northumbrian) Divisional Royal Engineers. Volume XLII September 1918		
War Diary	Martin Eglise	01/09/1918	15/09/1918
War Diary	Lucheux	16/09/1918	25/09/1918
War Diary	Montigny	26/09/1918	27/09/1918
War Diary	Combles	28/09/1918	30/09/1918
Miscellaneous	Central Registry		
Miscellaneous	C.E. Fourth Army/E. 260/6	09/11/1918	09/11/1918
Miscellaneous	C.E. XIII Corps No. 14/16/344	29/10/1918	29/10/1918
Miscellaneous	Bridging Of River Selle in connection with the Operations	26/10/1918	26/10/1918
Map			
Diagram etc			
Diagram etc	Sketch "B"		
Diagram etc	Sketch D		
Heading	War Diary Of C.R.E. 50th (Northumbrian) Divisional R.E. Volume XLIII October 1918		
War Diary	Combles	01/10/1918	01/10/1918
War Diary	Lieramont	02/10/1918	05/10/1918
War Diary	Epehy	06/10/1918	09/10/1918
War Diary	Guizancourt Farm	09/10/1918	11/10/1918
War Diary	Letrou Aux Soldats	12/10/1918	25/10/1918
War Diary	Le Cateau	26/10/1918	31/10/1918
Heading	War Diary Of C.R.E. 50th (Northumbrian) Division. Volume XLIV November 1918		
War Diary	Le Cateau	01/11/1918	03/11/1918
War Diary	Le Payt Farm	04/11/1918	04/11/1918

War Diary	Fintaine	05/11/1918	05/11/1918
War Diary	Hachette	06/11/1918	06/11/1918
War Diary	Monceau	07/11/1918	09/11/1918
War Diary	Dourlers	10/11/1918	30/11/1918
Heading	War Diary Of C.R.E. 50th (Northumbrian) Division. Volume XLV December 1918		
War Diary	Dourlers	01/12/1918	18/12/1918
War Diary	Le Quesnoy	19/12/1918	31/12/1918
Heading	War Diary Of C.R.E. 50th (Northumbrian) Division. Volume XLVI January 1919		
War Diary	Le Quesnoy	01/01/1919	10/01/1919
War Diary	Audignies St Waast Bry	14/01/1919	23/01/1919
War Diary	Le Quesnoy	25/01/1919	26/01/1919
War Diary	Herbignies	29/01/1919	31/01/1919
Heading	War Diary Of C.R.E. 50th (Northumbrian) Divisional Royal Engineers Volume XLVII February 1919		
War Diary	Le Quesnoy	01/02/1919	28/02/1919
Heading	War Diary Of C R E 50th (Northumbrian) Divisional R.E. Volume XLVIII		
War Diary	Le Quesnoy	01/03/1919	31/03/1919
Miscellaneous	Headquarters, 50th Divisional Packet, "A"	02/05/1919	02/05/1919
War Diary	Le Quesnoy	01/04/1919	31/05/1919
Miscellaneous	HQ 3rd Echelon	05/02/1919	05/02/1919

Army Form C. 2118

WAR DIARY
or
INTELLIGENCE SUMMARY
(Erase heading not required.)

Place	Date	Hour	Summary of Events and Information	Remarks and references to Appendices
WESTOUTRE.	27/5/16.		Took over from C.R.E. 3rd Division. Spent morning with G.S.O.I. 50 Div on attack scheme. C.R.E. moved to M.R.2. (Sheet 28) and 2nd South F.Co. to LOCREHOF FARM today.	
"	28/5/16.		Visited 1st South F. Co., KEMMEL DEFENCES, 2nd South F.Co., G.O.C. 150 Inf. Bde., also 50 Div HQ Offrs. Inspected new water supply at foot of MONT ROUGE.	
"	29/5/16.		Visited 150 F.Co., 7. F.W.Co., 253 Tunnelling Co Rd. & 136 A.T.Co, R. Visited 50 Div. HQ Offrs & inspected new water supply near CANADA CORNER.	
"	30/5/16		Visited 2nd Army HQ Offrs - went with Major Howard & see Mine Demonstration at Cassels School, 3rd Army - Visited 50 Div HQ Offrs.	
"	31/5/16.		Inspected Div. Battle HQrs. on SCHERPENBERG - Visited 7. & 1st South F.Co. Inspected water supply & new Bdgr. HQ Offrs. at NEPPMERE. Started nightshifts on caves at Mt. Park.	

O.S. Singer
M. Col. RE
C. RE 50 Div.

SECRET

Original

War Diary
of
C.R.E. 50th Div.

From 1/6/16
To 30/6/16

C.W. Singer
Lt. Col. the
C.R.E. 50th Div.

HARE 50 Div
VII 4

WAR DIARY or INTELLIGENCE SUMMARY

Army Form C. 2118

/15

(Erase heading not required.)

Place	Date	Hour	Summary of Events and Information	Remarks and references to Appendices
WESTOUTRE	1/8/16		Inspected Rd. Bdge. Head line with O.C. 2nd South W.G. Wk. Coy. Petri, C.E. 5' Corps called. Allied and Conference at 50' Div. H'd Qrs. H'd Qrs. of Brigadiers & C.R.A. Re arr. support line etc.	
"	2/8/16		Visited 7', 5th Cheshire Fd. Co. to arrange about work. Inspected our water supply on N. side of SCHERPENBERG, being made by 136 A.T. Co. Visited 50 Div. H'd Qrs.	
"	3/8/16		Went with G.O.C. & G.S.O.1 of 50th Div. to reconnoitre reserve lines on left of Div. Front. Inspected 50' Div. M.R. Park.	
"	4/8/16		Reconnoitred proposed switch from Subsidiary Line to Trench 24 with O.C. 2nd South A.C. alas "Overland Route". Visited 2.50' Tunnelling Co. & H'd Qrs 50' Div.	
"	5/8/16		Lt. Col. Shewel, G.S.O.1, 50' Div. Killed last night - attended funeral at WESTOUTRE today. Inspected water supply at WESTOUTRE	

Army Form C. 2118

116

WAR DIARY
or
INTELLIGENCE SUMMARY
(Erase heading not required.)

Instructions regarding War Diaries and Intelligence Summaries are contained in F. S. Regs., Part II. and the Staff Manual respectively. Title Pages will be prepared in manuscript.

Place	Date	Hour	Summary of Events and Information	Remarks and references to Appendices
WESTOUTRE	6/8/16		Inspected M.T. Park, SCHERPENBERG & water supply, LA CLYTTE Railway Siding. Inspected Laundry WESTOUTRE. Visited 50th Div. H.Q. Also.	
"	7/8/16		Reconnoitred WATLING STREET with G.O.C. 50th Div. & view the VIERSTRAAT SWITCH north ward to BRASSIERE. Inspected water supply near WESTOUTRE. O.C. 7th N.G.H.R. called.	
"	8/8/16		Visited 1st South H.Q. N.R. & inspected its Horse Lines; inspected new Brigade Hd. Qrs. at KEMMEL; visited 1st Entrenching Bn. Visited Canadian School of Instruction.	
"	9/8/16		Inspected VIERSTRAAT SWITCH, POPPY LANE and FOSSE WAY - also new Coy. O.Ps. at CAPTAIN'S POST and DESSINET I-PRM.	
"	10/8/16		Visited G.O.C. 153rd Inf. Bde. & O.C. 2nd South H.Q. - inspected KEMMEL DEFENCES. Visited 50th Div. H.Q. Also.	
"	11/8/16		Inspected M.T. Park, M.T.C. - Visited Flying Corps at BAILLEUL & view C.H.R. 2nd Div. & C.E. 5th Corps. Visited 50th Div. Hd. Also.	

Army Form C. 2118

117

WAR DIARY
or
INTELLIGENCE SUMMARY
(Erase heading not required.)

Place	Date	Hour	Summary of Events and Information	Remarks and references to Appendices
WESTOUTRE	12/8/16.		Visited Mt. Rout. 9nd C. Mt. 3rd Division at Klub of 20th K.R.R.C. (Temeins) 3rd Div. are engaged about work on VIERSTRAAT SWITCH, parallel to WATLING STREET and huts. Officers of 21 K.R.R.C. out there - marked out ground. Visited 50 Div. H.Q. Also.	
"	13/8/16.		Attended Conference at 50 Div. H.Q. Abo. with 5th Corps. Attended Memorial Service for Lord Kitchener. Visited Cheshire Fd.Co. & Mt. Rout.	
"	14/8/16.		With 50 Div. G.O.C. on scheme - visited G.O.C. 150 Inf. Bde., O.C. 2nd South. Fd.Co. & Kemmel. Attended Conference of Brigadiers & C.R.A. at 50 Div. H.Q. Abo.	
"	15/8/16.		Visited J.H.Q. & 1st South. Fd.Co. - inspected KEMMEL DEFENCES with Capt. Stevenson Nt. H.Q. Abo. 2nd Dismounted Cavalry Bde. C.E. 5th Corps, C.R.E. 2nd Div. & C.R.A. 50th Div. called.	
"	16/8/16.		Visited 20 K.R.R.C. (Teneiros) at work on VIERSTRAAT SWITCH; also O.C. Cheshire Fd.Co. on tracing on work on O.P.'s to Lieut. Busby MS, 1st North. Fd.Co. Inspected VIERSTRAAT LINE. Inspected water supply MONT. ROUGE.	

Army Form C. 2118

1/8

WAR DIARY
or
INTELLIGENCE SUMMARY
(Erase heading not required.)

Instructions regarding War Diaries and Intelligence Summaries are contained in F.S. Regs., Part II. and the Staff Manual respectively. Title Pages will be prepared in manuscript.

Place	Date	Hour	Summary of Events and Information	Remarks and references to Appendices
WESTOUTRE	17/8/16.		Inspected new Bdy. Hd. Qrs. Water Supply & Defences of KEMMEL. Inspected Subsidiary Line from LINDENHOEK to WATLING STREET & new land cart. Visited 1st South. F.C. & Div. Hd. Qrs.	
"	18/8/16.		Visited 20th K.R.R. (review) & 7th F.Co. - inspected O.P. at CAPTAIN'S POST & addresd new land at VIERSTRAAT. Visited 50th Div Hd. Qrs.	
"	19/8/16.		Took C.R.E. 2nd Div. round Right Regl. Sectn. with O.C. 2nd South. F.Co., travelling ovr. Attended Conference of Brigadiers & C.R.A. at 50 Div. Hd. Qrs.	
"	20/8/16		Visited O.C. 7 D.L.I. (review), 136 A.T. Co. R.E. & 20 K.R.R. (review). Inspected new Bdge. Hd. Qrs. KEMMEL. Defences. Inspected R.E. Park.	
"	21/8/16.		2nd South. F. Co. R.E. moved from "LOCKREHOF" to LA CLYTTE. N.T. a 9/c. Visited 2nd South. F.Co. & 1st Co. North. F.G. also 7 F.Co. R.E. Settled site for new Div. Hd. Qrs. on SCHERENBERG. C.E. 5th Corps called & settled various matters.	

1875 Wt. W593/826 1,000,000 4/15 J.B.C. & A. A.D.S.S./Forms/C. 2118.

Army Form C. 2118

119

WAR DIARY
or
INTELLIGENCE SUMMARY
(Erase heading not required.)

Instructions regarding War Diaries and Intelligence Summaries are contained in F. S. Regs., Part II. and the Staff Manual respectively. Title Pages will be prepared in manuscript.

Place	Date	Hour	Summary of Events and Information	Remarks and references to Appendices
WESTOUTRE			Visited 7 Fd. Co. & 2" South. Fd. Co. Inspected WEKSTRAAT SWITCH & new C.T. from	
"	22/8/16		POPPY LANE westwards; also proposed new 157 Bde. Batta. H? Qrs. Visited G.O.C. 50" Div. Fd. M.O.	
"	23/8/16		Visited works in SCHERPENBERG & 2" South. & 1" South. Fd. Co. Inspected works in KEMMEL HILL. Visited 50" Div. H? Qrs. & C.R.A. 50" Div. 12" Fd. G. Engineers marched to LACLYTTE, N.I.A. Stay for work on Art. O.P's.	
"	24/8/16		Visited G.O.C. 157 I.B. re working parties - inspected 12" Engineers Fd. Co., U.S. Park. Visited H? Qrs. 51" Div. Inspected new Div. H? Qrs. in SCHERPENBERG.	
"	25/8/16		Inspected POPPY LANE E.C.T. Cochran & proposed new Batta H.Q. of Left Btage. with A.A. Q.M.G. 50" Div., Col. M. Cartwright, C.B. - Visited 2" South. Fd. Co. W. C.R.E. 2nd Division & O.C. 20" K.R.R. (Pioneers) called.	
"	26/8/16		Attended Conference at Div. H? Qrs. of Brigadiers & C.R.A. Inspected R.E. Park - visited 2" South. Fd. Co., SCHERPENBERG & 20 Suths. Party Labour Bn. - visited 50" Div. H?Qro.	

WAR DIARY
or
INTELLIGENCE SUMMARY

(Erase heading not required.)

Army Form C. 2118

120

Place	Date	Hour	Summary of Events and Information	Remarks and references to Appendices
WESTOUTRE	27/8/16		Consultation with G.O.C. 53 Div re work in hand & proposed; got out Table showing Engr. Tasks required. Visited new Div HdQrs at SCHERPENBERG & 2" Bulth. HdQrs. Visited Water Supply, MONT NOIR.	
"	28/8/16		Inspected Mr. Park – visited 20" Siege, Derby Labour Bn., SCHERPENBERG & 2" Queen. Fd. Co. Took Lt Burge, 2" Bulth. HdQrs. to VIERSTRAAT-HALLEBAST ROAD to choose site for new Adv. Dressing Stn. Visited 53rd Div HdQrs.	
"	29/8/16		Inspected VIERSTRAAT SWITCH, new C.T. from POPPY LANE northwards & new Adv. Dressing Station with Col. Cartwright, A.D. & D.M.S. 53 Div. Gave lecture on Field Engineering to Army Officers School.	
"	30/8/16		Inspected VIERSTRAAT SWITCH & various Artillery O.P.s, also FOSSE C.T. & chose site for new Advanced Dressing Station at LAITERIE. Inspect Mr. Park.	

[signature] Lt. Col. RE
C. RE 53 Div

SECRET

ORIGINAL.

Vol 15

WAR DIARY.

C. R. E.
50th DIVISION.

JULY. 1916.

VOLUME. No. ~~XII~~

ORIGINAL.

Army Form C. 2118
/21.

WAR DIARY
or
INTELLIGENCE SUMMARY
(Erase heading not required.)

Instructions regarding War Diaries and Intelligence Summaries are contained in F. S. Regs., Part II. and the Staff Manual respectively. Title Pages will be prepared in manuscript.

Place	Date	Hour	Summary of Events and Information	Remarks and references to Appendices
WESTOUTRE	1/7/16		Visited 7 Fd. Co., 2nd Irish Fd. Co., 12th Anzac Fd. Co. re work in general. Visited Hd. Qrs. 149 I.B. reference reliefs & working parties - inspected work on SCHERPENBERG and R.E. Park. Attended Conference at 5th Corps Q with 50th Div. A.A. & Q.M.G.	
"	2/7/16		Inspected new Dressing Station and new Battle Bdgs. Hd. Qrs. with A.A. & Q.M.G. - inspected 148 Park & new Div. Hd. Qrs. at SCHERPENBERG.	
"	3/7/16		Visited 149 I.B. Hd. Qrs. re work, then saw O.C. 1st Irish Fd. Co., inspected new Regtl. Aid Post in Ridge Wood area & clone site for Heavy T.M. with O.C. T.M.O. Inspected new C.T. near PARRET FARM. Visited 50th Div. Hd. Qrs. Inspected R.E. Park.	
"	4/7/16		Visited 7 Fd. Co. & 2nd Irish Fd. Co. Inspected new Div. Hd. Qrs. at SCHERPENBERG, & O.P.o at VIERSTRAAT, also new POPPY LANE C.T. & adv. Dressing Station. Visited 50th Div. Hd. Qrs.	
"	5/7/16		Visited 1st & 2nd Irish Fd. Co. - Ry. Siding at LA CLYTTE - new Dressing Station at VIERSTRAAT. Selected site for new tramway at Bois CARRÉ. Inspected R.E. Ecean Park.	

WAR DIARY or INTELLIGENCE SUMMARY

Army Form C. 2118

122.

Place	Date	Hour	Summary of Events and Information	Remarks and references to Appendices
WESTOUTRE	6/7/16		Visited 1st North. Fd. Co. Inspected Regtl. Potgr. Front Line etc. with G.S.O.2, 50° Div. –	
"	7/7/16		Visited 2" North. Fd. Co. & H.Qrs. 50° Div. Inspected water supply MONT. NOIR. Inspected Rl. Potgr. Area Jerusalem with S.O.C. 50° Div, also Div. General Sir's Area. Dressing Station at LAITERIE; visited Rl. Bn. H.Qrs. Rl. I.B. at "YORK HOUSE." Inspected Rl. Park.	
"	8/7/16		Inspected new Div. H.Q. SCHERPENBERG – Visited 2nd North. Fd. Co. – inspected POPPY LANE C.IT. O.P. at VIERSTRAAT and Ads. Dressing Sta. at VIERSTRAAT, their new B: H.Qrs. Visited H.Qrs. 50° Div. Attended Conference at 5 Corpo BAILLEUL with 50° Div. A.A. & Q.M.G.	
"	9/7/16		Visited 1st Fd. & 2nd North. Fd. Co. Inspected Sigual Dug-out near Rt. Farm & new 15th H.Qrs. near VIERSTRAAT, also several new gun positions. Visited 50° Div. H.Qrs., 149 g. I. B. H.Qrs. & new water supply at MONT. NOIR.	
"	10/7/16		Inspected new Div. H.Qrs. at SCHERPENBERG & visited O.C. 7 D.T.S. (Marieca) – attendent for Recon Dumps near VIERSTRAAT with 50° Div. A.A. & Q.M.G. Inspected new Dressing Sta. at KEMMEL & new 15 dgr. H.Qrs.	

WAR DIARY or INTELLIGENCE SUMMARY

Army Form C. 2118
123.

Place	Date	Hour	Summary of Events and Information	Remarks and references to Appendices
WEST OUTRE	11/7/16.		Inspected new Div. H? Qrs. SCHERPENBERG - Visited 1st, 2nd & 1st South. Fd. Cos. - inspected new Adv. O.P.'s & various new gun emplacements, also new Dressing Stn. at LAITERIE. Inspected Rt. Pack & Canadian water supply in WEST OUTRE - CANADA CORNER ROAD.	2nd Lieut. W.F. BALDWIN (TC) 7th Fd. Co. wounded.
"	12/7/16.		Visited 1st & 2nd South. Fd. Co. Inspected POPPY LANE, FOSSE CT, LAITERIE Gen. Dressing Stn. Selected site for Grenade Dump at entrance to WATLING STREET. Visited 50th Div. H.Qrs. Attended funeral of 2nd Lieut. H. RUSSELL 7th Fd.G. at RIDGEWOOD.	2nd Lieut H. RUSSELL (TC) 7th Fd. Co. killed.
"	13/7/16.		Visited N.Z. Park & 2nd South. Fd. Co. - inspected water supply - new Div. H.Qrs. at SCHERPENBERG. Visited Canadian area water supply.	
"	14/7/16.		Inspected Rgt. Inf. Bgd. front trenches near 53 Div. G.S.O.I. - also heavy T.M. Emplacement. Visited 1st South. Fd. Co. & inspected Rt. Park.	
"	15/7/16.		Inspected POPPY LANE C.T. - RESERVE LINE, new Heavy T.M. Emplacement & new tramway in BOIS CARRE. Inspected Rt. Quarries, MONT. ROUGE & called on C.E. 9th Corps, Brig. Gen. SCHOLFIELD. R.E.	

WAR DIARY or INTELLIGENCE SUMMARY

Army Form C. 2118

124

Place	Date	Hour	Summary of Events and Information	Remarks and references to Appendices
WESTOUTRE	16/7/16.		Visited new Div. H⁰ Qrs, SCHEPENBERG - R.E. Park, CANADA CORNER - 253 Tunnelling Co. - 2ⁿᵈ South. Fd. Co. - 9ᵗʰ Fd. Co. Hd. Inspected new C.T. near WATLING STREET - new Adv. Dressing Station in Brewery, KEMMEL, visited G.O.C. 150 I.B. at KEMMEL. Visited 50ᵗʰ Div. H⁰ Qrs & water supply MONT NOIR.	
"	17/7/16.		Visited 2ⁿᵈ South. Fd. Co. & Rly. Siding at LA CLYTTE. Inspected new Adv. Dressing Sta. nr VIER-STRAAT - HALLEBAST ROAD, also various O.P.s, and Camouflage work at RIDGEWOOD. Attended Conference at BAILLEUL at 5ᵗʰ Corps (G) Office.	
"	18/7/16.		Visited G.O.C. 150 I.B. & their O.C. 4 Yorks at KEMMEL, 2ⁿᵈ South. Fd. Co., G.O.C. 149 I.B. O.C. 253 Tunnelling Co. - Inspected Wt. Park. Lectured at Young Officers School on Field Engineering.	
"	19/7/16.		Visited 2ⁿᵈ South. Fd. Co., 7ᵗʰ Fd. Co. - inspected new Signal Exchange Dug-out, new Reserve Bdge. H⁰ Qrs, new Adv. Dressing Station nr VIERSTRAAT ROAD. Inspected Wt. Park. Visited 50ᵗʰ Div. H⁰ Qrs.	
"	20/7/16.		Inspected site for new hutch Tramway fr. Heavy T.M. nr Ryd with O.C. 1ˢᵗ North. Fd. Co. - new Dressing Station at LAITERIE, new Div. H⁰ Qrs. SCHEPENBERG. Visited O.C. 7 Fd. Co. Wt.	

Army Form C. 2118

125.

WAR DIARY
or
INTELLIGENCE SUMMARY
(Erase heading not required.)

Place	Date	Hour	Summary of Events and Information	Remarks and references to Appendices
WESTOUTRE.	21/7/16.		Visited C.RE. 2nd Canadians & C.RE. 20th Divn. settling details of H.Coy. moves. Visited 7th Fd.Co. & 1st North. Fd. Co. Inspected Wt. Park & new Divn. Hd. Qtrs. at SCHERPENBERG.	
"	22/7/16.		Inspected new Divn. Hd. Qrs. SCHERPENBERG – new Adv. Dressing Station, VIERSTRAAT and LATERIE – POPPY LANE – C.T. – various Art. O.P's – new Divn. Grenade Store, entrance to WATELING STREET – Bridges on VIERSTRAAT – NEUVE EGLISE ROAD. Visited 2nd North. H. Co. Visited 50th Divn. Hd. Qrs. – 7th Fd. Co. moved to DAMOUTRE.	
"	23/7/16.		Visited 282nd A.T.Co. & 2nd Scott. Fd.Co. – Visited 7th Fd.Co. & new Dumps at LOCRE and DAMOUTRE – New Art. 18 idlrs of 7th Fd.Co. south of LINDENHOEK. Visited 50th Divn. Hd. Qrs. & MONT. ROUGE.	
"	24/7/16.		Inspected new Divn. Hd. Qrs. SCHERPENBERG – Visited 2nd North. Fd. Co. – inspected REGENT STREET & KINGSWAY C.T's and new Bridge Hd. Qrs. off VIGO STREET. Visited 50th Divn. Hd. Qrs. & new water supply MONT. NOIR.	

Army Form C. 2118

126.

WAR DIARY
or
INTELLIGENCE SUMMARY
(Erase heading not required.)

Place	Date	Hour	Summary of Events and Information	Remarks and references to Appendices
WEST OUTRE	25/7/16		Visited 2" North. F. G. Inspected Heavy T.M. Emplacement off ROSSIGNOL AVENUE, with a.a. & Q.M.G. 50" Div, also 2 Regt. Aid Post, new Grenade Store at WATEIN & STRONG and new cell Dressing Station at LAITERIE. Arranged for Bnf. party of 45 men to be attached to 1" North. F. C. fr new Tunnel Dug-Outs & 200 men to 171 Tunnelling Co. R.E. for preparation of Bdye.H.Q. sites etc in shaft at S.P.13.	
"	26/7/16		Inspected Rd. Bdye. area & cells N work with O.C. 7" F.A.C.H.Q. – Visited 2" North. H.Q. & 50" Div. Hd.Qrs. – arranged to proceed with 2 more Heavy T.M. Emplacements	
"	27/7/16		Inspected new Dressing Station, VIERSTRAAT-HALLEBAST-ROAD. also O.P.'o at "TOUCH-AND-GO and "TEA-HOUSE" – new Dressing Station at LAITERIE. also FOSSE C.T. Visited 50' Div. Hd.Qrs.	
"	28/7/16		Left G. Lo. I. 50" Div to BERTHEN to our Trench Mortar School – then to 7" A. Co. R.E. at DANOUTRE – thence to 149 I.B. Hd.Qrs. at NEUVE EGLISE. Inspected R.E. Park & new Div. Hd. Qrs. SCHEPENBERG	

WAR DIARY or INTELLIGENCE SUMMARY

Army Form C. 2118

Place	Date	Hour	Summary of Events and Information	Remarks and references to Appendices
WEST OUTRE	29/7/16		Visited 2nd Rock. Fd. C. & inspected O.Ps & Obs. Dressing Stn. Visited 1/2 & 1/3 K. H. G. and 1/4 T. & R. 1/5 - Visited 1st Snth. H. G. Attended Conference at 5 Corps H.Q. Wks. with A.A. & Q.M.G. 50th Div.	
	30/7/16		Inspected Rd. Park, CANADA CORNER. Visited 7 Fd. G. & inspected Rd. Bdge. Front Line also 2 new Heavy Trench Mortar Emplacements & work on Butts. Called on C.R.E. 36th Div. Visited 50th Div. H.Q. Wks.	
	31/7/16		Visited 1st Snth. Fd. C. - inspected two new Heavy T.M. Emplacements with O.C. Div. T.M. Capt. HANDS, R.F.A. - also Centre Bdge. Front Line. Visited 50th Div. H.Q. Wks. & Rd. Park.	

C. S. Tupper M. Col. R.E.
C. R.E. 50th Div.

Original.

SECRET.

CONFIDENTIAL.

WAR DIARY

of

C. R. E., 50th DIVISION.

Volume XVII.

From 1st to 31st August 1916.

WAR DIARY or INTELLIGENCE SUMMARY

Army Form C. 2118

Volume XVII.

128.

Place	Date	Hour	Summary of Events and Information	Remarks and references to Appendices
WESTOUTRE	1/8/16		Visited 289 A.T.C.Ms & 1st South Fd Co. — inspected new R.W. Dressing Stations in VIERSTRAAT — HALLEBAST ROAD & at LAITERIE, also various O.P's & Signal Dug-Outs. Visited by C.E. 5th Corps, attached 50th Divl Hd Qrs.	
"	2/8/16		Visited 2nd South & 7th Fd Cos. — inspected proposed Support Lines of Centre 157, 15th Bde. Attended Instruction of 2nd Gurkhas against consolidation of a Trench by 3rd Canadian Division at T.M. School. 2nd Army at BERTHEN. Lecture on Field Engineering at Young Officers School, 50th Divn.	
"	3/8/16		Visited 50th Divl Hd Qrs. Inspected Mt. Park & new Bridge. Hd Qrs. at KEMMEL, also O.P's on KEMMEL. Inspected new water supply.	
"	4/8/16		Visited 7th & 2nd South. Fd Cos. Inspected Rd 13 Bdge. Front Lines – Heavy T.M. Emplace. "Butts" etc. Visited 50th Divl Hd Qrs & new water supply.	
"	5/8/16		Visited 1st South Fd Co, with 50th Divl A.A. & Q.M.G. — inspected Adv. Dressing Stations at LAITERIE — VIERSTRAAT — also Signal Exchange Dug-Outs. Visited new water supply works	

WAR DIARY
or
INTELLIGENCE SUMMARY

(Erase heading not required.)

Army Form C. 2118

129

Place	Date	Hour	Summary of Events and Information	Remarks and references to Appendices
WESTOUTRE	7/8/16.		Visited 7th D.A.I. (Pinnero) & their work. C.W. XIX Division came to take over - took him round R.E. Park & 3 Fd. Coys. 15 illus - showed him various places.	
"	8/8/16.		Visited 1st & 2nd North H. Co., C.W. XIX Div came to take over - was going all places & reports on work. C.E. 5th Corps called.	
FLETRE	9/8/16.		50 Div. moved back to 5 Corps Rest Area today in relief by XIX Division. Fd. Coys. & Mtd. Bn. moved early to Billets occupied in April & May last. Visited Billets & our C.E. 5th Corps. Visited 1st & 2nd North H. Co.	
	10/8/16.		Visited Fd. Co., MON ROUGE & MONT. DES. CATS. C.E. 2nd Army called.	
BERNAVILLE	11/8/16.		50 Div. moved to 9 Corps area today.	

1875 Wt. W593/826 1,000,000 4/15 J.B.C. & A. A.D.S.S./Forms/C. 2118.

Army Form C. 2118

130

WAR DIARY
or
INTELLIGENCE SUMMARY
(Erase heading not required.)

Instructions regarding War Diaries and Intelligence Summaries are contained in F. S. Regs., Part II. and the Staff Manual respectively. Title Pages will be prepared in manuscript.

Place	Date	Hour	Summary of Events and Information	Remarks and references to Appendices
BERNAVILLE	12/8/16		7th Corps arrived this morning as follows: 1st H.Q. at BOISBERGUES, 1st Scott H. Co. at GRIMONT, 2nd Scott H.Q. at ST. HILAIRE. H'd Qrs. Wt. arrived 5.30 A.M. Visited 3 H. Co.	
"	13/8/16		Visited 50th Div. H'd Qrs. Allowed Conference at 50 Div. H'd Qrs. of Brigadiers, C.R.A. & Staff Officers	
"	14/8/16		Visited 50th Div. H'd Qrs. also 149 I.B. H'd Qrs. & interviewed various Officers who drove Transfer to the W.B. Collects various other items about the country by 1st Corps Stables. Mess at BERNAVILLE.	
VIGNACOURT	15/8/16		Opened H'd Qrs. today. Visited 2nd Scott. H.C.	
MONTIGNY	16/8/16		Opened H'd Qrs. today. Visited 1st Scott. H. Co.	
"	17/8/16		Visited C.E. 3rd Corps. Gen. Schreiber - also Mess H'd Corps. who marched to joint wells in test area today.	

Army Form C. 2118

131.

WAR DIARY
or
INTELLIGENCE SUMMARY
(Erase heading not required.)

Place	Date	Hour	Summary of Events and Information	Remarks and references to Appendices
MONTIGNY	18/8/16.		Visited Controller of Mines, 4th Army, at RIDEMONT & arranged for classes of instruction in Barrett's Hydraulic "Sentinel" Facing Jack. Saw one years of Labour Co. Nl. Visited 6" Dump, W. Park, 3rd Corps, near ALBERT & Manuel some material. Visited 1st A.G.W.L. & arranged to have targets made up for Snipers School of 50th Div. Visited 50th Div Hd Qrs.	
"	19/8/16.		Visited 2nd & 1st North. Fd Cos. & 1st D.L.I. (Pioneers) & arranged about having programme. Visited 50th Div Hd Qrs. C.E. 4th Army, Gen Buckland, called to see me.	
"	20/8/16.		Visited 1st & 2nd South. Fd Cos. & inspected their training. Visited 50th Div. Hd Qrs.	
"	21/8/16.		Visited 1st D.C. & 1st & 2nd South. Fd Cos. & inspected their training. Visited 50th Div Hd Qrs	
"	22/8/16.		Visited 2nd South Fd Co., 1st A Co. & 1st D.L.I. (Pioneers) & inspected their training. Visited 4th Army Hd Qrs. & saw D.D.A.S. who was out; inspected Snipers Range.	

Army Form C. 2118

132.

WAR DIARY
or
INTELLIGENCE SUMMARY
(Erase heading not required.)

Place	Date	Hour	Summary of Events and Information	Remarks and references to Appendices
MONTIGNY.	23/8/16		Visited C.R.E. 15th Div. near ALBERT - went up with O.C. 50th Div. Signal Co. M. to CONTAL- MAISON and MAMETZ WOOD. Visited 50th Div. Hd Qrs.	
"	24/8/16		Visited 3 R. Eng. & 7 D.L.I. (Pioneers) & inspected training. Drove into AMIENS - Visited 50th Div. Hd Qrs.	
"	25/8/16		Attended Div. Exercise in Air Contact Patrol work. Inspected training of 2nd South. Fd.Co. Arranged for work of 2nd South. H.G. & 2 Coys. Pioneers under C.R.E. 15th Div. Visited 50th Div. Hd Qrs.	
"	26/8/16		Visited 50th Div. Hd Qrs. Visited C.R.E. 15th Div. & C.E. 3rd Corps as to new work. Attended Inspection of Transport of 151st South. Fd. Co. by G.O.C. 50th Div.	
"	27/8/16		Went round 15th Div. Front Line Trenches with G.S.O's I & II, 50th Div. and C.R.E's of 15th & 47th Divs. Visited 50th Div. Hd Qrs.	

WAR DIARY
or
INTELLIGENCE SUMMARY
(Erase heading not required.)

Army Form C. 2118

133.

Place	Date	Hour	Summary of Events and Information	Remarks and references to Appendices
MOLLIENS	28/8/16		Inspected Transport & Training of 1st A. Co. etc. – Visited 2nd South. F.C. at work at "G" Dumps, also 1st South. F.C. at HÉHENCOURT WOOD on road making. Visited 50th Div. H.Q. Office.	
"	29/8/16		Inspected 1st A.C. & visited M.T. at BAZIEUX with a.a.Q.M.G. 50 Div. Visited C.E. 3rd Corps with reference to construction of huts at HÉHENCOURT. Visited 50th Div. H.Q. Office.	
"	30/8/16		Inspected new road at HÉHENCOURT WOOD – Visited 1st South. F.C. and Hydraulic Forcing Jack at work. Visited 50th Div. H.Q. Office.	
"	31/8/16		Inspected new road at HÉHENCOURT WOOD – Visited 1st South. F.C. and Hydraulic Jack at work. Visited 1st R.G. at BECOURT & 2nd South. F.C. near "G" Dumps. Visited 50th Div. H.Q. Office.	

[signature]
C.R.E. 50 Div.

50th. DIVISIONAL ENGINEERS

C . R . E .

50th. DIVISIONAL ENGINEERS

S E P T E M B E R 1 9 1 6.

ORIGINAL.   SECRET.

WAR DIARY

of

C. R. E.

50th (Northumbrian) Divisional

ROYAL ENGINEERS.

September, 1916.

Volume No. XVlll.

WAR DIARY or INTELLIGENCE SUMMARY

Army Form C. 2118

Vol. XVIII / 134

Place	Date	Hour	Summary of Events and Information	Remarks and references to Appendices
MONTIGNY	1/9/16		Started work on new Div. Hd. Qrs. with 1 section of 1st Scott. Fd. Co. under Adjutant Mt. — Visited 15th Div. Hd. Qrs. Inspected work on HEIHENCOURT WOOD ROAD. Visited 50th Div. Hd. Qrs.	
"	2/9/16		Visited 1st Scott. F.C. & new D.H.Q., also work on HEIHENCOURT WOOD ROAD. Attended Conference at 3rd Corps Hd. Qrs. with 50th Div. A.A. & Q.M.G.	
"	3/9/16		Inspected new D.H.Q. – Visited C.R.E. 15th Div. & arranged future work with him. Visited 50th Div. Hd. Qrs.	
"	4/9/16		Inspected new D.H.Q. – Visited C. R. 15th Div. – Visited 1st Scott. F.G. & 1st N.G. at BECOURT. 7th D.L.I. (Pioneers) moved to find today. Inspected new A.D.H.Q at BECOURT. RAILWAY WOOD – Visited C.R.E. 7 Div.	
"	5/9/16		Visited 1st, 2nd & 2nd Scott. H. Cos. who with moved today to BECOURT AREA. Visited G Dumps, 3rd Corps, also C. Rd. 15th Div., and C.E. & A.A. & Q.M.G. 3rd Corps re roads & tramways. Visited new D.H.Q. Visited 50th Div. Hd. Qrs.	

WAR DIARY or INTELLIGENCE SUMMARY

Army Form C. 2118.

135

Place	Date	Hour	Summary of Events and Information	Remarks and references to Appendices
MONTIGNY	6/9/16		Visited Front Line Trenches with C.RE. 15th Div. — Chose site for new Regt. Hrs. in QUARRY, BAZENTIN-LE-PETIT. Inspected work in CONTALMAISON ROAD. new D.H.Q. and HÉHENCOURT WOOD ROAD. Visited 50 Div Hrs.	
"	7/9/16		Visited C.R.E. 15th Div. Inspected new D.H.Q. and HÉHENCOURT WOOD ROAD. Visited 3 A. Corps, 50 Div. Visited 50 Div H.Q.	
"	8/9/16		Attended Conference of Brigadiers at 50 Div Hrs. in morning. Inspected new D.H.Q. & visited C.R.E. 15 Div	
"	9/9/16		Shewed D.H.Q. Visited & inspected work at BAZENTIN-LE-PETITE, CONTALMAISON etc. Visited 7.A.C. & 7.D.I.S. (Pioneers). Visited C.R.E. 15 Div. Visited 50 Div. H.Q.	
"	10/9/16		Held Conference with O.C. 7.D.I.S. (Pioneers); O.I.C. H.Co. and 7.Co. Bills re work etc. Inspected work of 7.A.G. & 7.D.I.S. on road at BAZENTIN-LE-PETIT. Visited 50 Div H.Q.	

BELLINGCOURT - ALBERT Rd.

WAR DIARY or INTELLIGENCE SUMMARY

Army Form C. 2118.
136.

Place: Dn. /BELLINCOURT - ALBERT ROAD

Date	Hour	Summary of Events and Information	Remarks and references to Appendices
11/9/16.		Visited To Co. & Pioneers & allied work. Inspected various works. Visited 50th Div. H.Q.	
12/9/16.		Inspected FRICOURT DUMP with Adjutant Rt. - recommended site for 2d Co. near LOZENGE COPSE - Visited 2nd South R.G. & arranged work on light Tramway. Visited "A" Dump with a.a. & Q.M.G., also 7th & 15th South. R. Co. C.R.E. 23rd Div. called. Visited 50th Div. H.Q. also.	
13/9/16.		Visited 7th A.C. Half of 128 Fd Co. M.S. & 1 Coy of South Staffords, work of 23rd Div. arrived today for work on light Tramway. Visited G.O.C. 15th I.B. & inspected work on CUTTING - BAZENTIN LE PETIT Road, near 15 Bgn. & Fd. H.Wks. & QUARRY. and 21st Dump at B.P. Visited 50th Div. H.Qrs.	
14/9/16.		Visited H.Co. & Pioneers, also 50th Div. H.Qs. Spoke with 50th Div. Staff. & advised D.H.Q. at RAILWAY. COPSE.	

WAR DIARY
or
INTELLIGENCE SUMMARY

Army Form C. 2118.

137

Place	Date	Hour	Summary of Events and Information	Remarks and references to Appendices
	15/9/16.		3rd Div. Hd.Qrs. moved to Old German Dug-outs at RAILWAY COPSE — adjutant to U/S. Relieved with R.V.9a. to look after them. 1st D. Co. went forward to Dug-outs on S.W. side of MAMETZ WOOD, 1st & 2nd South W. Cos. to bivouacs close to FRICOURT FARM.	
	16/9/16.		Div. attacked & secured left part of final objective & right half of second objective. One Coy of 1st, 7th D.L.I. (Pioneers) allotted to 149, 151 I.B'ds., 1st D. Co. employed as road from 13 A 2 cent. T.I.N. 65. to 57 I.T. under 1 Coy. Pioneers, 2 Coys. Pioneers & 2 D. Co. in reserve.	
	17/9/16.		Attack continued by Div. Coys. & Pioneers employed as yesterday with the addition of 1 Coy. Pioneers on roads from Th. CUTTING towards S.14.10.1/7 and 1st D. Co. & 2nd South W.C. 1 P.D. Co. & 1 Coy. Pioneers on road from S.14.10.1/7 towards HIGH WOOD.	
	18/9/16.		Consolidating positions won by Infantry. D. Co. & 2 Pioneer Coys. as road C. to Gwynnant. yesterday. 2 Pioneer Coys. as road as yesterday.	
	19/9/16.		3 D. Coys. & Pioneers as yesterday.	

WAR DIARY or INTELLIGENCE SUMMARY

Army Form C. 2118.
138.

Place	Date	Hour	Summary of Events and Information	Remarks and references to Appendices
	20/9/16.		2" Half. Fd. Coy. constructed Strong Point north of HIGH WOOD; remainder of Fd. Co. & 2 Coy. Pioneers on roads as before; 2 Coys. of Pioneers with R.E.'s on C.T.'s.	
	21/9/16.		1st half. F.C. with 2 Coys. Pioneers constructed gun trench, 5' deep & 3'0" long, joining up THE BOW with 47" Div on right - Very wet. Rem. employed on Fd. Coys. & Pioneers on roads as yesterday.	
	22/9/16.		7 F.C. started tramway with 16th. Decauville Track from junction of BETHEL SAP and HIGH WOOD - MARTIN PUICH Road towards PAVÉ COPSE. Remainder of Fd. Co. also 1 Coy. Pioneers on roads as before. 2 Coys. Pioneers on C.T.o.; 1 Coy. Pioneers on new trench joining STARFISH LINE and PRUE TRENCH.	
	23/9/16.		Fd. Co. & Pioneers employed as per yesterday assisted by parties of 2 Inf. Bdes. 200 men.	

RAILWAY COPSE

Army Form C. 2118.

139

WAR DIARY
or
INTELLIGENCE SUMMARY
(Erase heading not required.)

Place	Date	Hour	Summary of Events and Information	Remarks and references to Appendices
RAILWAY COPSE	24/9/16		2 Fd. Cos. & 1 Pioneer Coys. as per roster; 3 Pioneer Coys. on C.T.'s; 1 Fd. Coy. on Tramways. 2 N Inf. on Tram roads; 2 Bns. Inf. on roads. Visits all work & inspected old German M.G. Dumps in BAZENTIN LE PETIT – a large quantity of gun material of all descriptions still intact.	
	25/9/16		All working parties as for yesterday – intense bombardment of enemy by Div. Artillery at 12.35 P.M. Working parties little interfered by shell fire.	
	26/9/16		All working parties as for yesterday – intense bombardment of THIEPVAL at 12.35 P.M. Working very little interfered by enemy's shell fire.	
	27/9/16		All working parties as for yesterday – our front line advanced today. Visits all work, tramway had reached PRUE TRENCH and tin tail to STARFISH TRENCH.	
	28/9/16		All working parties as for yesterday, also commenced re-making road from BAZENTIN LE PETIT to MARTINPUICH – Reconnoitred this road & that thro' village northwards.	

Army Form C. 2118.

140

WAR DIARY
or
INTELLIGENCE SUMMARY
(Erase heading not required.)

Place: A.D.H.Q. RAILWAY COPSE.

Date	Hour	Summary of Events and Information	Remarks and references to Appendices
29/9/16		All working parties as for yesterday; road from BAZENTIN-LE-PETIT to MARTIN-PUICH brought up to within 50 yards of battle place. Consignment of rails received from "G" Dump.	
30/9/16		All working parties as for yesterday; road to MARTIN PUICH opened up to Church. Consignment of rails received from "G" Dump. Visited all working parties. Visited G.O.C. 157 I.B. with reference to marking out a jumping off trench tonight.	Appendices showing work done from 15-17 Sept 16th army orders 9 & 17, 1st Battalion = 2nd Battalion to G and 7 D 2 9 (Traces)

A.J. Turpin M.L.F.V.
C.R.E. 51st Div.

44

Summary of Doings of 7th F. Co. RE
during 15th – 17th Sept. inclusive.
———————————

15th Under C.R.E. Open Order No. 3 dt. 12/9/16 Supplemented by
C.R.E./1442 dt. 12/9/16 7th Co RE with 2 Plats: 7th D.L.I.(C(?))
were detailed to work from about Zero hour 15th on repair of road
from Pt: S.14.b.1.7 through "BAZENTIN-LE-PETIT" to Cross
roads at S.8.a.8.6 & thence on road leading to N.W. corner
of HIGH WOOD.

Work commenced 6.30 A.M. parties being organised as these:-

A. Party. 1 Sectⁿ R.E.   } 2 Forage Carts } repair of Section
           ½ Plat: Pioneers } 7 Wheelbarrows } S.14.b.1.7 – X roads
                            } 1 Handcart   } S.8.b.9.8.

B. Party. – do –   } 1 Forage cart   } repair of Section X roads
                           } 6 Wheelbarrows } S.8.b.9.8 for distance of
                                               200 x (Pt. S.8.a.8.4)

C. Party. – do –   } ~~Forage carts~~ } ~~200 x~~ Repair of Sectⁿ
                           } 6 Wheelbarrows   } 200 x Pt S.8.a.8.4 –
                           } 2 Handcarts   } X roads S.8.a.8.7.

D) Party. ½ Plat Pioneers :– { Debris Clearing.
E)   { Wood Cutting
                                { Metal loading #

By 1 P.M. road to S.8.a.8.7 X roads nearly completed.
(the road through BAZENTIN village being a series
of large Shell holes). Party rested 1 PM – 2 PM
                          & fed
At 2 PM – A, B, & C certain parties became available for work on
   Sectⁿ X road S.8.a.8.7 towards HIGH WOOD
By 6 P.M (when relieved by 1st Notts F.W. Co. R.E) the
road was readily passable as far as S.8.a.8.7 &
cleared (i.e. excavated to existing metal lying about
1'.6" – 2'.0 under ground level) and Shell holes ready for bricking
as far as S.8.b.4.8. – After 12 noon the village &

45

more especially vicinity of X roads at S.8.a.8.6 was intermittently shelled by 5·9" & 4·2", the latter being very inferior in quality. The work was not delayed – only 2 casualties occurred – Coy: returned to dug outs at SW corner of MAMETZ WOOD by 7.30 P.M, with orders to resume work at 6 A.M. – Later orders received to take over the work from the 2nd North Fd. Co. RE at 6 P.M. on 16/9/16.

(7th Co RE with 75 men 7th D.L.I. A (Coy))

16th / 17th At time of resuming work at 6 P.M on 16th inst: the road track had been cleared as far as S.3.c.6.4 but shell holes not bricked to within 300ˣ of this point. From S.3.c.6.4 a for distance of 270ˣ it was difficult to locate the road owing to a trench having been dug along it & crossing it in 2 places, consequently this portion took a considerable time to clear – By 6 A.M 17/9/16 the track had been prepared as far as S.3.d.2.7. & shell holes bricked as far as S.3.b.7.5, the "cutting" widened by 3' to avoid traffic blocks then occurring & metal laid on holes already bricked as far as S.8.a.9.4 –

The X roads at S.8.a.7.6 were intermittently shelled by 5·9" during the night somewhat delaying transport of material. Casualties 1 NCO. 1 man wounded – Work handed over to 1st North Fd. Co. RE at 6 A.M 17/9/16 when Coy: returned to dug outs at SW corner of MAMETZ WOOD. Coy: was not further employed till Dec 2/9/16.

James Dwain Carter
OC 7. Fd. Co. RE

C.R.E. 50th Division.

Reference your E.111.

Sept 15th
6 am to 4 pm. Coy stood to in readiness to move.
4 pm. Coy moved with Pioneer Working Party (140) and relieved 7th Field Coy at 6 pm on work of making road through Bazentin le Petit towards High Wood.

Sept 16th
6 a.m. Road made serviceable from S.8.b.1.7 to S.2.d.9.2 (Sheet 57c SW).
Shelling intermittently throughout night Sometimes very heavy.
29 Casualties in Party.
Relieved at 6 am by 2nd Field Coy.

Sept 17th
6 am. Relieved 7th Field Coy on above road.
Road made serviceable from S.3.c.6.5 to S.3.d.5.9 and cleared, but not bricked to S.3.b.7.2.
Very little shelling until 4 pm when very heavy barrage was put across road.
6 pm. Relieved by 2nd Field Coy.

NOTE. On night of Sept 18th New trench B.6.0 to M.34.c.7.3 laid out and dug by Coy assisted by 270 Pioneers.

C.E. Boast Capt
O.C.

C.R.E 50th Div.

ECB/66

REF: gen E111.

Brief Summary of doings of 2nd Northumbrian 3d Co R.E.
on Sept 15th to 17th inclusive.

15th 4 Sections with Tool carts & forage wagon standing
by at their billets H.Q. at (sheet 57d SE) X.28c.8.8.
Transport lining at X.27.b.5.2, in Divisional Reserve.
2 trestle wagons were at the disposal of ½ R.E. Coy & 1 pioneer coy
of 23rd Div. for transporting nails to MAMETZ WOOD.
O.C. received orders to relieve 1st North'n 3d Co R.E with
all 4 sections of Coy at 6.0 am on the 16th inst. & continue
with opening up road from BAZENTIN-LE-PETIT
towards HIGH WOOD.

16th Company paraded at 4-45 am at X.28c.8.8 &
marched to BAZENTIN-LE-PETIT with tools on
pack animals.
Officers present O.C. Lt T FORSTER. 2 Lt. NEILSON,
F.M.A. SMITH & PORTER.
Work continued where 1st N.R.E left off at
(Sheet 57d SW) S.8.a.8.7, where sappers filled up
shell holes with timber, which &c collected in
BAZENTIN-LE-PETIT working towards HIGH WOOD.
Party of Pioneers worked towards HIGH WOOD,
starting at (Sheet 57d SW) S.8.6.7.5, clearing earth &c
off surface of old road, which was cut up
with trenches & shell holes in many places.
24 D.A.C wagons were employed carrying material

from BAZENTIN-LE-PETIT, which was collected & loaded by No 3 section.

Road cleared to (Sheet 57°SW) S.3.d central by 6-0pm when Coy was relieved by 7th 30 CoRE with 2./2nd NAE Middlesex.
2 wagons at disposal of 28th Div detachment on tramway.

17th Rested until midday.
Moved camp to more suitable site near FRICOURT WOOD (Sheet 57°SE) X.28.C.9.3.

Coy Paraded at 4-45 pm & marched to road between BAZENTIN-LE-PETIT & HIGH WOOD where they relieved 1st Coy NAE at 6-0am & continued clearing road towards HIGH WOOD. D.A.C. wagons carting brick & loaded by No 3 section. Road passable to within 100 yds of HIGH WOOD. Road rather difficult to follow here owing to shell holes & trenches.

2 trestle wagons at disposal of detachment of 28th Div on tramway construction.

No casualties to men during this period. 2 horses wounded with Rifle Bullets.
Conditions generally, wonderfully quiet.

    U Burnup
    Major RE
    OC 2nd Northumbrian 30 CoRE

27/9/16.

Brief Summary of work done by 7th Bn. Durham Lt. Inf. (Pioneers) from 15th to 17th Sept. 1916.

At 6.20 am on the 15th the Battalion was distributed as follows:-

'B' Coy. attached 149th Inf. Brigade were in reserve trenches at S.8.b.3.3.

'D' Coy. attached 150th Infantry Brigade were in LANCS TRENCH and SEVENTIETH AVENUE

½ of 'C' Coy. were in dug-outs at X.29.b.5.8 with the 7th Field Coy. R.E.

The remainder of the Battalion were in reserve trenches - X.27.b. - X.28.a.

The Transport and Quartermaster's Stores were at F.1.b.9.0.

ROAD WORK. 'A' and 'C' Coys. These two Companies worked on the BAZENTIN-LE-PETIT, HIGH WOOD, MARTINPUICH road as under:-

The work consisted in clearing the mud off the road and filling shell holes with metal bricks etc. All the available transport assisted in leading metal from ROUND WOOD and CONTALMAISON DUMP. A party of 30 men from the Divisional Band acting as loading party.

DATE.	TIME.		COMPANY.	PROGRESS.
15th	7.30. AM	— 6. p.m.	½ of 'C' Coy.	Cleared to
15th	6. P.M.	— 6 AM.	'A' Coy.	JUTLAND
16th	6. AM.	— 6. P.M.	100. 'C' Coy.	ALLEY.
16th	6. P.M.	— 6. AM.	'A' Coy.	Cleared to
17th	6. AM.	— 6. P.M.	'C' Coy.	350 yards West
17th	6. P.M.	— 6. AM.	50 men 'A' Coy.	of HIGH WOOD.

17th 75 men from 'A' Coy with 2 sections 2nd Field Coy constructed a Cruciform Strong Point about S.3.b.8.7.

'B' Coy Attached 149th Inf. Brigade.
15th. 80 men were engaged in digging gun emplacements and trench for Howitzer Battery at S.8.b. Central.
16th. The Company connected up BETHELL SAP with German old line and cleared 800 yards of CRESCENT ALLEY to SUNKEN ROAD.
17th. The Company dug 400 yards of RUTHERFORD C.T. from Ground Level connecting EYE TRENCH with HOOK TRENCH.

'D' Coy Attached 150th Inf. Brigade.
This Company dug a Communication Trench 4' deep from PIONEER ALLEY to TANGLE TRENCH from S.2.b.2.6. — S.2.b.2.9.5.
16th. The Coy. moved to dug-outs at S.7.D.3.3. and joined up TANGLE NORTH with MARTIN ALLEY so as to establish a C.T. to the N.E of MARTINPUICH.
17th. 1 Officer and 30 men constructed a strong point in the crescent about M.33.b.8:4. The work consisted in consolidating the trench which was very much damaged for a small garrison. The remainder of the Company worked on clearing MARTIN ALLEY.

signature
Lt. Colonel
Commanding 7th Bn. Durham Light Infantry

27/9/16

(Original).

SECRET.

WAR DIARY

OF

C. R. E.

50th (NORTHUMBRIAN) DIVISIONAL R.E.

Volume XIX.

OCTOBER 1916.

Army Form C. 2118.

VA. XIX.
/4/.

WAR DIARY
or
INTELLIGENCE SUMMARY
(Erase heading not required.)

Place: A.D.H.Q. "RAILWAY COPSE"

Date	Hour	Summary of Events and Information	Remarks and references to Appendices
1/10/16		All working parties as before; consignment of rails arrived & Tramway being pushed on. Visited all working parties also C. RE 47 Div. FRICOURT FARM, 50 Div. RE Dump, FRI Coy R.T. Capture Front & Support FLERS LINE in conjunction with Div. on right. Capt Contacinus 28 AVENUE & RUTHERFORD ABOUT to FLERS SUPPORT.	
2/10/16		All working parties as usual – Visited work at ROZENTIN LE PETIT and MARTIN PUICH. Very wet from 11 A.M.	
3/10/16		3 F Corps. & Pinceiro as for yesterday. A.D.H.Q. moved back to MELLINCOURT and Mr. Higham to FRICOURT DUMP. 50 Div. relieved by 23rd Div. Today.	
4/10/16		3 Fr Corps. & Pinceiro as for yesterday. Visited C. RE 47 Div. & settled with Tramway; visited C.RE 23rd Div. & and C.E. 3rd Corps to arrange to take over road from CONTALMAISON to MARTIN PUICH. Visited Y 73 Co. RE	
5/10/16		3 Fr Corps & Pinceiro employed as fr yesterday. Visited all working parties & reconnoitred road from CONTALMAISON to MARTIN PUICH.	

WAR DIARY
or
INTELLIGENCE SUMMARY

Army Form C. 2118.

142.

Place: FRICOURT

Date	Hour	Summary of Events and Information	Remarks and references to Appendices
6/9/16		3 Fd. Co. & Pioneers on work as for yesterday, visited all working parties. Visited C.R.E. 47th Div. & was visited by C.R.E. 23rd Div.	
7/9/16		3 Fd. Co. & Pioneers as for yesterday, visited all working parties, also C.R.E's 23rd & 47th Divs. Myself C.E. 3rd Army permission to extend Tramway S.W. from HIGH WOOD & BAZENTIN LE PETIT. Visited by G. S. O. I, 50th Div.	
8/9/16		3 Fd. Coys. & Pioneers as for yesterday. Visited C.R.E's of 47th & 23rd Divs. who are being relieved today by 9th & 15th Divs. respectively. The C.R.E's came to see me.	
9/9/16		Work as usual – Roads very bad owing to heavy traffic & wet weather.	
10/9/16		3 Fd. Coys. & Pioneers as for yesterday – slightly easier day.	
11/9/16		Works as for yesterday. 1st Sect. Fd. Co. & 3 Coy. Pioneers to be attached for work to 15th Div. & J.B.C. & 1 Coy. Pioneers to 9th Div. for Tramway. 2 Sect. Fd. Co. with 9th D.A.D.	

Army Form C. 2118.

143

WAR DIARY
or
INTELLIGENCE SUMMARY

(Erase heading not required.)

Instructions regarding War Diaries and Intelligence Summaries are contained in F. S. Regs., Part II. and the Staff Manual respectively. Title Pages will be prepared in manuscript.

Place: TRICOURT CIRCUS.

Date	Hour	Summary of Events and Information	Remarks and references to Appendices
		and the 5th Yorks put under C.R.E. 50th Div. for work on roads as follows: from CONTALMAISON to BAZENTIN-LE-GRAND, and from MAMETZ to BAZENTIN-LE-GRAND.	
12/10/16		Inspected both roads mentioned above and parties at work on. Visited C.R.E. 9th & 15th Divs. & O.C. 7 F.G.	
13/10/16		Inspected both roads & arranged for future work. Visited C.R.E. 15th Div. & conv with H. Corps.	
14/10/16		Inspected both roads. Visited H. Co. C.E. 3rd Corps came to see me with reference to roads generally - also G. S.O.I. 50th Div.	
15/10/16		Inspected both roads & tramway from BAZENTIN-LE-PETIT. Visited Q. 9th Div. & C.R.E. 30th Div.	

War Diary or Intelligence Summary

Army Form C. 2118.

144

Place: FRICOURT CIRCUS

Date	Hour	Summary of Events and Information	Remarks and references to Appendices
16/10/16		Working hours on roads altered to:- 6 A.M. – 11 A.M.; 12 noon – 2.30 P.M. Stopped being clipped as far as period between 12 – 2 P.M. Visited all working parties, also rides & camps of 3 A. Coys + Pioneers of 5" Div. at 5.13.D.	
17/10/16		Working parties as usual. Met C.E. 3rd Corps & Staff Officer at 8a.25 N.7.W. STATION on question of roads. Visited all working parties + O.C. 7" F.C.	
18/10/16		Extra Bn. of Infantry awaiting 3 Pro. & 2 F. Coy H.Q. on roads – visited all working parties & inspected BEAVER, ROAD and new camps of F. Cos (Pioneers). C.E. called to see O.C. 7" F.Co. H.Q. with reference to rotating on Tramways. Visited C.R.E. of 9" Div	
19/10/16		Very wet – inspected all working parties on roads. G.S.O.I. II of 51 Div called late A.M. & P.M. J.	
20/10/16		Fine & cold – inspected all working parties on roads. Saw G. S.O. 2 of 3 Corps & CRES of 9" & 8" Australian Div.	

Army Form C. 2118.

WAR DIARY
or
INTELLIGENCE SUMMARY

(Erase heading not required.)

145.

Instructions regarding War Diaries and Intelligence Summaries are contained in F. S. Regs., Part II. and the Staff Manual respectively. Title Pages will be prepared in manuscript.

Place	Date	Hour	Summary of Events and Information	Remarks and references to Appendices
FRICOURT	21/10/16		Attended meeting at "B" Office 3rd Corps with A.A. & Q.M. & 50th Div. re outposts & reliefs & route holding. Visited C. re. 9th Div with reference to taking over also O.C. 15 Siege A.C.	
	22/10/16		Commenced new Advanced D.H.Q. All parties on roads as before; visited all working parties. Visited 9 Div G. Office & inspected new shelter of 50 Div D.A.C.	
	23/10/16		Working parties on roads as before. Inspected dug-outs in MAMETZ WOOD had found them not suitable for Adv. D.H.Q. Visited C. re. O. of 9th & 15th Div.	
	24/10/16		Working parties on roads as before. 50th Div take over line from 9 Div. Today - 2/Lt W.E.R R.N. relieves me in charge of roads tomorrow. Inspected roads as usual. Visited 1/Portland Ft. Co. and attended Conference of Brigadiers of 50 Div at 9 Div H.Q. Ars. Visited C. re. 9th Div	

Army Form C. 2118.

WAR DIARY
or
INTELLIGENCE SUMMARY
(Erase heading not required.)

Place	Date	Hour	Summary of Events and Information	Remarks and references to Appendices
FRICOURT FARM.	25/10/16		Moved D.H.Q. to FRICOURT FARM. Orders received today for 1st & 2nd South. Fd. Cos. & 7 D.L.I. (Pioneers) to return to 50 Div. tomorrow, 23rd, 26th & 1st Scottish Fd. Co., also 6 Welsh (Pioneers), all of 1st Div. attached to 50 Div. Arranged with new units.	
	26/10/16		Visited BAZENTIN LE PETIT and HIGH WOOD with A.D.C.R. Engrs 50 Div. & chose sites for huts for Reserve Infantry Brigade at former place. Visited O.C. Corps Tramways & 7 D.L.I. (Pioneers).	
	27/10/16		Visited 7 D.L.I. (Pioneers) & 2 Fd. Co. - O.C. Corps Tramways - Actg. D.H.Q. - BAZENTIN LE PETIT - HIGH WOOD Road, CLARKE's and B.P. Dumps. Visited C.R.E. 15 Div.	
	28/10/16.		Visited 7 D.L.I. (Pioneers) & 2nd South. Fd. Co. & O.C. Corps Tramways - Actg. D.H.Q. - BAZENTIN LE PETIT - HIGH WOOD Road, CLARKE'S & B.P. DUMPS.	
	29/10/16		Very wet. Visited new site for horse lines at BAZENTIN LE PETIT, also O.C. Corps Tramways & C.H.E. 15 Div. Major G.C. Pollard D.S.O. has arrived from 1st Scottish Fd. Co. & is i/c West Riding Fd. Co.	

WAR DIARY
or
INTELLIGENCE SUMMARY

(Erase heading not required.)

Army Form C. 2118.

147

Place: FRICOURT; PARIS

Date	Hour	Summary of Events and Information	Remarks and references to Appendices
30/10/16		Very wet. Inspected new Camp Sites & Bath Room at BAZENTIN-LE-PETIT, also road from thence to HIGH WOOD & new camp site near HIGH WOOD. Visited 149th Bde. Coy. of Division and of D.T.S. (Pioneers).	
31/10/16		Finer day. Inspected work on new Camps, Bath Room, BAZENTIN-LE-PETIT. also new Advanced D.H.Q. Visited 5th Div. A.Q.	

J. Turgin Lt. Col. M.
C.R.E. 50' Div

(Original).

S_E_C_R_E_T.

WAR   DIARY

O F

C. R. E.

50th (NORTHUMBRIAN) DIVISIONAL R.E.

Volume No: XX.

November 1916.

Army Form C. 2118.

Vol. XX. 148

WAR DIARY
or
INTELLIGENCE SUMMARY
(Erase heading not required.)

Place	Date	Hour	Summary of Events and Information	Remarks and references to Appendices
FRICOURT FARM.	1/11/16		Wet. Visited sites for Camps at BAZENTIN-LE-PETIT and HIGH WOOD, inspected roads from HIGH WOOD to BAZENTIN. CIRCUS, also met Col. D.H.Q. Visited 2 Fd. Co. & Pioneers.	
do.	2/11/16		Very wet. Visited all working parties as for yesterday. Also 2 Fd Co. & Pioneers and arranged future work. Visited 23 Fd. Co. & details saw Officers & 1 section to work on 2 machine guns emplacements under Corps.	
do.	3/11/16		Dry. Visited all working parties & sites for Camps. Bathhouse with a.a. & H.H. G. 50 Div. Inspected road from BAZENTIN-LE-PETIT to HIGH WOOD & took S. of HIGH WOOD. Visited C. Rt. 48 Div.	
do.	4/11/16		Dry. O.C.9 D.2.I came to see me about work in C.T's done last night saw Corps Commander & G.S.O.I of 3 Corps. Visited FRICOURT. Went to 150 I.B. H! Qrs. to meet all Bn Commanders with reference to working parties.	
do.	5/11/16		Dry. Spent day at R.E. D.H.Q. near SABOT COPSE with G.O.C. Staff. 50 Div. were attacking GIRDLINE. Visited HIGH WOOD Road, site for new Camps &c.	

Army Form C. 2118.

149.

WAR DIARY
or
INTELLIGENCE SUMMARY
(Erase heading not required.)

Place	Date	Hour	Summary of Events and Information	Remarks and references to Appendices
FRICOURT FARM.	6/11/16		Fairly dry. Visited all working parties near A.O. & A.M.G. - Huts South of HIGH WOOD - road from S.E.A. 9/1 to HIGH WOOD - new huts near BAZENTIN LE PETIT - Visited C.R.E. & C.R.A. of 4th Div.	
do	7/11/16		Very wet & stormy. Visited all working parties near A.O. & A.M. of 3rd Corps - cleared MISSEN huts from BAZENTIN LE PETIT Ry. Station. Visits of D.A.D.S. (Finucis) and 2nd Smith H.Q. - arranged to start 2 "rest and bath" tramway routes to trenches, also for 1st South H.Q. & log planks over wire-netting on no tram line.	
do	8/11/16		Incl. arrangts. for 2nd 21 to Mill. Mains Rd & 1st South H.Q. & appropriated siding of Pioneer Lund with 157 Cavalry under Corps orders. Visited 2 South H.Q. & 7 D.R.G. (Finucis) - Visited all working parties.	
do	9/11/16		Fine. Visited all working parties near A.O. & A.M.G. 50th Div. - selected site for huts for 2nd Bn. near HIGH WOOD. Visited F. Welch (Finucis)	

Army Form C. 2118.

WAR DIARY
or
INTELLIGENCE SUMMARY
(Erase heading not required.)

Place	Date	Hour	Summary of Events and Information	Remarks and references to Appendices
FRICOURT FARM	10/11/16		Fine. All working parties as usual. Instrns to HASDEN & Staff Sergt to put a lecture on "Experiences of a field Company Commander". Genl. Kenyon & Staff present. Instrns to 4th Army School at FLEXICOURT later.	
do.	11/11/16		Fine - all working parties as usual. Gave new lecture to 4th Army School. Genl. Buckland present. Returned to D.H.Q. by 2 p.m.	
do.	12/11/16		Fine - all working parties as usual. Visited MISSEN HUTS camp - roads near repair - CLARKE'S and B.P. DUMPS - new Bath Houses - new advanced D.H.Q. and O.C. 2nd A.T. Co. M. re water supply. CLARKE'S DUMP.	
do.	13/11/16		Fine - visited all working parties near Q.A. & R.Pr. of 53rd Div. Visited C.R.E. 2nd Australian Div. & relieved new site for 2nd Austr. Horse Lines.	
do.	14/11/16		Fine - visited all working parties. F.I.O 2. 1st Div called upon reference to relief of Div.	

WAR DIARY or INTELLIGENCE SUMMARY

Army Form C. 2118.

Place	Date	Hour	Summary of Events and Information	Remarks and references to Appendices
FRICOURT FARM	15/11/16		Gen¹ - Visited all working parties selected site for R¹ Dumps at BAZENTIN STATION, visited 7 D.L.S. (Vinieres) C.R.E. 1ˢᵗ Div. Called about tasking over.	
do	16/11/16		Gen¹ - visited all working parties, saw C.R.E. 1ˢᵗ Div. at BAZENTIN, explained alteration to him. Visited new Transport Lines, 2ⁿᵈ South W. G.	
do	17/11/16		Gen¹ - Visited all working parties. Inspected 23ʳᵈ H.C. and 7 D.W.G. Horse Lines.	
do	18/11/16		Handed over all papers, maps etc. to Lt. Col. C. Russell-Brown, D.S.O. R.E. C.R.E. 1ˢᵗ Division. Two Fuis Coys. & Pioneer Bn. of 51ˢᵗ Div. to remain in present camps, come under C.R.E. 1ˢᵗ Div. to work as follows:- 1ˢᵗ South. W. G. to complete "AMIENS" Huts near HIGH WOOD, 2ⁿᵈ South. W. G. to continue work on Adv. D.H.Q. and SABOT COPSE. 7 D.L.S. (Vinieres) to work on road from BAZENTIN CIRCUS to S.6 A9/6.	

WAR DIARY or INTELLIGENCE SUMMARY

Army Form C. 2118.

152

Place	Date	Hour	Summary of Events and Information	Remarks and references to Appendices
FRICOURT			Visited BAZENTIN STATION to see M.T. Dumps; and Col. Vaux, 7 D.L.I (Pioneers)	
FARM	19/11/16		& went over his work on road with him. Visited 150 I.B. H.Qs. also at BECOURT.	
ALBERT. 12 RUE DE BARAME			Several Div. M.T. H.Q. Offrs. head h Corps H.Q. Offrs. h see D.G.M.S. i.c.t. was advised	
	20/11/16.		to approve contract of Construction of Reserve Defence Line.	
	21/11/16.		To FRICOURT h see C.R.E. 1st Div. & Mess. & BAZENTIN LE PETIT h see M. Gen. and Division - arranged h take over the billets at FRICOURT FARM tomorrow. In a.m. & p.m. h inspected 1 sqdn I.B. Transport Lines at ALBERT- BAZENTIN ROAD	
FRICOURT FARM.	22/11/16		Returned here today h take over work with 2d Cavalry Division at Reserve Line, Arranged with for interviews with Cavalry & 2 Lieut Wilkinson, 1st South. Lt. Co. Visited C.R.E. 1st Div	
do.	23/11/16		Spent Capt DUDGEON Inniskillen Dragoons, & 2 Lt WILLIAMS at LANGUARD CIRCUS at HAPP - Visited C.R.E. 1st Div. & made arrangements for moving Corps Reserve Line. Visited "D" 1st Div & Cavalry Lieuses M.U	

Army Form C. 2118.

153

WAR DIARY
or
INTELLIGENCE SUMMARY

(Erase heading not required.)

Instructions regarding War Diaries and Intelligence Summaries are contained in F. S. Regs., Part II. and the Staff Manual respectively. Title Pages will be prepared in manuscript.

Place	Date	Hour	Summary of Events and Information	Remarks and references to Appendices
FRICOURT - FARM	20/9/16		Inspected road, BAZENTIN CIRCUS to S.B. A 9/6 with O.C. 7" D.L.S. (Pomeira) & decided on what work should be done. Visited HIGH WOOD Road and its DUMP, BAZENTIN STATION. Visited C. Rct. 15 Div re provision of wiring material for Enemy Barriers employed on Reserve Line.	
	25/9/16		Visited 126 Battery R.F.A. 4 Div near GINCHY. Went on wiring Corps Second Line by Cav Pioneer Bn. conferred with	
	26/9/16		Inspected road from BAZENTIN CIRCUS to S.B. A 9/6 with O.C. 7" D.L.S. (Pomeira) & acted as with him above. Visited O. R. Corps Tramways, 1st South R. Co and 2nd South R. Co. R.E.	
	27/9/16		Job ALBERT 4 50 Div. H.M. Also, to make arrangements for cont. for supply of R.E. Stores where Div goes into Training Area in 30 mile. To Div. Corps in afternoon to present "Sporting Gazette" Ribbons 2 3 N.C.O's of 1st South R. Co and 2 of 2nd South R. G.	

Army Form C. 2118.

154

WAR DIARY
or
INTELLIGENCE SUMMARY
(Erase heading not required.)

Place	Date	Hour	Summary of Events and Information	Remarks and references to Appendices
	28/11/16		To ALBERT to give lecture to class of Officers — outposts — Supply of R.E. Stores; Employment of R.E. with Infantry; Employment of R.E. & Pioneers in the attack. Visited O.C. Cav. Pioneer Bn. & C.R.E. 1st Div.	
	29/11/16		Visited 4th R.E. in charge of spare accommodation. With C.E. 3rd Corps and 2 Lieut. Wilkinson R.E. to reconnoitre 3rd Corps Second Line of Defence	
	30/11/16		All working parties as usual. Selected N.C.O. & act as P.W. & also Instructor to Div. School. MONTIGNY. 3rd Div., two Mt. Pioneers moved back to Keep Reserve Area — 17th Div. BAIZIEUX. C.R.E. proceeded on leave	

[signature]
Lt. Col. R.E.
C.R.E. 50' Div.

SECRET.
Original.

WAR DIARY

OF

C. R. E.

50th Divisional R.E.

---------oOo---------

Volume XXI.

December 1916.

WAR DIARY
or
INTELLIGENCE SUMMARY

Army Form C. 2118.

Vol. XXI

Place	Date	Hour	Summary of Events and Information	Remarks and references to Appendices
FRICOURT FARM	1/12/16		Finished working party of 1 7" Q.L.I. on road between BAZENTIN LE PETIT & HIGH WOOD. Finished 7" Q.L.I. + 1st Fd. Coy. - also C.O. when Pioneer Battn. Fair. Much fog & frost.	
	2/12/16		Finished working party at HIGH WOOD. Fair - frost.	
	3/12/16		Finished Pioneer Stables at MILLENCOURT. Finished C.O. when Pioneer Battn. also C.R.E. 1st Div. fair	
	4/12/16		Finished U.S. Coy & discussed with O.C. the question of reduction of transport. Fine -	
	5/12/16		Finished working party at HIGH WOOD. Snowy -	
	6/12/16		Finished new Horse Lines for Coy. Also working party on road between BAZENTIN LE PETIT and HIGH WOOD, and the old Long line -	
	7/12/16		Finished D.A.C. fine -	
	8/12/16		at AMIENS Snowy	
	9/12/16		fair wet. Finished Field Stables at MILLENCOURT	
	10/12/16		Ploroning. Finished Field Stables & horselines & finished two camps at BAZENTIN LE PETIT.	
	11/12/16		fair. Finished the Field Coys & horselines	
	12/12/16		Wet.	
	13/12/16		fair. Finished Field Coys new Horse lines.	
	14/12/16		Snowy. Finished work on BAZENTIN LE PETIT and HIGH WOOD road -	

Army Form C. 2118.

15

WAR DIARY
or
INTELLIGENCE SUMMARY
(Erase heading not required.)

Instructions regarding War Diaries and Intelligence Summaries are contained in F.S. Regs., Part II. and the Staff Manual respectively. Title Pages will be prepared in manuscript.

Place: TRICOURT FARM.

Date	Hour	Summary of Events and Information	Remarks and references to Appendices
15/10/16		C.Wr. returned from leave. Visited new Laundry at AMIENS and new Rest Station for Div. near MILLENCOURT.	
16/10/16		Visited T.I. 1st South. and 2nd South. F.As., inspected huts at BAZENTIN LE PETIT, also road to HIGH WOOD. Visited C.Wr. 1st Div., and Lt. Col. Vansey who has now retnd proposed scheme for Fd. Ey. Commanders at HQrs DIV. Lt. Col. Evans, K.R.R.C. 3rd Corps M.G. officer called with reference to selection of N.G. Emplacements on Cops 3rd Line	
17/10/16		Inspected 1st South. & 2nd South. Fd.Cos. Visited Lt. C. Mattre. Visited 3rd Corps HQrs and G.S.O.2 re laying Corps 2nd Line, also Major Evans, 3rd Corps Sr. G. Officer. Visited 50 Div. HQrs. at BAZIEUX & inspected 50 Div. D.A.C. Camp.	
18/10/16		Visited 1st and 2nd South. Fd Cos. inspected huts & roads at BAZENTIN LE PETIT and Horse Lines of 1st D.A.C. (Senior) Visited C.W.R 15th Div	

Army Form C. 2118.

157

WAR DIARY
or
INTELLIGENCE SUMMARY
(Erase heading not required.)

Instructions regarding War Diaries and Intelligence Summaries are contained in F. S. Regs., Part II. and the Staff Manual respectively. Title Pages will be prepared in manuscript.

Place	Date	Hour	Summary of Events and Information	Remarks and references to Appendices
TRICOURT FARM	19/12/16		Very cold with some snow. Inspected wiring of 3rd Corps 2nd Line in morning. Saw H.I.G.H. Ward. Inspected 50" Div. D.A.C. Stables.	
	20/12/16		Inspected Corps 2nd Line with Major Balfour, Corps G. Co 2, Lt. Col. Evans, Corps M.G. Officer and 2nd Lt. Williams Rt. & selected position of wire entanglement.	
	21/12/16		Inspected 2 Fd Coy, & D.A.C. Stables. Lt. Col. Pawley R.E., Assistant to E. in C. and Major Henderson R.E. called – latter to become temporary C.R.E. 50" Div. Called at 50" D.H.Q.	
	22/12/16		Visited 3 Fd Coy. & 7 D.L.I. (Pioneers) with Major Henderson R.E. Visited Stables of 2 Fd Coy. & C.R.E. 1st Div.	
	23/12/16		Major E.C. Henderson R.E. took over duties of C.R.E. 50" Div. from Lt. Col. C.W. Singer R.E. Saw O'Sullivan and went over wiring completed and proposed in 2nd Corps Line. Showery.	
	24/12/16		Accompanied C.R.E. (on to Hudson Lees, Bazenton le Petit. Attended his Conference. Works Montaun Fd Co and 6 Welch (Pioneers). Fair.	

Original.
C.R.E., 50th Division.

SECRET.

WAR DIARY

OF

C. R. E.

50th (Northumbrian) Divisional R.E.

Volume No:XXll.
****

January 1917.

Army Form C. 2118

Vol XXII 159

WAR DIARY
or
INTELLIGENCE SUMMARY
(Erase heading not required.)

Instructions regarding War Diaries and Intelligence Summaries are contained in F. S. Regs., Part II. and the Staff Manual respectively. Title Pages will be prepared in manuscript.

Place	Date	Hour	Summary of Events and Information	Remarks and references to Appendices
FRIGURT Farm.	Jan 19th	1 pm	Went with Captain GIBSON, 2nd Nth'd Co. to see excavation in bank of 3 deep dug outs proposed Bn Batt. HQ. Visited Cough DROP - Left Bgde HQ. Saw G.O.C. met G.O.C. Rifle Bde at Factory Corner. Cloudy - slight mist. Paid my first call on G.O.C. Division.	
		2 pm	Visited Hutting Office and went over advanced HQ. Accommodation. Saw 6/0 Bde and arranged about Nissen huts for his HQ. Saw O.C. 1st Nth'd Co. Went over B.P. Siding. Visited Major McQueen's office and 9th D.L.I. Cloudy and warm.	
		3 pm	Question of shifting HQ Rear of Bde settled. Q. orders Mr Chuck blue hints to sit below Adv. H.Q. on opposite side of road. Cloudy - slight rain and drizzle. R.O.E. works question of Lt Railway between at Factory trench finished and at Fancourt L'Abbaye.	
		4 pm	Visited forward area. Saw shells to Luxembr. M.G. Bn & A/B in Trenches ¼ in and firing Pruisian of Hohenzollern Colour. Big met S.L.T. and at head of Trick Ave. Reconnoitred tramway Railway behind Fancourt L'Abbaye and from Railway Corner to new line up along Combies road to bank behind YARRA Support. Walk on 3 dug outs Rear HQ. & back began tonight.	
		5 pm	9/L.S. Midland Co. came under orders 1/50th Division for work. O.C. cheerful. Brained work. Went and saw huts proposed for the trains by him near Courtalvacson. Arrived & display. Saw a repairing Ambulance place in Q.Ng.B. in place of 9th D.L.I. to be C.T., only 1st see Mannetz Wood Camp - G.O.C. came to my Office. Telephones & about & long bile for revetting. Told chief to give some of franzers.	

WAR DIARY
INTELLIGENCE SUMMARY
(Erase heading not required.)

Army Form C. 2118.

Vol XVII

160

Place	Date	Hour	Summary of Events and Information	Remarks and references to Appendices
FRICOURT Farm.	January.			
	6.		Went with G.S.O.I. Brunwell and I.O. Crichton Potts across open ground facing Road. Visited 23rd Pitts. m/s. Indiants. Col. Lawrence at HQ in Wood.	
	7.		Sunday. Visited Dump to be about empty. Found shelves & B.P. Dump. C/E (acting) called at my Hqrs. Dined in Ctn (acting) at Corps Hd.	
	8.		Blank V.O.T., 7 D.L.I. Called. Q.S. decides to replace Pioneer Labour for facing & Power Avenues.	
	9.		Remonstrated and under protest, I leave part on line until a.c. – Captain McLellan with him. Saw h.Q. P. of A. also testing line Hays wire. Whitebrook examined tunnels enquiring for tunnellers 1st and 2nd Pl Cnys. Saw O.C. M.S. Hustanks rebuilding a tramway at Hertford Road.	
	10.		Tramway completed. Granton 20" & Halton Road. Artillery bombardment & German lines.	
	11.		Heavy shell fire. Blank Vaux & D.L.I. Called.	
	12.		Saw Q.O.E. and was informed (verbally as to dug. out policy). Complaints from Coldham & Lunnen that 12 tunnelling by was withdrawing proving available without his labour. A little snow. Capt. McLellan left for Ben Command of Reinforcements.	
	13.		Coys all without Infantry Coy. 1st N. Cn., 2nd N. Cn., & P/S Hustanks & wire screen. Enquiries M. Potiers. Visited all 3 Coys. Saw Capt. Powell about workshop supply.	

2449 Wt. W14957/M90 750,000 1/16 J.B.C. & A. Forms/C.2118/12.

WAR DIARY or INTELLIGENCE SUMMARY

Army Form C. 2118.

Place	Date	Hour	Summary of Events and Information	Remarks and references to Appendices
France	Jan. 1917.			
Farm	14.		Showed line of posts to Capt. Cockburn of 1/S. Midd'sex Co. - also Hessian Road & M.G. huts B.H.A.	
	15.		Inspected 1/5 S. Entrance to Dug out. Yarra Bank Tunnel. will as usual be Winches.	
	16.		Visited B.P. Dump, 23rd Co, B de HQrs R. Mess Bdr. also Factory Avenue & Dug out Yarra Bank.	
	17.		Office - have given [illegible] W.S. in relief of March.	
	18.		A letter own Shortland to H.Machine -	
	19.		Office - Visited Compagnie M.B.P. Dump. Orders received in re Relieving 1st Aust. Div. (25-29)	
	20.		Snow - Cold - Prepare new Trench report chew in 1/1. Informed 1/5 Midd's relieve us 27.	
	21.		Visited Compagnie - Received orders to move to RIBEMONT on 29 & 30 - Thursday new.	
	22.		CRE 1st Australian Div. called and was shown papers re work in hand. Moved 4 to 5 pm in 12 Feb.	
	23.		Visited R.E. Bde HQ in area also Intermediate (Capts.) lines, Pierre ave, Kerkum Road	
	24.		Charles dump & H.Nabn, 2 Nabn & 7 Div HQ. (See 1/ S.M. Quilts.	
	25.		Hour for [illegible] on arrival to RIBEMONT (Du HQ on 28-) acct 1st Aust. Engineer Coun and our find having our bit of all work. Conference & 5th Div 1st Aust. Div. les Commanders re forwarding work Completion over to 3rd Co Aust. Engineer WE are all Halting. See 1/ S. Midd'sex Left.	
	26.		Handed over all labour to CRE, 1st Aust. Engineer (Col. Markin). 23 - 26 History reprint 1st Div for work	

Army Form C. 2118.

Vol XII 162.

WAR DIARY
or
INTELLIGENCE SUMMARY
(Erase heading not required.)

Place	Date	Hour	Summary of Events and Information	Remarks and references to Appendices
FRICOURT	Jan 27/17		Conference handed over work to 1st Aust. Engineers in forwards.	
	28th	4 pm	Reconnoitred a C.R.E. of work in forward area taken over by C.R.E. 2nd Aust. Engineers. 2/S. Hudland Bos (H.Q. m'kn) returned under order of 1st A. Div. C.R.E. 2nd Aust. Bros. left Fricourt.	
	29th	11 am.		
RIBEMONT	29th		Visited 4 dumps to state numerio and in bullets. Also visited H.Q. 1st Anzac Corps and ar ranges where work done at [SEAULT?] Nowhipa while we was working.	
	30th		Visited dumps, 1st Anzac Corps C.E. also French area. H.Q. 18th C.E. d'Armée very Silvue Matthew at Estrun and Cdm. pr. Bolor. Saw CRE 36th (French) Div. and a CRE 35th (French) Div. at LA BARAQUETTE & Pole à Commandant Gabriele Sub lieut?. Mais correction to plan & dump & railways in this area. Visited CE III Corps and informed French were not apparently (owing to enemy scarce supply at all their dumps.	
	31st		Visits him at a. Picked up CRE 136th (?) Div. at 10.20 am (Commandant HABERT): Continued Sous-Secré BERNY - Bayeux IV en Infant-back to H.Q. & French Cmd'n to also much him in return trip. Called at C.R.E. 35th Fr. Div. in evening & advis lite about blow. In	

RIBEMONT.
1.2.17.

E.C. Henderson Major R.E.
C.R.E. 1st Div.

Original. SECRET.

WAR DIARY

OF

C.R.E., 50th Division.

Volume XXIII.

February, 1917.

Army Form C. 2118.

Vol. XXIII. 163.

WAR DIARY
or
INTELLIGENCE SUMMARY

(Erase heading not required.)

Instructions regarding War Diaries and Intelligence Summaries are contained in F. S. Regs., Part II. and the Staff Manual respectively. Title Pages will be prepared in manuscript.

Place	Date	Hour	Summary of Events and Information	Remarks and references to Appendices
RIBEMONT.	Feb 1917 1st		Visit P.M, R.T.O, O & M.T.O, Called also Mons the Queen, 2nd Mo. E. a Division Eau. Received orders a transfer in 8th unit to MERICOURT. Obtained a 3rd Co. about further transfer of lorries in area. 60 Foden light in our area. Began attachment of materials required from La Hayue (III Corps) dumps.	
	2nd		Visited hrs area and went over BERNY section with all CRE 35th & Div - Shrine & vild. Engaged in task of Tubing Planks and Resting required in our area. Subsection Out of St Simeche Gode - daily required for 10 days. Saw 7th E, D.L.I. at BAISIEUX. Saw 446 - 7078.	
	3rd			
	4th			
	5th			
	6th			
	7th		O.C. 446 M.T. Co, brought and material & new area - reinforced for relief of March 11-13th.	
	8th		arrange orders and Canvas was being - Saw O.C. 7th M.T.Co.	
	9th		To our area with Capt Watkins on Saturday and Platoon Dumps.	
	10th		Siftens area - passing by MERICOURT to the Sign boards - much delay.	
	11th		To our area to water through - Saw 446 may Coys at FOUCAM COURT arranges for with Watkins BERNY sector.	
	12th		To our area - Mareulan les Buffay, la Hayne and then to later one Mt stn 36-oes Rail Cut. 446 M.T Co Relieve French Corps 35th & 36th Div -	
LA BOIRSELLE Reg C 5.6 Sheet 62D).	13th		To Minister P.C Gabrielle self to Quartier CRE 36th Div-	
	14th		La Marcelcan - RE 3rd Corp WSWS - La Hayne and Meaulte. Sent in reports distribution of work for RE to Picardie.	

Army Form C. 2118.

VOL XXIII

164.

WAR DIARY
or
INTELLIGENCE SUMMARY

(Erase heading not required.)

Place	Date	Hour	Summary of Events and Information	Remarks and references to Appendices
LA BARAQUETTE	Feb 15	1417	Sent in work reports for 12th M.U.	
R.qe 85 (Sheet 62d)	16		Saw Lt. VAN & arrangements requirements for hutting, camps etc. THAW begins	
	17.18		THAW still in progress.	
	19		Roads came in as to Roads which kept in repair by sevens and trunk.	
	20		Visited Roads water Dumps at BOIS TOUFFO with Captain K'Ella. Saw CRE 1 Div. Dron harn Program and Thence Officer in charge (Wells) Pumps on area.	
	21		Visited BERAY Suter - CTs on bus. - Saw drawings of CT. II also have proposed Tramway to Petroleum Trench. Orders given to GABRIELLE, 2nd & 3rd Section. No Tramways for evening. Hutting definitely blue scale, 6 at Piccinini Battalion under orders of CRE. 1st Place Plans at Authors (Hutting Areas).	
	22		Tramway Col. own dining out work. Lunch in Officer Q.S. & hen Q.S. at P.C. Gabrielle (Tudoth).	
P.C. GABRIELLE M2c a Corbie-ont (Sheet 62c)	23		Visited Sw Hop. - Preliminary warnings received by SG Dir.	
	24		Travel HQ to P.C. Gabrielle. Touchline hurricane-lamps will (So II from t.	
	25			
	26		Rearranges for House Officer the Central House. Instruction for relief issues more in detail. Reliefs all afternoon.	

Army Form C. 2118.

WAR DIARY
or
INTELLIGENCE SUMMARY

(Erase heading not required.)

VOL XXIII
1655

Place	Date	Hour	Summary of Events and Information	Remarks and references to Appendices
P.C. GRIBEAUVAL	27		Attended CO's III Corps conference of CREs at CHUIGNOLLES. Major Luc Queen returned.	
	28		Bew round & CofR's line with Capt'n Glubb. Saw Thurs. line between with as also explosion of Bois Bismarck. Recons. reverse preparation in view of an advance. Events are entitched to tours. Salvage work, bathing. Thunder. Taking in hostile but-ends thin.	
			J Anderson Maj. R.E. CRE 50th D.	
			1.3.17	

Vol 23

Original

SECRET

War · Diary
Of
C·R·E
50ᵀᴴ (Northumbrian) Divⁿ R·E
Volume · XXIV

March. 1917.

Army Form C. 2118.

WAR DIARY
or
INTELLIGENCE SUMMARY
(Erase heading not required.)

Vol XXIV   16G

Place	Date	Hour	Summary of Events and Information	Remarks and references to Appendices
P.C. BARRIERE (Mond Central) Sheet 62c.	March 1st.		Lt. Col. Roberts OC 7 Sqdn. D.L.I. called 9.30 am. Shewed him detailed front, work reports etc. Afternoon shewed him our trench maps OC 7 Bn. 1st (Pioneer) also heard him — saw afternoon but briefly — tried properly to discuss heavy mist. Lt. Col. Roberts to stay. Received men to relieve 6–9.	
	2nd.		Stones places at our disposal for company stores. Work began on road to Bde. H.Q. Francis heap, he queen ware [?] Batt. Commanders even at ADERSTOT. Old and new capbells went towards BOEN & Chevaliers Bumps.	
	3rd.		Went round R.Bd. front with OC 1st Sqdn. — Saw all work in hand — Brig ordered replacements. Introduced him, Huttor, GS, road to BOEN and Gauthier. Received order that Pinelin up as a trench tomorrow. Visited 7 D.L.I.	
	4th.		Visited 1st Bn a-fresh with ONE Sqdn. Do. — Saw all work in hand and men whilst intermediate him in trenches. Saw Major the Captain Heycock, OC hs.3 Sec. returned by ambulance. Letters and Capt. he Entier Commanding half that 7 D.L.I. was taken into hospital. Damaged knee very clear. Returned in bad spirits and stays by Captain.	
	5th.		Saw in morning — Too little rain. Thrice he [?] was in warning from Seven Huey[?] at Aubers. Adjt. Lt. D.L.I. Crees. Lieutenant. Lt. Varey 7 D.L.I. acting report to Lord Stores to A.Seuillie trash, which shell heard to 9th 7 D.L.I. has been taken to — sent to train. O.Q.S. & transport to come 1.0 Common and 6th D.L.I.	

Army Form C. 2118.

WAR DIARY
or
INTELLIGENCE SUMMARY
(Erase heading not required.)

Vol XXIV. 16?

Place	Date	Hour	Summary of Events and Information	Remarks and references to Appendices
P.C. GABRIELLE	March 6.		Completed arrangement for handing over to CRE 59th Div.	
	7.		Dumps handed over - also plans for the C.W. line.	
	8.		Sent in memorandum scheme for roads, tramlines, water supply and hutting in the event of an advance.	
	9.		Moved to CHALLOI. MERICOURT - 0/S on (M)S. Rather all composed along 7" D.L.I.	
MERICOURT S/SOMME	10.		Saw Tom Major BAYONVILLERS, WARFUSSEE and MORCOURT - some leave. Saw GE at Corps HQ. He liked him completely. Saw 446 Co. and went to Petit Blangy to see 7th D.L.I.	
			447 Co. - 7th R.D.L.I. - Cadres at Belloy Dompierre(han) Nesson (huts). Saw Tom Major BAYONVILLERS - Cadres in CE and Mahmoud Wares Sir Robt Blangy huts. Saw Billy Foster.	
	11.		Roads very bad. Sam all Company Commanders re Training Programme - also Haven 16 in 157 Bde. Saw Tom Major HAMEL in 3 Nissen huts - rain to Nottie Board drinking water etc. Fine but cloudy - mild. Lorry traffic stopped.	
	13		Wrote day - visits Petit Blangy - Huts in occupation; saw all Companies except 446. Returns at Div Q School MORIGNY - visited Bocan Rifle range.	
	14.			
	15.		Rode round and saw all 3 Companies.	
	17.		Fine showery day - Heard S.E. Div had advanced to Marshall A. Villes Carbonnel Road. Eqs.	

Army Form C. 2118.

168

WAR DIARY
or
INTELLIGENCE SUMMARY
(Erase heading not required.)

Place	Date	Hour	Summary of Events and Information	Remarks and references to Appendices
MERICOURT SUR SOMME	March 18"		Visited 7" D.L.I. & completed arrangements for hym dismantling 6 Adrian huts at Camp 57 & 25". Informed C.E. III Corps accordingly. Saw 50th Div Q.M.G. & made arrangements for premises & transport required. Fine.	
	19"		Fan. Vid. Mull. Visited 7" Pld. Coy.	
	20"		Cold & showery. Visited Camp 57 with Capt. 11" D.L.I. to see progress being made with dismantling huts.	
	21"		Attended address given by G.O.C. 18th Corps to Officers 50th Div.	
	22"		Cold.	
	23"		Cold. Snow showers. Visited Camp 57 & arranged for Shyrne Dump.	
	24"		Fine. Vid. cold. Visited all Pld Coy & field Coys.	
	25"		Fine. Cold. Held Reunion & 7" Pld Coy.	
	26"		Fine. Lt. Col. C.W. SINGER, C.M.G., D.S.O., N.Z. returned & resumed duties C.R.E. 50" Div.	
	27"		Wet. Visited all 3 Fld. Coys. and Pioneer Bat.	
	28"		Wet, showery. Making arrangements for move.	
	29"		Cold, fine. Inspected 7" Fld. Co. Advance Class of Instruction on Pontoon Bridges.	
	30"		Wet. Visited 4/5 & 1st Divisional Areas.	
	31"		Wet. Visited 3 Fld. Coys.	
MORLIENS HQ 10013			Div. H.Q. arrived.	

A. Singer
Lt. Col. R.
C.R.E. 50" Div

Original.

SECRET.

WAR DIARY
of
C. R. E.,
50th (Northumbrian) Divisional Royal Engineers.

Volume No. XXV.

APRIL, 1917.

WAR DIARY
or
INTELLIGENCE SUMMARY

Army Form C.2118

Vol. XXV.

169

Place	Date	Hour	Summary of Events and Information	Remarks and references to Appendices
MOLLINS.	1/4/17.		Visited all three field Companies in morning.	
AU BOIS.	2-4-17		Visited O.C. 150 I.B. in afternoon.	
	3-4-17		Moved to BEAUVAL. Visited 7th Fd Cy.	
	4-4-17		Moved to BUQUEMAISON. Lt Col Aspin M.V.O. newly appointed as C.E. XII Corps.	
RAMECOURT.	5-4-17		Moved to RAMECOURT.	
RAMECOURT	6-4-17		Nothing to report. Visited 7th Fd Cy.	
	7-4-17		Moved to ROELLECOURT. Major McLaren R.E. O.C. 7th Fd Cy moved to assume duties of 2nd I/C C.R.E.	
	8-4-17		Going to LE CAUROY.	
LE CAUROY	9-4-17		Visited C.E. XVIII Corps and Corps dump at LAHERLIERE. Lt Col Robbins R.E. arrived and assumed duties of C.R.E. Major Hughes returned to his Coy.	
BERNAVILLE	10-4-17		Moved to BERNAVILLE.	
ARRAS	11-4-17		Moved to ARRAS: visited C.R.E. 14th Divn at MERCUS, div'l dumps at DAINVILLE, and FOSSEUX-RONVILLE.	
Do	12-4-17		Reconnoitred forward roads, + visited WANCOURT. 7th Field Co. allotted to 151st Inf. Bde. Visited work in hand on roads, overland track WANCOURT etc: issued orders to prepare dugout + shelter accomm. for 1 Bde. in + near WANCOURT.	
	14-4-17		Visited C.E. VII Corps re roads, water + stores. Motor Corps dump at SAULTY: R.E.	
"	16-4-17		Battalions intended to each Inf. Bde. for liaison services.	

WAR DIARY or INTELLIGENCE SUMMARY

Army Form C. 2118.

Place	Date	Hour	Summary of Events and Information	Remarks and references to Appendices
ARRAS	16-4-17		Visited work in progress on roads and shelters; rec'd orders to prepare supply at N.7 to 4-7 for adv'd Div'l H.Q. Weather bad.	
do	17-4-17		Visited works in progress on roads & shelters - weather bad.	
do	18-4-17		do do do do do	
do	19-4-17		Conference at Div'l H.Q. in m'ng; Office in afternoon: then conference at office of C.E. VII Corps 5.30 - 7.30.	
do	20-4-17		Visited works in progress.	
do	21-4-17		Office: preparing orders for R.E. & Pioneers for spading: conference of Field Co. Cmdrs & O.C. Pioneers, to explain work to be done.	
do	22-4-17		Visited works in progress during night 21/22. Lt CHAPLIN RE killed on duty: 6 O.R. killed and 5 O.R. wounded during night 21/22.	
Advanced Div'l H.Q.	23-4-17		To adv'd D.H.Q. for early m'ng attack & afternoon attack on the line east of WANCOURT. 3 Companies R.E. & Pioneers continued work on Hellers cellars on dugout WANCOURT, 2 Ft H.Q., 2 R.A.P. aid Posts TILLOY-WANCOURT road, and Approaches thereto, construction of large rest stakes Nr. Pratzel, lengthening trenches EE of WANCOURT, running alongside above & demolition road approaches thereto, repair of track WANCOURT, & widening of corpse scout pond-line & construction of road E.E. of WANCOURT and Examination of dugouts; reconnaissance of road to overhead mile, & railway track; dug outs found at night in B.19.a (650x) Dullidry men to to Col. 16th Gun collector of work dealing LOUVERVAL.	
do	24-4-17			
do	25-4-17		Night 24/25, completion of Morse passes for use by Pioneers on Hillside and to Col. 16th Gun collection of work specifying LOUVERVAL, 8 p.m. self to MONT Péréire on night 25/26 Péréire tunnel 650' trench 3rd Company next Gillett at COUTERELLE East of WANCOURT Tower.	
COUTERELLE	26-4-17			

Army Form C. 2118.

WAR DIARY
or
INTELLIGENCE SUMMARY

(Erase heading not required.)

Instructions regarding War Diaries and Intelligence Summaries are contained in F. S. Regs., Part II. and the Staff Manual respectively. Title Pages will be prepared in manuscript.

Place	Date	Hour	Summary of Events and Information	Remarks and references to Appendices
COUTERELLE	27-4-17		Rest billets, writing up report on operations April 13th - 26th: copy attached marked "Z".	1/1.
do.	28-4-17		Rest billets	
do.	29-4-17		Meeting of field Cn Commanders: to discuss lessons of recent operations and instruction to be carried out during the future of rest.	
do.	30-4-17		Visited 7th Field Co. R.E. at HUMBERCOURT. Forwarded A.F. W.3121 to Div H.Q. for immediate reserves in connection with operations during period April 13th to 26th —	

H. Rathbone
Lieut Col.
CRE 38th Divn.

38/4/17

REPORT on part taken by R.E. and Pioneers in OPERATIONS near WANCOURT between April 14th and 26th, 1917.

Head Quarters,
    50th Division.

1. On April 13th, R.E. work in WANCOURT area was taken over from C.R.E., 14th Division.

    On April 14th, the 3 Field Companies moved from ARRAS into bivouac, 446th and 447th (Northumbrian) Field Coys near BEAURAINS, 7th Field Coy, between NEUVILLE VITASSE and WANCOURT.

2. The work executed on the Division's programme included the following jobs :-

ROADS.

(a) Formation of new road for horse transport at West end of TILLOY - BEAURAINS Road, where for ¼ mile the original road was non-existent, by reason of enemy having dug a traversed trench down it.
    In order to get the road open for H.T. at the earliest moment possible, stone and brick from ruined buildings in BEAURAINS were used; Road was used by traffic after 2 days work. The work involved in maintenance was very heavy, owing to wet weather and the soil upon which the roadway was formed being earth.

(b) The completion of diversion round the crater on the above TILLOY - BEAURAINS Road and its widening to take double line of traffic.

(c) The filling in of shell holes, trenches, strengthening of bridges, drainage and general repairs to road and the scraping of mud off surface.

(d) Similar work to above on the TILLOY - WANCOURT Road. This was heavy work, owing to wet weather during the first week, the use by Heavy Artillery and H.A. ammunition lorries of the Northern half of the road, and enemy shell fire, which was particularly severe in and near WANCOURT.

(e) Maintenance of the RONVILLE - BEAURAINS Road for the first week, viz; until C.E., VII Corps assumed responsibility and even then the Division continued to supply 2 Companies of Infantry on this work.

WATER.

(a) A little work was done at the Water Point on the RONVILLE - BEAURAINS Road, before responsibility was assumed by C.E., VII Corps.

(b) 7 Wells were found, opened up, repaired and pumps put in order in WANCOURT.

ACCOMMODATION.

(a) Cellars and dug-outs were located, cleared and repaired in WANCOURT, thereby providing accommodation for 850 men.
    As WANCOURT was under enemy observation and shell fire, the above was a trying job and as about 8 cellars and dug-outs were damaged daily by enemy shell fire, the maintenance of the work was arduous and involved a fair number of casualties.

(b)............

(b) 59 Splinter proof shelters, each to hold 12 men were constructed ½ mile West of WANCOURT, thus providing accommodation for 708 men.

(c) A (double entrance) small deep dug-out was made in bank East of WANCOURT for H.Q. of 2 Battalions.
This site was under enemy observation from GUEMAPPE; and the party executing the work, suffered heavy casualties.

(d) 4 small shelters were constructed near the above dug-outs for use as Regl. Aid Posts.

(e) 2 dug-outs were converted for use as Advanced Divisional Hd. Quarters, and huts built for C.R.E., "G" and R.A. clerks, cookhouses, etc.,

COMMUNICATION, other than roads.

(a) Overland tracks were marked out from BEAURAINS to Adv. Divl. Hd Qrs and thence to TILLOY - WANCOURT Road.

(b) 3 Overland tracks were marked out East of WANCOURT, after the advance of 23rd/24th April, to facilitate movement.

(c) All Overland tracks notice-boarded and provided with illuminated box signs.

(d) Road and Track/Junctions, East of WANCOURT signboarded and marked with location map co-ordinates.

DEFENCE WORK.

(a) 200 Knife rests were provided for use East of WANCOURT after battle of 23rd April, and materials for 1,000 yards of double apron b.wire obstacle and transported to vicinity of TOWER.

(b) 2 Strong Points were made and good wire obstacle put up in front of these and along whole Divisional width of VII Corps Strong Point line, i.e., NIGER Trench from N.16.b.3.2. to N.22.b.0.4.

(c) 220 Infantry and 6 Sections R.E. dug 650 yards Support Trench (4 to 4½ ft. deep) on night 24th/25th April from 0.19.c.9.9. to 0.19.a.9.7.
Most of the R.E. had done a full days work prior to going out on this job.

(d) 1,100 yards of b.wire obstacle was put out by Pioneers in front of old German Support trench 0.19.a.2.9. - N.30.b.6.8. on 25th/26th April.

(e) Traced out a jumping off line for infantry assembling for attack on night 13th/14th April, 1,000 yards long.

BRIDGING.

(a) The masonary bridge over River COJEUL having been shaken by shell fire, was strengthened with timbering, while under enemy observation.

(b) As the above bridge was narrow and carried the only road available for use by the Division, it was decided to build a diversion alongside it, to allow of double way traffic and prevent interruption of traffic should the other bridge be destroyed.
This involved the building of two bridges to carry the road diversion over ditch and stream alongside the old road.(Span 15 feet and 22 feet)
The collection and transport of the necessary materials had

to be done at night; the Bridges, R.S.joists on a crib work centre support were constructed in 16 hours and a total of 120 yards approach road on each side of stream thereto completed with corduroy, (and partly bricked over) in another 9 hours.

Both these new bridges are fit to carry any wheeled traffic including tractors and heaviest Artillery.

The strengthened masonary bridge will carry any wheeled or motor traffic up to and including 6" guns.

(c) 3 footbridges for Infantry were made over R, COJEUL and approach tracks formed and marked.

RECONNAISSANCE.

R.E. Officers made reconnaissances in area captured from enemy on 23rd/24th April, of roads, railway track, dug-outs, bridges, etc.,

Notice boards erected at road junctions.

DEMOLITIONS.

An enemy M.G. Emplacement in Farm adjoining WANCOURT TOWER was blown up by 1l Lieut. LITTLEWOOD, R.E. on the afternoon of 16th April; a charge of 70 lbs guncotton was needed to destroy this M.G. Emplacement, which was a strong reinforced concrete structure.

By a counterattack on night 16th/17th April, the enemy regained possession for a short time of the Farm and TOWER, and eviction by the Infantry Brigade was certainly facilitated by the previous destruction of this M.G. Emplacement.

MISCELLANEOUS.

Repairs were effected, during operations, to cellars and roads near Reserve Brigade H.Q. at RONVILLE, damaged by shell fire.

3.

TRANSPORT and MATERIALS:

The lack of lorry transport, combined with the distance behind the line of Army R.E.Park (at MONDICOURT), and Corps R.E. Depot(SAULTY) and Corps forward Dump (DAINVILLE) made the supply to the Division of R.E. Stores and materials a matter of difficulty.

Consequently, the Division had to depend chiefly on Stores, etc., available locally e.g., captured German Stores and for road work, on bricks and soft stone from ruined villages.

For the conveyance of such Stores and materials, the transport available was that belonging to the Field Companies and Pioneers, supplemented by 20 G.S. and Limbered Wagons from the Division.

It is thought that under such circumstances, responsibility for maintenance of roads that are used by M.T. and Heavy Artillery should not fall upon a Division in the line.

It is accordingly suggested that Divisions in the line should be responsible for roads forward of "lorry limit" only, and it would tend to greater efficiency of the road repairs effected by Divisional labour, if the Corps would undertake to deliver to the "lorry limit", such road repair materials as are needed and available

e.g........

4.

   e.g., Road metal,
      Fascines,
      Sleepers or beech slabs,
      Split pitprops or poles, (for corduroy).

  It is thought that the same principal is applicable to the supply of R.E. Stores generally: viz, that the Corps should get them forward to Divisions in the line, to avoid Divisions having to send back for Stores.

4. ATTACHMENT OF SMALL INFANTRY PARTY TO FIELD COMPANIES.

  A platoon of the 8th Bn. D.L.I. was attached to the 7th Field Co, R.E. with great benefit to that Company.

  It is thought that the attachment of 2 Infantry Platoons to each Field Company during operations is most desirable.

  The principal has received G.H.Q., approval, vide pamphlet G.S.145 page 14, Section VIII and page 8, Section 111 (e).

5. CASUALTIES.

  During the period under review, the following casualties were incurred :-

Unit.	Killed, Officers.	O.R.	Wounded & Gassed. Officers	O.R.	Total.
7th Field Co,	1.	7.	1.	22.	31.
446th (Nbn) Fd Co, R.E.	-	-	-	-	-
447th (Nbn) Fd Co, R.E.	-	1.	-	2.	3.
TOTAL.	1.	8.	1.	24.	34.

6. RECOMMENDATIONS.

  The services of the undermentioned are brought to notice for the excellence of the work done by them, in order of merit in each Company :-

    11 Lieut. H.A.Baker, R.E.)
    Sergt. Farrer,   )
    Corpl. Cutts,   ) 7th Field Co, R.E.
    Sapper Southern,   )
     " Edwards,   )
    11 Lieut. Littlewood, R.E.)

    11 Lieut. Williams,   )
    Sapper M.Burn,   ) 446th (Nbn) Field
    11 Lieut. Law,   )   Co, R.E.
    Corpl. Foreman,   )

  For the above A.F.W.3121 are being submitted for consideration for bestowal of immediate reward.

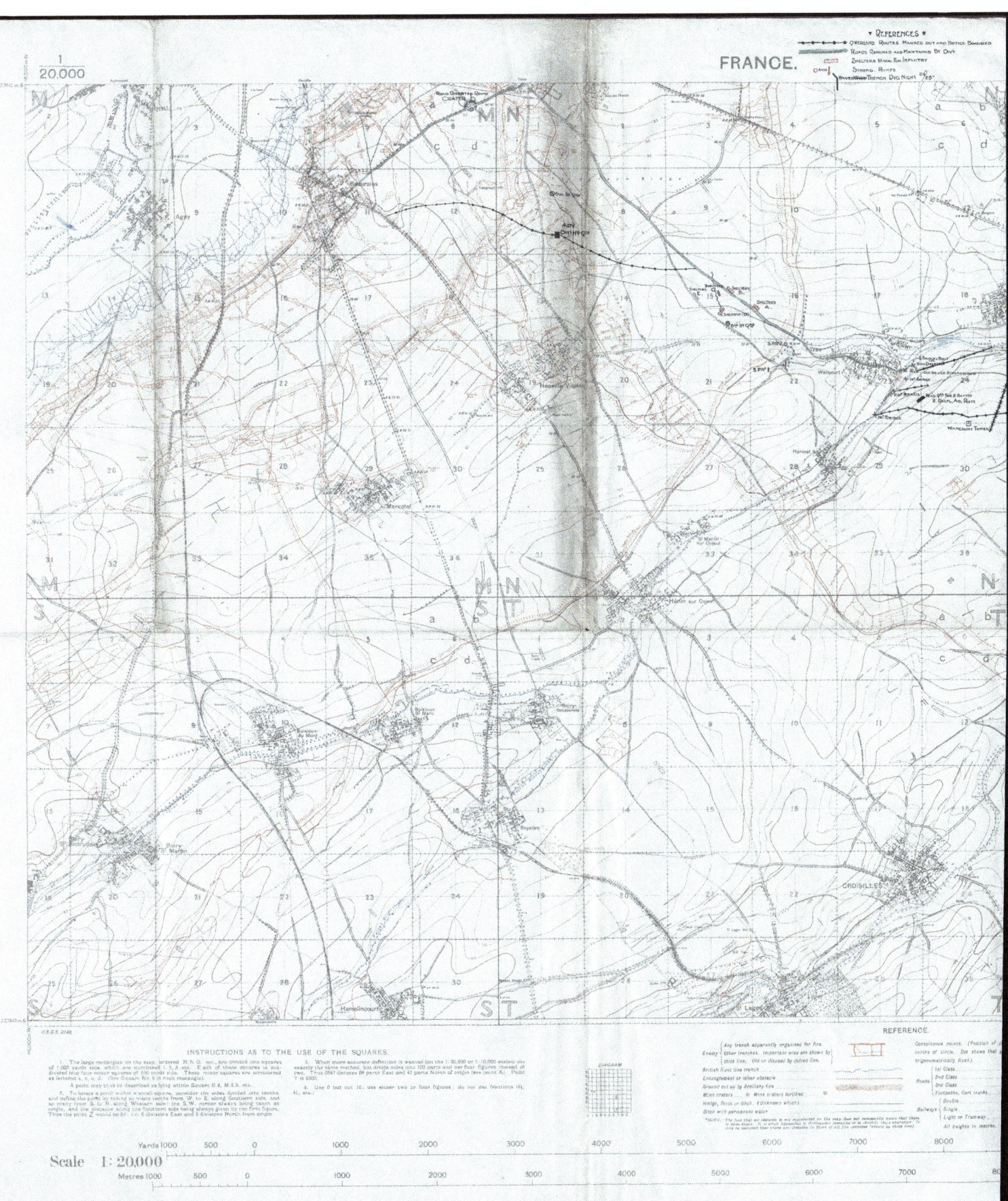

Original.

SECRET.
****

WAR DIARY

OF

C. R. E.

50th (Northumbrian) Division.

Volume No: XXVI.

May, 1917.

Army Form C. 2118.

WAR DIARY or INTELLIGENCE SUMMARY

(Erase heading not required.)

Vol. XXVI. 1/2

Place	Date	Hour	Summary of Events and Information	Remarks and references to Appendices
COUTURELLE	1-5-17		Received: Visited Corps H.Q. BRETENCOURT with H.Q. VII. & more Corps H.Q. to NEUVILLE-VITASSE & then went to NEUVILLE-VITASSE to select site. Arranged for finish of 2 Armstrong huts & 16 tarpaulin shelters from RIVIÈRE to SHOLTY. O.C. 7 Field Co. R.E. called to have account returned for. D.H.Q. explained to him.	
COUTURELLE	2-5-17		Moved to Adv. B.H.Q. at M.18.d. 6/4 east of BEAURAINS – NEUVILLE VITASSE Road, where camp was established by 7th Co. R.E. in very quick time, & was 1/4 mile march. Accounts provided as follows :– 16 tarpaulin shelters / 10 bell tents / 1 marquee / 2 Armstrong huts / 4 cookhouses / 4 latrines	
NEUVILLE VITASSE	3-5-17		At 3.45 a.m. attack by VII Corps in conjunction with an attack by I Corps of 5th Div. in Reserve. Morning & evening attacks unsuccessful. 3rd Army.	
do	4-5-17		Reconnoitres to return to COUTURELLE leaving 7 Field Co. R.E. to take care of camp. Sir. H.Q. fitted NEUVILLE VITASSE in afternoon.	
COUTURELLE	5-5-17		Regt bills: 446 HQ field Company marching back to left table at CAMBARN and POMMERA. 11th POTTUS RE. & left of O.R. arrived MONDICOURT.	
do	6-5-17		Visited 3rd Field Survey Co. R.E. for maps & inform. about survey road etc.	
do	7-5-17		Afternoon visited DENT and GRIEVE for Commanders in R.E. Visited the 3 Field Companies at NEUVILLE VITASSE (7th), POMMERA (447) and CAMBARN (446). 7th F.Co. closes to HUMBERCOURT.	
do	8-5-17		Weather wet: 7th Field Co. on move to HUMBERCOURT.	
do	9-5-17		Field Co. Commander to H.Q. to discuss proposal to replace platoon Officers by Camp' Sarjeants, Officers Class I. 7th Field Co. R.E. arrived HUMBERCOURT.	

WAR DIARY
or
INTELLIGENCE SUMMARY.
(Erase heading not required.)

Army Form C. 2118.

Place	Date	Hour	Summary of Events and Information	Remarks and references to Appendices
LUCHEUX	10-5-17		Oxford to LUCHEUX. Weather fine.	
Do	11-5-17		Visited the 3 Companies. Weather fine.	
Do	12-5-17		Weather fine, but oppressive. Circulars issued re Sanitation, to Companies.	
Do	13-5-17		Do Do Discussed training with O.C. 7th C.F.R.E.	
Do	14-5-17		Inspected billets of 446th and 447th Field Companies, at CHAUMESNIL and POMMERA.	
Do	15-5-17		" " 7th Field C.R.E. at HUMBERCOURT. Park visited at inspection. Weather cooler. Lt.Col. BAKER R.E. Summoned to explained to Field Coy Commanders. O.C. 7th Field C.R.E. from Hospital. Corps Commander awarded Military Medals, 2 to 7th and 3 to 446th Coy.	
Do	16-5-17		Weather colder. Used in afternoon: arranged for making of 2000 Evidence Support sticks for dist at A.T.C.oy workshops SAULTY, 447th Coy supplying Labour.	
Do	17-5-17		Visited A.T.C. workshops at SAULTY, where Evidence Sticks were being made. 446th and 447th Field Companies moving to SOUASTRE and FONQUEVILLERS areas. H.Q. BAKER to H.Q. R.E.	
Do	18-5-17		Visited by O.C. 7th Field C.R.E. 7th Field Co. putter HUMBERCOURT: 446th Field Company putter SOUASTRE FONQUEVILLERS area for DOUCHY: 7th C.oyand MONCHY: 447th Coy re SOUASTRE	
Do and BEAUMETZ-les-LOGES	19-5-17		Self H.Q. quitted COUTURELLE and moved to BEAUMETZ-les-LOGES. Weather fine. 30th Divn. temporarily at disposal of VII Corps.	

Army Form C. 2118.

WAR DIARY
or
INTELLIGENCE SUMMARY.
(Erase heading not required.)

Instructions regarding War Diaries and Intelligence Summaries are contained in F. S. Regs., Part II. and the Staff Manual respectively. Title pages will be prepared in manuscript.

Place	Date	Hour	Summary of Events and Information	Remarks and references to Appendices
BEAUMETZ -les-LOGES	20-5-17		Accompanied by A.D.V.S. inspected the animals of 447th Field Co. R.E. (horse) at SOUASTRE & circular embodying results of inspection to all Co's.	14/4
do.	21-5-17		Visited 7th Field Co. at MINCHY-au-BOIS. Rain at night	
do.	22-5-17		Visited 446th Field Co. R.E. with A.D.V.S. and inspected horses. Co's at DOUCHY. Wet day	
do.	"		ii Lt BAKER proceeded on 21 days leave, & Capt McLELLAN on 10 day leave.	
do. and COUIN	23-5-17		Division less 149th Inf. Bde, reverts to XVIII Corps. Div. HQ. move from BEAUMETZ-les-LOGES to COUIN. Visited 447th Field Co. R.E. at SOUASTRE. Weather fine	
COUIN	24-5-17		7th Field Co. at GOMARCEMETZ and 446th Field Co at COIGNEUX. Visited 446th Field Co's and 447th Field Co. at COIGNEUX and SOUASTRE. 7th Field Co. moved from GOMARCEMETZ to SOUASTRE.	
do.	25-5-17		Capt. BOWMER to GE XVIII Corps: remained at HQ awig to strained leg. weather fine	
do.	26-5-17		Lt No 7 R.E. Advanced park visited the 3 Field Companies - weather fine. Military Cross awarded by F.M. CinC to ii Lt BAKER & LITTLEWOOD of 7th Field Co.R.E. and to ii Lt LAW and WILLIAMS of 446th Field Co. R.E.	
do.	27-5-17		Weather fine. Companies on church parades. SUNDAY.	
do.	28-5-17		" " Visited the 3 Field Companies.	

Army Form C. 2118.

WAR DIARY
or
INTELLIGENCE SUMMARY.
(Erase heading not required.)

Instructions regarding War Diaries and Intelligence Summaries are contained in F. S. Regs., Part II. and the Staff Manual respectively. Title pages will be prepared in manuscript.

Place	Date	Hour	Summary of Events and Information	Remarks and references to Appendices
COUIN	29-5-17		Inspection of Mounted Section & Transport of 7th Field Co. R.E. visited 447th Field Co. R.E. ½ Porter to R.E. H.Q. during absence on leave of the adjutant Capt POTTS [to ENGLAND 29-5-17]. Weather fine after rain at night.	
COUIN	30-5-17		Inspection of Mounted Section & Transport of 446th Field Co. R.E. visited Rifle range work in hand for 151st Infy Bde. Some showers.	
COUIN	31-5-17		Inspection of Transport of 447th Field Co. R.E. visited MONCHY-au-BOIS with S/Offrs re water supply. Arranged to fix one section of 447th Field Co. R.E. to MONCHY to improve water supply in 1-6-17 Weather fine	

Matthews
Lt Col R.E.
C.R.E. 50th Divn

1-6-17

Original.

SECRET.

WAR DIARY

OF

C. R. E.

50th (Northumbrian) Divisional Royal Engineers.

Volume XXVII.

June, 1917.

Army Form C. 2118.

WAR DIARY
or
INTELLIGENCE SUMMARY.
(Erase heading not required.)

Volume XXVII

Instructions regarding War Diaries and Intelligence Summaries are contained in F. S. Regs., Part II. and the Staff Manual respectively. Title pages will be prepared in manuscript.

Place	Date	Hour	Summary of Events and Information	Remarks and references to Appendices
COUIN	1-6-17		Inspection of dismounted pltoon of Signal Company, billets, harness &c in a.m. Visited 131st Inf. Bde Rifle Ranges cantonedes by 7th Field Co and Bde in valley N of COIGNEUX, & inspected drivers of 447th Field Co. R.E. at SOUASTRE. Weather fine.	
COUIN	2-6-17		Inspection of Signal Company Transport in a.m. at COUIN	
COUIN	3-6-17		Visited MONCHY-au-BOIS with OC 447th Field Co. R.E. re water supply; visited OC 7th Field Co. R.E. at SOUASTRE. Meeting at HQ of Field and Signal Company Commanders in afternoon. Notes TARRAN GIRDER BRIDGE at COIGNEUX.	
COUIN	4-6-17		Visited 7th & 447th Field Companies. 2 sections of 447th to MONDICOURT for bridging instruction. Lt SLATTERY to ENGLAND on leave.	
COUIN	5-6-17		Visited SOUASTRE, BAYENCOURT and COIGNEUX. Lt INGLIS to ENGLAND on leave. Lt Col RATHBONE and Maj MCQUEEN awarded D.S.O. in King's Birthday Honours list. Visited 2 sections of 447th Field Co. bridging at MONDICOURT. Latest night ree? Orders to detail a Field Co. for employment under OC. VII Corps: 446th Co detailed.	
COUIN	6-6-17		CE VII Corps telephoned 2 sections will suffice for work of dismantling Nissen huts at MONCHET. Nos 1 & 2 sections of 446 C. marched off in afternoon. Visited 7th Coy in afternoon.	

A6945 Wt. W1142/M1180 350,000 12/16 D. D. & L. Forms/C, 2118/14.

Army Form C. 2118.

WAR DIARY
or
INTELLIGENCE SUMMARY.
(Erase heading not required.)

Instructions regarding War Diaries and Intelligence Summaries are contained in F. S. Regs., Part II. and the Staff Manual respectively. Title pages will be prepared in manuscript.

Place	Date	Hour	Summary of Events and Information	Remarks and references to Appendices
COUIN	6-6-17 (continued)		Capt: Thelewan 5/446th C° and Lt PYEMONT of Signal C° awarded Military Cross in King's Birthday Honours list. Weather sultry: thunderstorm & rain.	
Do.	7-6-17		Visited 7th and 446th Field Companies. Do. Do. Do. Do.	
Do.	8-6-17		Visited Dentist at GAUDIEMPRE; visited 2 sections of 447th R.E. Bridging at MONDICOURT. Some rain in p.m.	
			MONDICOURT: attended 7th C° Sports at SOUASTRE.	
Do.	9-8-17		Visited 2 sections of 447th C° Bridging at MONDICOURT with O.C. 7th C°. & visited section of 447th C° at MONCHY-au-BOIS. Visited 446th C° R.E. at COIGNEUX. Weather fine.	
Do.	10-6-17		Visited H.Q. 18th Div. with G.S.O. I	
Do.	11-6-17		Visited MONDICOURT. Heavy thunderstorm in early morning.	
Do.	12-6-17		Visited 18th Div. H.Q. and trenches with A.D.O.S. and C.R.E. 18th Div.	
Do.	13-6-17		Capt: CUMPSTIE returned from leave to U.K. Visited 446th Field C.R.E. stores.	
Do.	14-6-17		Visited 7th, 447th & 446th 7.6.a.m. Shewed round aft. of 28th Div. meeting of Field C° Commanders in p.m. re taking over from 18th Div.	
Do.	15-6-17		Saw 447th and 7th Field Companies re lines of march to MENIN, with Div. Comdr. & 3 Companies move to 15th Div. area near HENIN. Weather hot. Do. Do.	
Do.	16-6-17		Visited C.R.E. 18th Div. re taking over. Do. Do.	

Army Form C. 2118.

WAR DIARY
or
INTELLIGENCE SUMMARY.
(Erase heading not required.)

Instructions regarding War Diaries and Intelligence Summaries are contained in F. S. Regs., Part II. and the Staff Manual respectively. Title pages will be prepared in manuscript.

Place	Date	Hour	Summary of Events and Information	Remarks and references to Appendices
COUIN	17-6-17		Rest billets. Coys in 8th Divl H. Area.	
BOISLEUX-AU-MONT	18-6-17		Marched from COUIN to BOISLEUX-au-MONT. Inspected the 3 Field Companies in p.m.: showers & some thunder.	
Do	19-6-17		Thunderstorm early. No infy working parties for 3rd Coy. No infy working parties for 3rd Coy. Visited Left Picquets. Brigadier saw CO Cmdt of 446 & 447, & OC Pioneers & OC Tunn. Coy. Recon.	
Do	20-6-17		Walked this "Second" (= Corps) line. Visited 7th Coy dump for R.F.A. Visited J.O.C. Right Bde. Visited 446 & 7th Companies. Rain in evening.	
Do	21-6-17		To see OC Pioneers, then to Right Bde H.Q., then round trenches with OC 446 Coy, then to Left Bde H.Q., then to S.H.Q.	
Do	22-6-17		Visited water points with McWhort & inspected dump. Saw OC 446 Coy re his share in operations of 25/26 June.	
Do	23-6-17		To Right Bde HQ in Hindenburg Line later fwd piece re Coy demolition party for operation of 25/26, & detailing of 2 trained men to him for prettipping etc of front & support lines. Then round trenches. Visited SP No 28, then to meeting of OC Pioneers & Field Companies: discussed progress of works, future plans & necessity for concentration of effort on CTs etc.	

WAR DIARY or INTELLIGENCE SUMMARY

Army Form C. 2118.

Place	Date	Hour	Summary of Events and Information	Remarks and references to Appendices
BOISLEUX-au-MONT	24-6-17		Accompanied CE. VII Corps in his inspection of Corps Defence Line and of HQ HENINEL-SWITCH. Weather fine.	
do	25-6-17		Visited attack demonstration at NOYELLE-CHATEAU with GSO II. Weather fine.	
do	26-6-17		Visited Dump Right Bde HQ with report to Demolition during Night 25/26. w/ which a RE demolition party took part (4th 6 Cs). Inspected trenches and all 3 Companies. Way Damp Dump & Trench Timber.	
do	27-6-17		Kill Lune at HQ all day till evening, then by car to CE VII Corps to discuss proposal to shut Corps Workshops. Ribemy.	
do	28-6-17		Stay home - at HQ till afternoon, then by car to ARRAS to see CRE 56th Divn re taking over. Huidertram (Army in evening).	
do	29-6-17		Kill Jone; by motor car to see CE VII Corps re RITZ Dump & have interior trenches near MERCATEL, then to LA HERLIERE Dump. Saw OC Pioneers in afternoon.	
do	30-6-17		Saw OC 7th Field Co. re new area to be taken over. Maj McEwan fixed for 1 Months Leave. Lt. BALDWIN joined 7th Field Co. Weather well. Awaited visit by Corps Works Supply Officer & CRE 21st Divn; neither arrived.	

Mattone
Lt Colonel
CRE 50th Divn

1-7-17

Original.

S E C R E T.

W A R D I A R Y

O F

C. R. E.

50th (Northumbrian) Divisional Royal Engineers.

Volume XXVIII.

July, 1917.

WAR DIARY
or
INTELLIGENCE SUMMARY.
(Erase heading not required.)

Army Form C. 2118.

Volume XXVIII

160

Place	Date	Hour	Summary of Events and Information	Remarks and references to Appendices
BAILEUL-au-MONT S.17.a.8.4.	1-7-17		Worked by a/s OC 7th Field Co. & by O/g CRE 21st Div.: explanation of takeover & work handed over in area transferred to 21st Div. Then by car to HQrs to get Hurling over notes etc. from CRE 36th Div. Dull & showery.	
Do	2-7-17		Quit handed over part of Southern Subsector to 21st Div. & took over part of 36th Div. front on our left. 7th Field Co from Back area Work to new Left Subsector, and the 446th Field Co. from old Right Subsector to Back area work.	
Do	3-7-17		Visited Left Subsector, & 7th Co. H.Q., both camps of Henry & Dunya ex MARLIERE. Coy slew practice. Weather fine.	
Do	4-7-17		Laid up. Went to 151 Bde H.Q, — 2 Reconnaissances of workland front at Left Subsector. Major PRATT resumed from leave to U.K.	
Do	5-7-17		Visited by CRE VII Corps. Troops. Water Supply Officer re taking over RITZ dumps, handing over La HERLIEZE dump & Water Supply Mercatel etc. Was laid up.	
Do	6-7-17		Cuff to La HERLIEZE to hand over dump to CRE Corps Troops & ditto to RITZ dump, also MERCATEL in Water front for horses. Weather fine but windy.	
Do	7-7-17		French Tramway Scheme prepared. Attended conference at Corps HQ with Mr. OLMS. Visited by Deputy J.D. Co. reference works. Thunderstorm during night 7/8th	

Army Form C. 2118.

WAR DIARY
or
INTELLIGENCE SUMMARY.
(Erase heading not required.)

Place	Date	Hour	Summary of Events and Information	Remarks and references to Appendices
BOIS-SUR-au-MONT	8-7-17		Wet Day. Major Plane & escort generally. Saw T.M.O re bed for heavy T.M.	151
Do	9-7-17		Worked in all morning for Army Tramway officer. On his arrival to MARICOURT & worked with him & OC 446 2nd Coy over route of proposed tramway	
Do	10-7-17		Visited 18th G.S. commanding Right & Reserve Bdes & broken front at MERCATEL. Visited by OC Pioneers. OC Twn's Coy re programme of work.	
Do	11-7-17		Visited new Left Bde HQ (under construction) at N.13.d. 5/3. Visited RF Commander Left Subsector MERCATEL waterfronts & 447 & 2nd Co broken lines. In afternoon held meeting of Coy Commanders re works. W/O LITTLEWOOD RE killed (shell) night 10/11 July.	
Do	12-7-17		Visited horse lines of 447 and 7th Field Company with SABWC. Preparing stations for RE work in event of an advance.	
Do	13-7-17		Visited Right Bde HQ. Mo Wan of # FOSTER Inn Suppin ? Sincere. Mc Bdeg # 34H HQ. Down RECESSES & visited Bde HQ on return	
Mooreyng				
Do	14-7-17		Visited Left Subsector, & inspected progress made in clearing route for tramline. Also inspected work done at Left Bde HQ. Wrote this summary.	
Do	15-7-17		Visited by SC 447 2nd Co RE. Visited OC Com's Reserve Bde re construction of connections. Visited water points on BEAURAINS - MERCATEL road. Reviewing schemes for advance.	

Army Form C. 2118.

WAR DIARY
or
INTELLIGENCE SUMMARY.
(Erase heading not required.)

162

Place	Date	Hour	Summary of Events and Information	Remarks and references to Appendices
BOISLEUX-au-MONT	16-7-17		Went round Companies HEADQUARTERS with ADKS VII Corps. Visited HENIN-HANCOURT LR and OC Pioneers	
Do	17-7-17		Visited OC FA Bde HQ. Inspected work in hand. Rifle subsectors, new trench dug from DEAD BOCHE RAP to BYKER SAP. Visited OC Pioneers, also 3 Field Co Cmdrs	
Do	18-7-17		Arranged with Pioneer programme for new trench diggings BYKER-OTTO and SWIFT & CHICKEN C.T. Met Div RE Officer. Rifle emplacements & dugouts.	
Do	19-7-17		447th Field Co to Back Area work from Right Subsector, changing places with 446th Field Co RE. Visited Left Subsector N of COJEUL R. & walked along Tramway tracks cleared to date. Visited Left Bde HQ.	
Do	20-7-17		Discussed MG dugouts with WE Bde R.O. Mailed in for Officer to Third Army Tramway. Office work. Visited by OC 447. 2 C of RE Reps. Work taken over & Rep's matters.	
Do	21-7-17		To WANCOURT. Noted work in progress in Left Subsector Right of R COJEUL. Visited Right Bde HQ, OC Pioneers, & also visited by OC 446 2 Co RE.	
Do	22-7-17		Visited broken down cast water pipes near INFANTRY hutting in ARRAS BATHHOUSE (?) hose lines of 447 and Div Signal Co RE.	
Do	23-7-17		To Left Bde HQ. Inspected work in hand, & saw OC Cmdrs. Met CE VII Corps. General TANNER by appt at 11·00 am with him looked at Louve Avre (?) of	

A6915 Wt. W14422/M1160 350,000 12/16 D. D. & L. Forms/C.2118/14.

WAR DIARY or INTELLIGENCE SUMMARY

Army Form C. 2118.

Place	Date	Hour	Summary of Events and Information	Remarks and references to Appendices
	23-7-17 (cont.)			
BOISLEUX-au-MONT			the Corps Defence Line; then walked towards SOUTHERN ⊥ with a view to his inspection of trenches near CAVALRY FARM. When within 50 yds of the way station at MORLIERE a HE Shell fell & burst within a few yards of Lieutenant Francis Charles TANNER behind right ear, penetrating deeply & mortally wounding him. He died within a few minutes. Reflex occurrences. I went to Corps & went to Corps HQ and forward effects & reported what had happened to Corps Commander. May return to 3rd Rear Station. Office; preparing report on defence alterations to pamphlet etc. Went to funeral of General TANNER in afternoon.	
Do	24-7-17		Visited left Bde H.Q. & Right Bde H.Q. Then to see OC 446 C⁰ and trenches then to trenches, thunderstorm in afternoon.	
Do	25-7-17		OC 447 3⁰ C⁰ re work in hand thunderstorm in afternoon.	
Do	26-7-17		Visited by OC 238 A.T.C. Rly. then to MERCATEL etc re winter holding sites for field Companies. Visited OC 7th D.L.I Pioneers. HENIN Rd dump. any to trenches + H.Q. Visited by OC 446 and OC 7 Field Companies.	
Do	27-7-17		To MARLIERE re tramway. then to trenches. Visited OC 446 2 ole C⁰ visited OC Pioneers & met Field C⁰s Commanders at HENIN dump. Visited by OC 181 Tun⁰ C⁰ Rly.	

WAR DIARY
or
INTELLIGENCE SUMMARY.
(Erase heading not required.)

Army Form C. 2118.

Place	Date	Hour	Summary of Events and Information	Remarks and references to Appendices
BOIS LEUX-au-MONT	28-7-17		OC 107 Field Co & OC Tramway tracklaying to HQ re special arrangements Organisation Recommitted by OC re Supply from Army Stores of recovered track of various lengths for jun[c]t[io]ns in Europour & the Collection from said different places, visited by OC of 7th F. Co. accompanied Matron to inspect Border camp sites & new water points near MERCATEL	
Do	29-7-17		Took S.M.C. to inspect animals of 446th, 7th May 14 and Civil Signal Coin RE Thunderstorm & train	
Do	30-7-17		Visited trench tramway & works N of R COJEUL; visited Rfylt BdeHQ & OC Pioneers; also inspected making of trench crossings at HENIN then to SHQ; visited by OC 32 LR operating Co & VII Corps F.E. re winter hutting. Held a meeting	
Do	31-7-17		Maj McQUEEN returned from leave; handing over to him before going on leave	

Maurice
Lieut-Col
CRE 56th Divn

Original.

SECRET.

WAR DIARY

of

C. R. E.

50th. (NORTHUMBRIAN) DIVISIONAL ROYAL ENGINEERS.

Volume. XXIX.

August 1917

WAR DIARY
or
INTELLIGENCE SUMMARY. AUGUST 1917. Vol. XXIX

Army Form C. 2118.

165

Place	Date	Hour	Summary of Events and Information	Remarks and references to Appendices
N. ROUSSEAUX DETACHMENT	1st		Visited 7th & 9th Corps: OC Reserve Army ships on 8th by Ed Wash in hand & Red Jewel when Labour available - Visited sites of Keep & ask Total 9th of Church & Forest Res: Plan inspection at 8th Corps	
	2nd		Visited Rd Construction & Water Sully at Bronson Siding - Visited OC 107 Ry Reinforcements WE - Supervision of Survey Parties & said the work first done if not as Eng DS should return the relaid to replacements - Visited Thornton Spur & Frostville Ey Sidings - Survey Parties July on Rd Congn Approx Seat on no further work tonight - Visited Power Station FOSTER. AM & OC Reserve family interviewed RE Powers	
	3rd		Wrote history site for RE Corps & Powers Charges by Labo - Received work & ordering Water RE?	
	4th		Inspected - Visited New Site which is inundated by OC 7th Corps & Infantry Tribunal re shortage found - Visited attempts at Impoverishing Father on of 764 Co of Relief 2	
		4.45 to 6.45. Railing Walker visit (7 & 1246) on 3rd site - Demonstration received pleased	
		5.00 pm - to 5th Tank Arm re Colin Rodentisement -	
	5th		Selected new site for RE Corps Powers into that immediately NE of Doney Reservoir & Amersen Tribunals - Visited RE 2nd Line Inspection on new Station sent out to 10.30 am - home to Luit - Brosnan Damm water connected safe to left down with night 9th July Jobs Damn up Belgian Maghiston: Received his letter gives I Daniason by: asked write Shelly & take on Laying Flame 6 Sept 14th -	
	6th		Visited 87th No. 107th Co re Labo Army were priorly on arrangements of OC Ry Co re location for Ry & administration of Forest of Dormancy?	

Army Form C. 2118.

WAR DIARY
or
INTELLIGENCE SUMMARY.

(Erase heading not required.)

August 1917 — Vol. XXIX

Place	Date	Hour	Summary of Events and Information	Remarks and references to Appendices
Nr. BOISLEUX AU MONT	7/8		Sgt Downs & 2 pupils went out on patrol & saw patrol of one officer & four Germans — killed 2 O.R.s & 4 O.R.s O.C. Pioneers — See 2 Co. 1 Pioneering Co's commit to blue on Drumnock — Trench relaid on right of 78/85 commit to Pts. O.13.d.3.3. E.P. CLUSMORE. (It. Laid by A.E. Coys. 8200.)	
	8/8		Visited O/c Drummy's but went into it 7th Coy. decided on siting reported as unsuitable. Reid O.C. Lysis Parkways a.d. Boomshorp tracks. He walked over the length of (20 M) and from 3/16 NIMROD — notions pointed arrows where necessary & showing wire views O.C. 7/8 BN. (Queens) it week is land. It next week 8/c 8 Coys — 8 O.I. Affair a considerable development of TACKROW (Front line) in regard also reported extentor to whaler now was this known Pts. were over too familiar — Coy. duties carried out by Nr. McMath in supervision of the whands by Nr. attributed to No. 1 lowe bridge to Nr. 1 mark & left Pts. been in R. C. 53511 taken over Pts. 8/3/16 — recent causes a similar yvork & left Pts. been in R. C. 53511 taken over Pts. 8/3/16 —	
	9/8		Reconnoitre purposes have been carried out to move the R.C. Pts. & found an alignment used to nr. 5.19.b. — Instructions given to 247 Co. to remove the now alignment. Increases to be 5.0. of 150 Nrs. 9 report to keep Concerning work — the Nolen 181 Nrs. = loy & 782/76 — tests work is — Coy. filed reminiscing Seen these lives & the Pts. were — Nochia Pioneers unit reported	
	10/8		Nochia Que — Sept and Sgt. Johnsmann from St. to Bl. Thurnelling 2 Sgt. 78 Kh (Queens) obtained information had Bl. Cwh obtained instruments to the Test bound a Bl. Bonk 1/32WARRANTE — also that patents of the Rev. We believe locations of a Bonlr 1/32WARRANTE — also that patents to the Rev. We believe locations of ordnance, & men into there.	
	11/8		NEALATTE was reported the occupied the occupied shortly referred collections of mens into there. Particulars visited the Minor R.G. Pts thoroughly to have an arrangement for company of the evr. — also water — for North Party — Wm. Col. (signature) Lily TRESORM	

Army Form C. 2118.

WAR DIARY
or
INTELLIGENCE SUMMARY.
(Erase heading not required.)

Place	Date	Hour	Summary of Events and Information	Remarks and references to Appendices
GOSLENY-au-MONT	12=8-17		Lieut Rathbone returned from leave, & took over from Major McQueen.	
Do	13-8-17		Visited by OC 132 AT Co RE & took over instruments from him as S.11 and M.12 etc. Selected site for hold in instruments near GOREY BECQUEREL	
Do	14-8-17		Visited dump; visited OC 446 R.Co. R.E. re trenches re screening; visited Regt. офr. & Reserve Bde H.Q. re screening. Weather wet. Visited OC Train re horse standings.	
Do	15=8=17		Visited OC 7th Field Co RE and B.G. Comndg Reserve Bde re course of instruction of hf. officers & NCOs in trench intee engineering; then to WANCOURT re screens. Visited OC 7th St.L. (Pioneers); then to D.H.Q. to meet CE VI Corps who put off visit till 16th Augs.	
Do	16-8-17		Visited HENIN Dressing Stn with ADMS after waiting in to meet CE VI Corps. Then to OC 447 Co HQ re wotks, & to hear an appeal by OC of that Co. then to Reserve Bde HQ reference a complaint, range, & trench intee covers of instruction. then to 4/7 Co have been inspected hitres.	
Do	17-8-17		Office all day preparing scheme & schedule for screening proposals for VI Corps.	
Do	18-8-17		To HENIN and then with OC 7 Field Co R.E. to site of proposed tram line Reft. Intruders	

WAR DIARY or INTELLIGENCE SUMMARY

Army Form C. 2118.

Place	Date	Hour	Summary of Events and Information	Remarks and references to Appendices
BOUZINCOURT	18-8-17 (Cont)		then to new dug out H/Qrs re improvements. Then to B.H.Q. in p.m. to see Capt Kerr Hay. Arr at 6pm to meet O/C Army Tramway Co.	
	19-8-17		Visited Res Bn H/Q re trench tram. Saw Curran of Instructors torpedoes of various sizes. To O.C.M O.C. 7th Bn S. Lancs, then W.E.N.N. dressing Sta. the two O.R. trn. S Co. re by dugout schemes.	
	20-8-17		Visited y held C.R.S. then to trenches, then to O.M.Q.R. Right Bde, then to O.C. Hdqr. y.j. C.S.R.L. then accompanied B.B.M.G. in his inspection of armoury of H.Q. 3 Field Co=	
	21-8-17		To see O.C. Pioneers re new work in VENUE, then to trenches re Capt line to new trench tramway, railed work in dressing Stn. arranged for tram transport for wounded. Capt Glover severely wounded right arm near WENN.	
	22-8-17		To new dressing stn with Col. W.L., then to R.E. dump, then to 10.10 Co re Capt field, then to Gen Rest Stn. Met O.C. 101 & 174 Tun. Cos re new dugout work in F.L. wasted in the funeral H'ls. who asaid accompanied him to M.D.S. Buried the brother of new tramway line to Corps line, visited left sheech N.y R.C.Field. rated proposed site for B.H.Q. winter huntments.	
	23-8-17			
	24-8-17		Visited O.C. 7th and 4.6.6th Field Co re Trench Tramway command Routers sewer work. Visited Hill of the 3 Huzard re revetting etc. visited workmen hand at NEW VIRUS-VITRAIZ	

WAR DIARY
or
INTELLIGENCE SUMMARY.
(Erase heading not required.)

Army Form C. 2118.

Place	Date	Hour	Summary of Events and Information	Remarks and references to Appendices
BOESEUX-au-MONT	25-8-17		Accompanied CE VI Corps on a visit to trenches & an inspection of proposed tramway in right subsector.	
Do	26-8-17		With OTC to SAC lines; picked out a site for new forward map & Field OC's. Visited Moral line of 74th in connection with above. Probably 07th Army Tramway Co will assist in & proposed trench tramway with SAGHO to inspect animals of 6th Spraf Co. Meeting of OC Pioneers & Field Co Commanders at DHQ reference preparation of trenches for winter. Wet in evening - stormy.	
Do	27-8-17		Rec'd orders to make OP for RA in PIONEER alley. Visited OC 101 Tun'd Coy. visited 27 MO & hutting site at BOIRI-BECOURELLE. Very wet & stormy	
Do	28-8-17		To YSERNSILLE with Cl. VI Corps Re screening high road zone tram.	
Do	29-8-17		To trenches, Right Subsector, then to Right Bde HQ. Then visited all three field Co. HQ's. Stormy & wet.	
Do	30-8-17		With OC 46 D II to reconnoitre for new rifle range. Visited new Rag Rifle HQ. visited range at MERENTIE being improved: visited site for winter DHQ. Visited by OC Pioneers, OC 181 Tun'd Co and OC 2nd Delocht. 174 Tun'd Co.: interviewed Officer nominated as 2nd Trench Tramway Officer. Showery & windy.	

Place	Date	Hour	Summary of Events and Information	Remarks and references to Appendices
BOUZLEIR-AU-MONT	31-8-17		Visited by GO to CE VI Corps. With APOI to next BDE Commanding 151 Inf.d Bde at site selected for a "replica" of a portion of enemy branch system. then with the GO to Broncky, walked over part of Branchine. then to OC 446 field Co. re layout of the "replica", & setup of new rifle range. Weather showery.	

A. Rathborne
Lt Col RE
CRE 50th Divn

31-8-17

WAR DIARY
of
C. R. E.
50TH. (NORTHUMBRIAN) DIVISIONAL ROYAL ENGINEERS.

—*—*—*—*—*—ooooOOOOOOOooo—*—*—*—*—*—

VOLUME XXX.

SEPTEMBER 1917.

WAR DIARY or INTELLIGENCE SUMMARY

Army Form C. 2118.

SEPTEMBER 1917 No. 50th Div. RE — Vol XXX 101

Place	Date	Hour	Summary of Events and Information	Remarks and references to Appendices
BOISLEUX-AU-MONT	1-9-17		Met OC 446 Field Co re new Rifle Range S.5 & S.11. Settled combs line inspected. Visited bullring of 7.M. Battery & Field Co's. Visited Hindenburg & bullring of Reserve Bde. 3 Bde Transport lines, 2 Field Ambulances, RFA DAC Train, SAAC etc.	
do	2-9-17		To MERCATEL re proposed junk tram line to Brass Bde Transport lines. Visit 352rd to inspect animals of 3" Field Coy RE. Visited by OC 352 E&M Co RE re practice lifting of Hindenburg tunnel. Visited by Div'l Tramway Officer and OC 446 Field Coy RE re timber hutting.	
do	3-9-17		Visited by OC Pioneers re broken hand. Lost 4 PM & 7. Marching to Western and Hindenburg lines. Met OC 352 E&M Co RE and later Supply Officer Third Army re reference E.L and winter supply of Hindenburg tunnel.	
do	4-9-17		To OC 446 Co HQ re "practice" then & 447 Co HQ then to LO Right Pale, then to visit work in Right Section then to 7th Field Co HP.	
do	5-9-17		Visit SAA.I. Walked over 2nd (top line) pocketed by OC Detail 17 + Tens 3 Co RE, OC 446 Field Co RE + American L.R. Co Briefing Officer.	
do	6-9-17		Office then to Arras, cloudy, overcum in pm.	
do	7-9-17		To Hindenburg BAPAUME	

Army Form C. 2118.

WAR DIARY
or
INTELLIGENCE SUMMARY.
(Erase heading not required)

H.Q. 50TH DIV R.E. Vol XXX

Instructions regarding War Diaries and Intelligence Summaries are contained in F. S. Regs., Part II. and the Staff Manual respectively. Title pages will be prepared in manuscript.

Place	Date	Hour	Summary of Events and Information	Remarks and references to Appendices
BOISLEUX-au-MONT	8-9-17		To tea OC Pioneers. B.Q. Commanding 151 Bde to OC 447 Field Co H.Q., & then to ridge re horse lines etc.	
do	9-9-17		To MERCATEL to mt Range. Pole transport lines 446, 2nd(?) Co,(?) & 2nd O C 7th Field Co R.E., to 447 Res Bde; presented several New ribbons to NCOs & Drivers. Visited 2nd Co R.E.	
do	10-9-17		To trenches N. of COJEUL - to left Bde H.Q. then to MEPRUN to H.Q. 16 Divn. re Hindenburg line water supply - In pm. re Hindenburg line water supply -	
do	11-9-17		To trenches S. of COJEUL. Visited H.Q. of Right & Left Brigades. Visited by O.C. 446 Field Co. and OC 7th Field Co.	
do	12-9-17		Visited Dump & OC Pioneers: Army Office all day.	
do	13-9-17		Met CRA: 9 & II Corps Water Supply Officer at S.A.C. & Rept Horse lines reference new water point: visited hutting in progress: visited by OC Detach 174 Tun'g Co R.E. & OC 181 Tun'g Co R.E.	
do	14-9-17		Visited Trenches Rifle Section. Visited dumps.	
do	15-9-17		Visited OC 7th Field Co R.E. Reserve Bde H.Q. & Rifle Range work at S.T.C. Visited by Major Gibon R.E.	
do	16-9-17		Visited trenches in pm. by Water Raid. Visited by Major Gibon R.E., visited raiding party JR.E. visited here lines of 447th, 7th & 446 Field Companies R.E. Visited by OC 7th Field Pioneers	

Army Form C. 2118.

WAR DIARY
or
INTELLIGENCE SUMMARY.
(Erase heading not required.)

Place	Date	Hour	Summary of Events and Information	Remarks and references to Appendices
BAISIEUX-au-MONT	17-9-17		To Hoffrichs HQ then to trenches N/E of Cojeul then to right Rt. Bn HQ then to Bn HQ then to Sop Q. Saw 3rd Div. offrs at work.	
Do	18-9-17		Office in morning. In p.m. to USA RE, parties in camp, re LR guarding & new camp site to improve work.	
Do	19-9-17		With OC E.E. VI Corps + CRA 16th Div. to Hindenburg Line re water supply scheme (route) then to Heninel-Le huc + E.E. chambers. Visited 1st Field Coy R.E.	
Do	20-9-17		Noted progress of 153 Bde in work proposed to be done during that Bde's tour of duty in left section. Visited Rifle Range. S.C. Ready. They filtrate of M.P. seen by ADMS, Motors to be sent for duty at the front.	
Do	21-9-17		Indexing most of day. Then Cinema: Scala.	
Do	22-9-17		Office till 10.0 am then to Division etc returning in pm.	
Do	23-9-17		To Rifle Bde HQ then to Salvation W J Cozens re RAP change of site then to left Bde HQ.	
Do 24-9-17			More or less day revisits & depots.	
Do 25-9-17				

Army Form C. 2118.

WAR DIARY
or
INTELLIGENCE SUMMARY.

(Erase heading not required.)

Place	Date	Hour	Summary of Events and Information	Remarks and references to Appendices
BETHUNE or MONT	26-9-17		Notes by CRE 51 Div re taking over May fletcher handed over they CE to Capt McLellan.	
	27-9-17		Office: Notes by Maj McQueen OC 2nd Field Coy R.E. hand in Reports & Returns Reconnaissance for G. for fujites.	
	28-9-17		Movements from Divn 3.4 & 5 M. All Ment rec from Divn 57th Divn took over. Rand Anster hulking & Notes by CRE 57th Divn. Handing over to Maj McQueen horse standing. In gun to GIVENCHY- & Route to Lectures to Students. II Corps School. Maj McQueen various duties to Corps Rest Station at BEUGY.	
	29-9-17		to CRE.	
	30.9.17		Lt Col Fleming DSO CRE 51 Divn taken over Rights Div. ditto & hirer. Arrangements made for T.B.W. (Russian) & Indian Forts in Job Rivers.	

J.M.McQueen Maj R.E.
Acty C.R.E. 50th Divn

Confidential.

ON HIS MAJESTY'S SERVICE.

Officer i/c A.G's Office at the Base.

War Diary. A.D.P.S., Canadian Forces.
1-10-17 to 31-10-17.

No. 42.

POST OFFICE.

Original

WAR DIARY

of

C. R. E.

50TH. DIVISIONAL ROYAL ENGINEERS.

VOLUME XXXI.

OCTOBER 1917.

WAR DIARY or INTELLIGENCE SUMMARY

Army Form C. 2118.

VOL No XXXI 195
HQ.R.P. 50 Div R.E. — OCTOBER 1917

Place	Date	Hour	Summary of Events and Information	Remarks and references to Appendices
BOISLEUX ST MARC	1st 2nd		Visited Filoys: reference handing over of works to Filoys of 51st Divn. Information heard through all papers relative to probable work with C.R.E. 51st Divn. Bound hurriedly over preliminary movement orders for units. Officer of morning for Coys: F.S.I. & Div. Bond on units. After tatting up purposes — Received necessary Efad that 2 Filoy Coys were to be employed in littering of 51st Divn. Reinforcement Camp under the C.R.E. to receive Divns being out of the Line — G.M. & GOC 51st Div. & GSO 1 informed these news.	
	3rd		With GSO. Visited CRE (Lt Col. Dodge.) E. Coffee & B.S. S.S. E. Office. He would be informed. Met 2 Section RE. and 60 Pioneers. J. DL 1 the employed on hutting on Place F. 2 Coys RE. Visited quarries with GSO. + issued orders to 446 G. & RE. 22. Anti-Aircraft Visited the John Reinforcement Camp with Mr Bonst R & 416 & 417 RE. & police of hutting work & start on 5th. Dir. Pontage & correspondence camp site of Mr Bonst. F.S.I. Div. Shewed he kheud 50 Dr. Pontage & correspondence camp site & critical keep him etc.? Felt our kheud only Was satisfactorily the fitted hut to accomodate Coys as at hard shelters. That unfortunately side put to us to decide but to accomodate Coys as at his own farmer be in this are even till he had better a visited all groups an afternoon.	
	4th		Interesting so into purposes of had mentioned — I heard that hearting on purposes completed — 446 Feld RE. to ACHIET LE PETIT. Last 7th F.G. RE marched to GOMIECOURT — 446 Feld RE to ACHIET LE PETIT. Last both Coys in the march. Visited by Lt Col. FLEMING. 5.0. (RE 51st Div.) ad Major wishes us to remain bound by A) 51st D-R.E. — C.E. D. Office (Gen Hull 10 B) called on 4th L. Engine to keep in of C R.E. 50 Div. at the last ape.	
ACHIET LE PETIT	5th		50th Div H.Q. Marched to ACHIET LE PETIT. 447 F.J.G. R.E. marched to COURCELLES — Saw the latter on the march. In columns seen, weather broken)	

WAR DIARY or INTELLIGENCE SUMMARY

Army Form C. 2118.

Vol No XXXI

50th DIV. R.E. H.Q.rs — OCTOBER 1917.

Place	Date	Hour	Summary of Events and Information	Remarks and references to Appendices
ACHEYLE PETIT.	7th		Received orders for certain divisional engineering targets required by 13th inst. Which allotted to 446 F.C.R.E. — 7th & 446 C/o been inoculated — Continuous rain.	
	8th		Visited all Fd. Coys. re training — Fine morning — Units doing drills & lectures — 447 Coy: Inoculation — Appx. & Shows: heavy rain — No likely training into.	
	9th		Training & recreation — Appx. Rent. H.Q. Units continue training. Visited C.R.E. (at Athetabre D.S.O.) at 41 Jake Road H.Q. Units continue training.	
	10th		F. 7. Fd. Co. R.E. Units training picquets much hampered by continued bad weather.	
	11th		Reconnaissance & 2 D/s of 10 hours leave for duration sent to W.O. (M.3)	
	12th		Visited 76, 447 & 7.D.S.I.	
	13th		Lieut Rathbone returned to duty from VI Corps Rest Station.	
	14th		Visited 447 & 7 F.C. Field Companies.	
	15th		Visited 447 & 7 to II Corps area. Zeggero-Capelle & Labeyelle.	
	16th		Took Fd.S.O.II to II Corps area. allotted to 50th Div.	
	17th		Visiting training areas in II Corps area & H.Q.	
	18th		Visited XIX Corps Army H.Q.: & Fetcher Major Caniers from near ELVERDINGHE.	
LEBEZELE S/o	19th		Moved self & 447th Co. in Command. Visited 3 field companies, 7th Army. Major Caniers to 447th Co near Railroute west near Arneke.	
PROPEREN S/o			Zeggero-Capelle moved to PROVEN. Visited H.Q. XV Corps at St. SIXTE.	
PROVEN	20th		D.H.Q. moved to PROVEN.	
	21st		Took AA d'Oury to H.Q. 35th & 17th Div re looking over.	
	22nd		Free all day. No car available — Saw CRE 57th Div.: Attended conference (C.R.E.)	
	23rd		7 & 20 to ELVERDINGHE. 447th Co to Hull's Farm: 446 F.N.G. ELVERDINGHE.	

Army Form C. 2118.

194

WAR DIARY
or
INTELLIGENCE SUMMARY.
(Erase heading not required.)

Place	Date	Hour	Summary of Events and Information	Remarks and references to Appendices
PROVEN	23–10–17 (continued)		To SNDANK, ELVERDINGHE and BOESINGHE, to dumps.	
ELVERDINGHE	24–10–17		To 35th Divn H.Q. Gave C.R.E. then to new Divl H.P. at ELVERDINGHE, to conference at XV Corps H.Q. re communications, hutting & fuel — to conference at XV Corps H.Q. re communications, hutting & fuel — to conference with D.E. Pontoons & O.C. Pen cars & Jd Co. Commanders — Meetup in evening with O.C. Pen cars & Jd Co. Commanders etc.	
do	25–10–17		To KOEKUIT by road & back by HUNTER St. duckwalk track: met S.E. Bfs. Army at BOESINGHE dumps fine & dry. Weather wet.	
do	26–10–17		Battle began 5.40 a.m. 1810th duckboard track laid on 25th (night). 2d Co cancelled working parties of infantry for Pioneer & 2nd Lt. Co's to C.R.E. XIV Corps. Troops on duckboard deficiency (anticipated) replacements to C.R.E. XIV Corps. Troops on Celap Sneline, noting duckboards tracks, inspecting road to W of NEY X-Roads.	
do	27–10–17		St Corps Trench Tramway C.R.J. & Cpl Corp Trops. ORDARK dumps. to H.P. To XV Corps H.Q. to see C.E. & Aerog Officer. Meeting in p.m. took Jd Co. After Army to see C.E. O/C.T.b.&. to Report on Communication Camp. Chief & relieved of O.C.T.b.&. to BOESINGHE dumps then to MARSOUIN Camp. With Adjt & O.C.T.b.&. to BOESINGHE then to 74 Co HQ & line —	
do	29–10–17		Re Shelter for 2 Bns at Camp.	
do	30–10–17		To see C.E./XIX Corps. + C.R.E. XIX Corps. Troops.	
do	31–10–17		To line, visiting BOESINGHE R.E. dumps Nulaa B.Q. Camps? Bde in F.L.	

MMatterson
Lorance
C.R.E. 50th Divn.

31/10/17

1.   50th. Division took over the sector from 18th. Division on 15 - 17th June 1917.

2.   Since that date the Sector was diminished by handing over to 21st Division of a portion of the Southern Section (this was temporary, for the area in question reverted to 50th Division a few weeks later), and was increased by taking over from the 56th Division all that portion of the Sector which lies North of SHAWK AVENUE, i.e. about 2000 yards of front.

3.   At the time of taking over there was a fairly extensive trench system, but front trenches were narrow and shallow in most cases, none were revetted or properly fire-stepped, there were few cubby holes, no shelters, and not more than half a dozen deep dugouts in the front system.

4.   There were two fairly good C. T's:-

    FIRST AVENUE and
    FOSTER AVENUE

both duckboarded, and 4 indifferent C. T's:-

    SHAWK.
    KESTRAL.
    SHIKAR.
    SOUTHERN.

the greater part of them was duckboarded, but all narrow and shallow as to forward portions.

All these 4 C. T's. were widened, deepened, sumped, bermed, and provided with passing places and ramps out, working from Front Line backwards, and provided with duckboards throughout.

New C. T's. were dug, viz:-

    PIONEER ALLEY + CUCKOO.
    DURHAM ALLEY.

In September the work of revetting C. T's. was begun, and following were dealt with, working from Front Line rearwards:-

FOSTER	back to	NEST.
PIONEER	"	FOSTER.
SHIKAR	"	STAG.
SOUTHERN	"	RAKE.

5. A considerable amount of new trench digging was done in the front system, as shewn in red on plan marked "C" herewith, as well as reclaiming of "dud" or bad trenches, as shewn by broad blue lines on same plan.

The bulk of the Front Line (excluding portion excavated in chalk) was revetted and duckboarded, and most of the alleys between Support and Front Line were also revetted.

Work in hand in revetting of Support Line, and good progress has been made.

6. During its tour in the line the Division has, with the assistance of its Field Companies and 2 Sections of 181st. Tunnelling Company R.E., constructed 60 dugouts, i.e:-

Electric Light Chambers.	1.
Regtl. Aid Posts.	1 & 2 in hand.
O.Ps.	8.
M.G.	7.
Brigade Headquarters.	1.
T.M. Emplacements (Heavy).	3.
Battalion Headquarters.	4.
Company Headquarters and Platoon Dugouts.	24.
R.E.	2.
R.A.	9.

The above figures include 9 dugouts made for, or by, R.F.A., most of which were built by R.A. labour with some technical R.E. supervision.

4 old dugouts were repaired and strengthened.

7. Besides the construction of R.A.Ps. for R.A.M.C. in the trench system, extensive improvements, amounting to re-construction, were effected to Advanced Dressing Stations at MARLIERE CAVES and HENIN.

8. 2 wells were sunk in the trench system, at one of the dugouts in MALLARD TRENCH and in PANTHER TRENCH. A Hun well and pump in N.35.d. were also repaired.

Work was begun on a scheme for water supply of HINDENBURG LINE jointly with 16th. Division.

-3-

The water supply at MARLIERE CAVES was also improved.

9. A considerable amount of work was done on roads, the Division being responsible for the maintenance of 9 miles of roads.

10. A good many shelters were erected for accommodation of personnel at 2 Brigade Headquarters, for rations at ALBATROSS ROAD, and for Left Brigade Reserve Battalion.

11. 2 Rifle Ranges, 16 targets (windmill) were constructed at M.23 and S.5.

12. The majority of the dugouts in the trench system were protected against gas.

13. A good deal of work was done in repairing and erecting screens.

14. Owing to falls of trench in wet weather, the consequent rise of trench level caused flow of water and mud down the adits of SHAFT TRENCH.

Special work was undertaken to exclude mud from adits, involving the employment of much labour and material.

15. Several short courses of instruction in Field Engineering were held for Officers and N.C.Os. of Battalions in Reserve Brigade.

16. The RIVER COJEUL TRENCH TRAMWAY was begun by the Division, and about two-thirds work was done prior to Army Tramway Company taking over the work.

The bulk of the labour was supplied, and the collection, sorting, and repair of the track was performed, by the Division. Length of track over 2 miles.

A second Trench Tramway to serve the Right Section was put in hand; the Division furnishing from 60 to 100 men, supervision being exercised by the Army Tramway Company.

17. A considerable amount of miscellaneous work was done, including such items as:-

Provision of lorry standings.
" ironing sheds.
" settling tanks for baths affluents.
" dressing rooms at baths (3).
Notice boards.
Sign boards.
Map boards and easels.
Joint boxes for signals.
Map boards for R.A.
Assistance to Y.M.C.A.

18. In the trench system a number of improvements of a minor character were carried out:-

Traverses were made in straight trenches.
Overhead traverses were provided in some trenches.
Some hundreds of boxes of various kinds, e.g.

for S.A.A.
Bombs.
Very lights.
Rifle grenades.
Latrines.

were provided and fixed.

Firebays were marked with number plates.
Numerous notice and sign-boards were provided.
Many steel and timber cubby holes were constructed.
Artillery bridges were placed over trenches.
Block "gates" were provided to protect a number of front line posts.
A considerable number of firebays were made, and steps revetted.
Bridges were made over streams and trenches to carry roads or trench tramways.

19. 9110 barbed wire concertinas were made under R.E. supervision and 8000 placed in position by Infantry.

20. 373 "dud" shell were destroyed.

CAMPS AND HUTTING ETC.

Work done may be divided into two classes:-

(a) Miscellaneous accommodation.
(b) Winter Hutting.

(a) (i) Divisional Headquarters was enlarged and improved, see para. 6 of attached Summary "B".

(ii) 2 Water points were installed, 1 at MERCATEL, and 1 on the MERCATEL-BEAURAINS road; 8 troughs (600 gall.) each.

(iii) R.E. stores, distributed amongst some 7 or 8 dumps, were collected and concentrated at 2 dumps, HENIN and MARLIERE.

(b) Midway through August, the Division was informed that it must carry out its own Winter Hutting; up to that date an Army Troops Co. R.E. and Labour Battalion had been employed on preparing Winter hutted camps, and had erected about 180 huts; of these, however, many were deficient of lining, and one-third were not immediately habitable.

These camps were worked upon by a small R.E. party while the scheme for Winter Hutting was being prepared, sites selected, etc.

When this had been done, the work was taken in hand, September 2nd., seriously, and to the execution of the work were allotted one Field Co. R.E., and about 400 R.F.A., Infantry, A.S.C. etc.

By the end of September all hutting, to number allotted by the Corps was completed: All horse standings (99) were bricked, and all roofing over ditto was finished.

Standings for further 400 horses were bricked, but no superstructures were erected on these.

SUMMARY OF WORK DONE

BY R.E. FIELD COMPANIES AND PIONEERS OF

50TH. DIVISION, FROM JUNE 19TH. TO OCTOBER 4TH. 1917.

1. **TRENCHES.**

    (a) 5616 yards of New Trenches, Front Line and Communication, were traced and dug to correct dimensions.

    (b) 15593 yards of existing Trenches, cleared, widened and deepened.

    (c) 57 traverses made in trenches (exclusive of those in (a) New Trenches).

    (d) 170 Firebays made with Firestep.

    (e) 212 Cubby Holes excavated.

    (f) 11350 Duckboards fixed + about 10000 put in trenches unfixed.

    (g) 39 Sumps dug out and fitted with Boxes.

    (h) 329 Boxes made and fixed in Trenches, for Bombs, Very Lights, S.A.A. Hand and Rifle Grenades.

    (j) 12193 yards Berm made on both sides of Trenches.

    (k) 12216 yards of Revetting on both sides of Trenches made.

    (l) 386 Notice Boards fixed at Trench Junctions, and Dugout entrances shewing accommodation etc.

    (m) 35 Ramps made out of C. T's.

    (n) 10 Daylight Dumps levelled and completed.

    (o) 13 Stretcher Rests made and Revetted in C. T's.

    (p) 14 Passing Places made in C. T's.

    (q) Blocks caused by Shell Fire cleared in all Trenches by Maintenance Parties.

    (r) (30 Blocks in Trenches (Front System) made.
        (38 Gates made and fixed in Front Line.

2. DUGOUTS.

60 Dugouts were completed giving 17536 square feet of Superficial area and occupied as follows:-

   (a) Brigade Headquarters.   1.
   (b) Battalion Headquarters.   4.
   (c) Company Headquarters.   11.
   (d) Platoon Dugouts.   5.
   (e) Infantry Dugouts.   8.
   (f) Machine Guns and Crews.   7.
   (g) Trench Mortars and Crews.   3.
   (h) R.F.A. Batteries.   9.
   (j) R.E. Dugouts.   2.
   (k) Electric Plant.   1.
   (l) R.A. Observation Posts.   8.
   (m) Regimental Aid Posts.   1.

3. GAS-PROOFING DUGOUTS.

62 Dugouts rendered Gas-proof by fixing frames, blanketed at entrances.

4. TRENCH TRAMWAYS.

   (a) Left Section. River COJEUL Tramway. 3800 yards of formation was completed and rails laid; Tramway in full working order.

   8 sidings constructed.

   3 bridges over River COJEUL built.

   880 yards Mule Track cleared and bricked.

   4 large German trucks were salved.

   10 trucks were converted to 2 feet wheelbase.

   (b) Right Section. 4010 yards of formation completed and 3415 yards of rail laid.

   6 bridges over trenches were built to carry tramway.

5. WATER SUPPLY.

Trenches. Well dug 40 feet deep below floor level in deep dugout MALLARD TRENCH. Excavated for and fixed 2 tanks in trench. Pump, tanks and delivery hose placed in position. Island traverse dug for traffic. Well dug 30 feet deep below floor level in deep dugout PANTHER TRENCH. Pump fixed and 250 feet pipe (part of scheme to carry water to water point in SHIKAR AVENUE a distance of 500 yards). 2 water tanks placed in position

<u>Back Area.</u> 2 Water Points made, each with 240 feet run of troughing, brick bottoming etc., complete.

2, 50 gallon tanks erected at MERCATEL Water Point.

General repairs carried out and a sure and efficient water supply kept up throughout the area.

Sleeper roadway built for lorries.

Concrete platform and stand for water carts completed.

6. <u>HUTTING.</u>

255 Nissen huts, 12 Pup huts and 17 Adrian huts erected in accordance with Winter Hutting Scheme. Also 2 Barracks to accommodate 24 Officers, house for G.O.C. and building for "A" Mess erected at new D.H.Q.

Erected at old D.H.Q., on taking over from 18th Division:-

    3 cook-houses, 3 huts R.E. pattern. 2 Nissen huts and 3 Armstrong huts. 4 latrines.

Y.M.C.A. NEUVILLE VITASSE, 1 Allin hut erected.

Machine Gun Company 2 Allin huts.

Signal School 4 Allin huts and 4 Nissen huts.

Gas School 2 huts R.E. pattern.

R.E. Field Company Offices 2 huts R.E. pattern.

Divisional R.E. Dump 1 Nissen and 2 R.E. pattern huts erected, also a dugout was constructed covered with French shelter and sandbagged.

Right Brigade Headquarters Hut for Staff Captain erected.

Trenchboards were laid in all camps amounting to about 9500 yards run, laid and fixed on piles. These were salved boards brought up from Back Area in about 60 lorry loads.

7. <u>HORSE STANDINGS.</u>

99 Horse Standings were erected to accommodate 4356 horses, and other Standings made for use as Forage Sheds, Q.M. Stores, Farriers Shops and Repair Shops,

which if used for horses would accommodate a further 800 or 900. 9 Standings for 400 Horses were laid but no superstructure fixed.

All were paved with broken brick or chalk and cemented, and roofs covered with corrugated iron. This work has involved the carriage of 730 motor lorry loads of materials, 29160 G.S. wagon loads of broken brick and chalk, and the following materials were used in erection:-

>42000 sheets of Corrugated iron.
>5700 Poles, and
>1400 Roof trusses with about 122000 feet run of purlins.

8. SHELTERS IN TRENCHES.

53 small steel shelters completed, excavated and sandbagged.

2 large shelters for rations ALBATROSS ROAD.

7 large shelters for accommodation.

2 emergency steel Elephant shelters as ration stores at entrance to FOSTER and SHAWK Communication Trenches.

9. ROADS.

9 miles of Roads repaired and kept going, and 870 loads of brick and 465 loads of road metal were put down.

GUEMAPPE-CHERISY ROAD. Brick arch bridge demolished and re-constructed.

Shell holes were filled in on Overland Tracks and white posts fixed to enable roads to be used at night time.

10. SCREENING.

D.H.Q. 13 screens erected for shading light.

A total of 1730 yards screening made and fixed in forward area.

All screens repaired and re-erected after damage by shell fire and gales.

11. RIFLE RANGES.

Rifle Range for Reserve Brigade at BOISLEUX ST. MARC completed. Trench excavated and revetted for Targets and used as a markers' trench.

8 girders salved from WANCOURT raised and bases concreted and 8 revolving targets made and fixed.

Firing Points at 350, 300, 250, and 100 yards made and revetted.

Rifle Range at MERCATEL in hand.

8 Revolving Targets constructed and fixed in trench dug for markers. Firing Point at 310 yards revetted.

12. BATHS.

Work on Baths at BOIRY BECQUERELLE, BOISLEUX-AU-MONT and NEUVILLE VITASSE.

6 settling tanks dug and lined with cement, and 4 filter tanks constructed. Dressing huts and Ironing sheds erected and stoves, with brick chimneys, built. Sump pits and drains dug.

Open Air Baths, HENIN. 3, 2300 gallon Tarpaulin Baths put in after excavation.

13. DRESSING STATIONS.

Dressing Station shelter constructed; roof strutted and 2 layers of sandbags added in BOOTHAM TRENCH.

MARLIERE CAVES. New shaft sunk. Blocks cleared and weak places strutted. Caves ventilated. Water supply improved. 4 new shafts constructed.

HENIN. 2 Nissen huts erected after clearing sites. Concrete floor laid in out-building and breast work erected protecting dugout entrances. Cellar roof strengthened, props removed and girders substituted: Large improvements, 40 yards of seating made, 4 stretcher shelters for 19 stretchers. Pump repaired. Painting, whitewashing, and general improvements carried out. Cook-houses erected.

14. RAIDS.

20 dummy figures were made up into sets with appliances for raising and lowering, and one dummy tank was made. All were used in operations - 2 raids on enemy trenches on 15th. September 1917, when 1

Officer and 12 Other Ranks R.E. were employed in conjunction with Infantry. 11 dugout shafts were blown in by placing boxes of guncotton on the dugout steps; for this purpose 17 mobile charges were made up and used (as reference para. 18(b)).

15. COURSES OF INSTRUCTION.

A series of Pioneer Courses of Instruction was given in revetting and trench construction generally, lasting altogether 32 days, during which time 128 Officers, and 256 Other Ranks attended.

16. "DUD" DESTRUCTION.

373 of various calibres destroyed.

17. CONCERTINAS AND WIRING.

9110 constructed and 8000 taken up by brigades in the line for fixing.

2000 yards Intermediate Line wire put out.

200 yards BOOTHAM TRENCH wire put out.

8040 yards wire on Corps Line put out.

3800 yards of this double apron.

18. MOBILE CHARGES.

(a) 12 mobile charges made up and taken up to be used in July Operations with Infantry if required (not used).

(b) 17 made and used in raids on enemy trenches 15/9/1917 (see para. 14 "RAIDS.").

19. BANGALORE TORPEDOES.

6 were made.

20. MISCELLANEOUS.

(i) Pump at N.35.d.8.5. dismantled and plunger rod repaired.

(ii) Pump at MALLARD WELL repaired.

(iii) Wire netting fence round D.H.Q. put up.

(iv) Miscellaneous work for offices, messes, etc., at D.H.Q; tables and forms made.

(v) Anti-aircraft mounting for Lewis Gun made.

STORES ISSUED FROM HENIN DUMP DURING PERIOD 1/7/17 to 30/9/17 INCLUSIVE.

Articles.	No. issued.
Sandbags.	870000
Trenchboards.	26539 (about 30 miles).
Shovels G.S.	563
Picks G.S.	651
Corrugated iron, sheets.	8066
Shelters, small, English.	488 sheets.
" large. "	655 "
" Trench.	387 "
X.P.M., sheets.	21551 (about 24½ miles).
Wire, barbed, coils.	12467
" plain, "	487
" netting, rolls.	652
" square mesh, rolls.	87
" French.	50
" Concertinas.	8232
" staples, French wire.	5828
Pickets, wood, long.	4514
" " short.	5364
" angle iron, long.	38640
" " " short.	3939
" screw, long.	17039
" " short.	7080
" " medium.	994
Hurdles.	427
Tapes, tracing.	301
Nails, 1", 2", 3".	77 cwts.
" 4", 5", 6".	88½ "
" clout.	24½ "
Canvas, green, rolls.	15½
" hessian "	108
Felt, rolls.	472
Rope, fathoms.	693
Tar, barrels.	60
Tanks, water.	31
R.S. Joists.	130
Dugout, entrances, cases 5' 3" x 2' 7½"	347*
" chamber " 6' x 4'	1323 *
Round timber (pit props).	759
Cement, barrels.	148
Paint, drums.	11
Timber 1" boarding.	84350 ft.
" above 4" x 2" scantling.	18599 ft.
" less than " "	89398 ft.
" 2" x 1" for barbed wire concertinas.	144302 ft.

*Excludes those salved from Back Area by Tunnelling Co. RE.

Hutting stores drawn from various Corps Dumps and issued direct to the work are not included in above table.

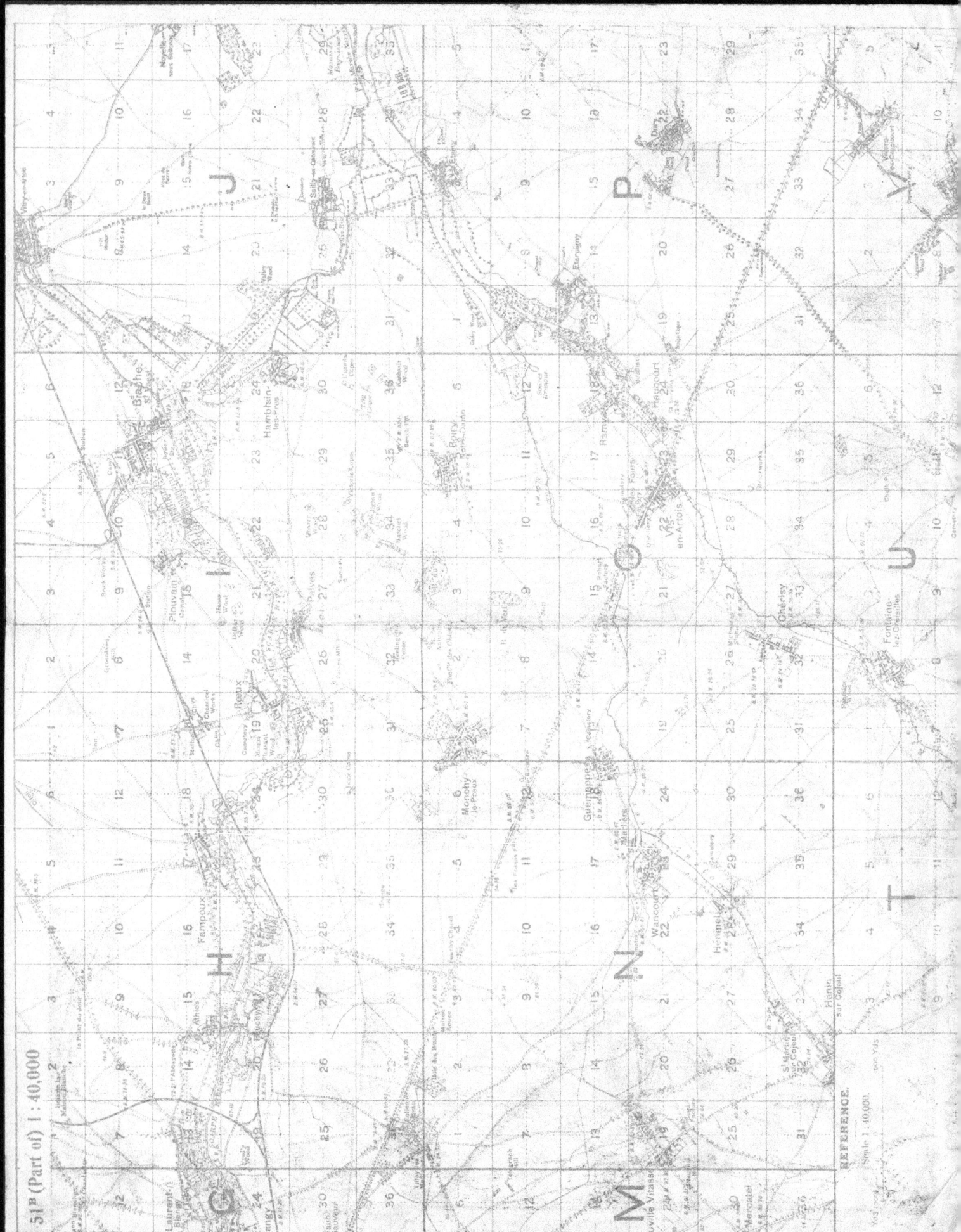

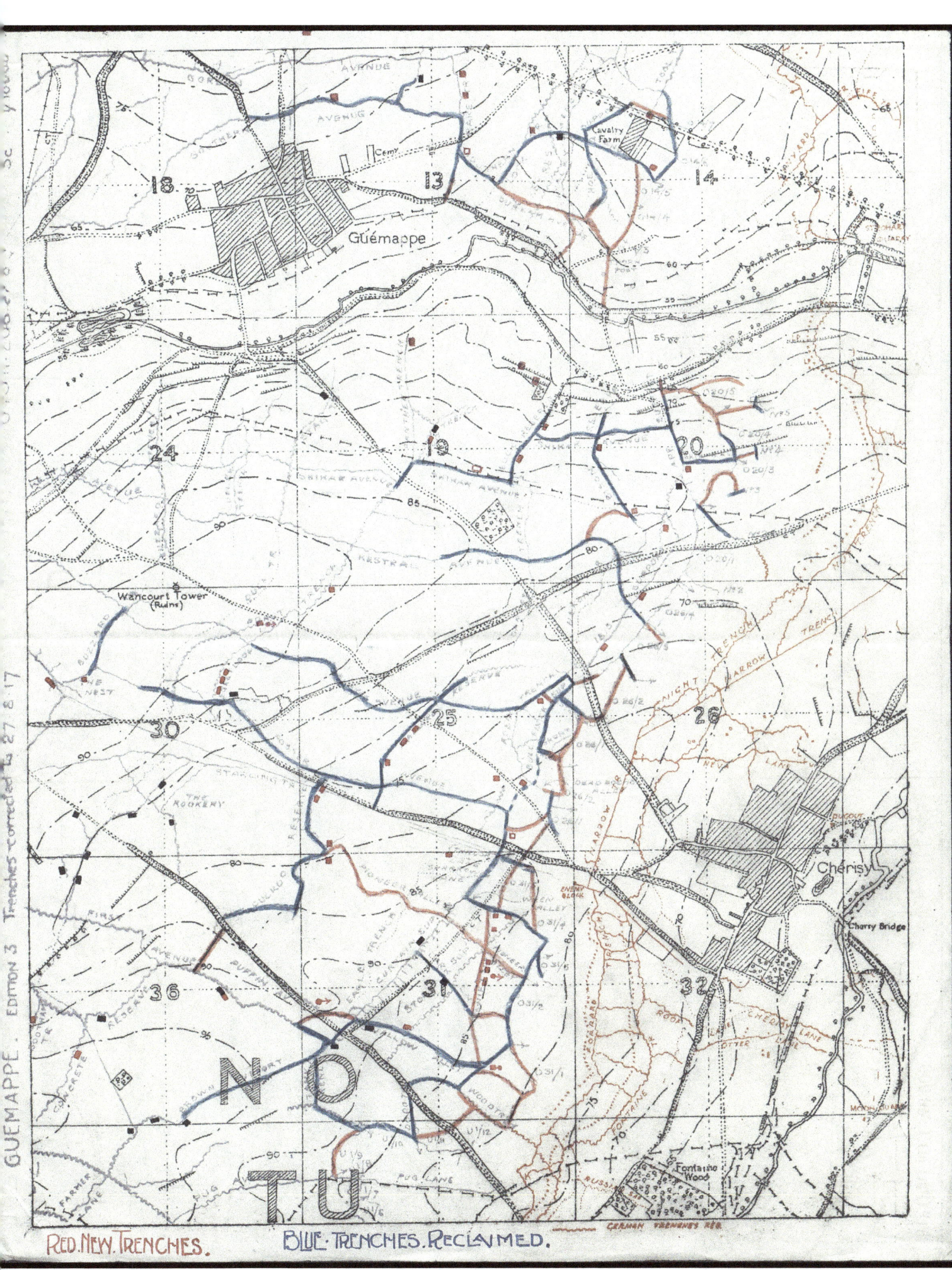

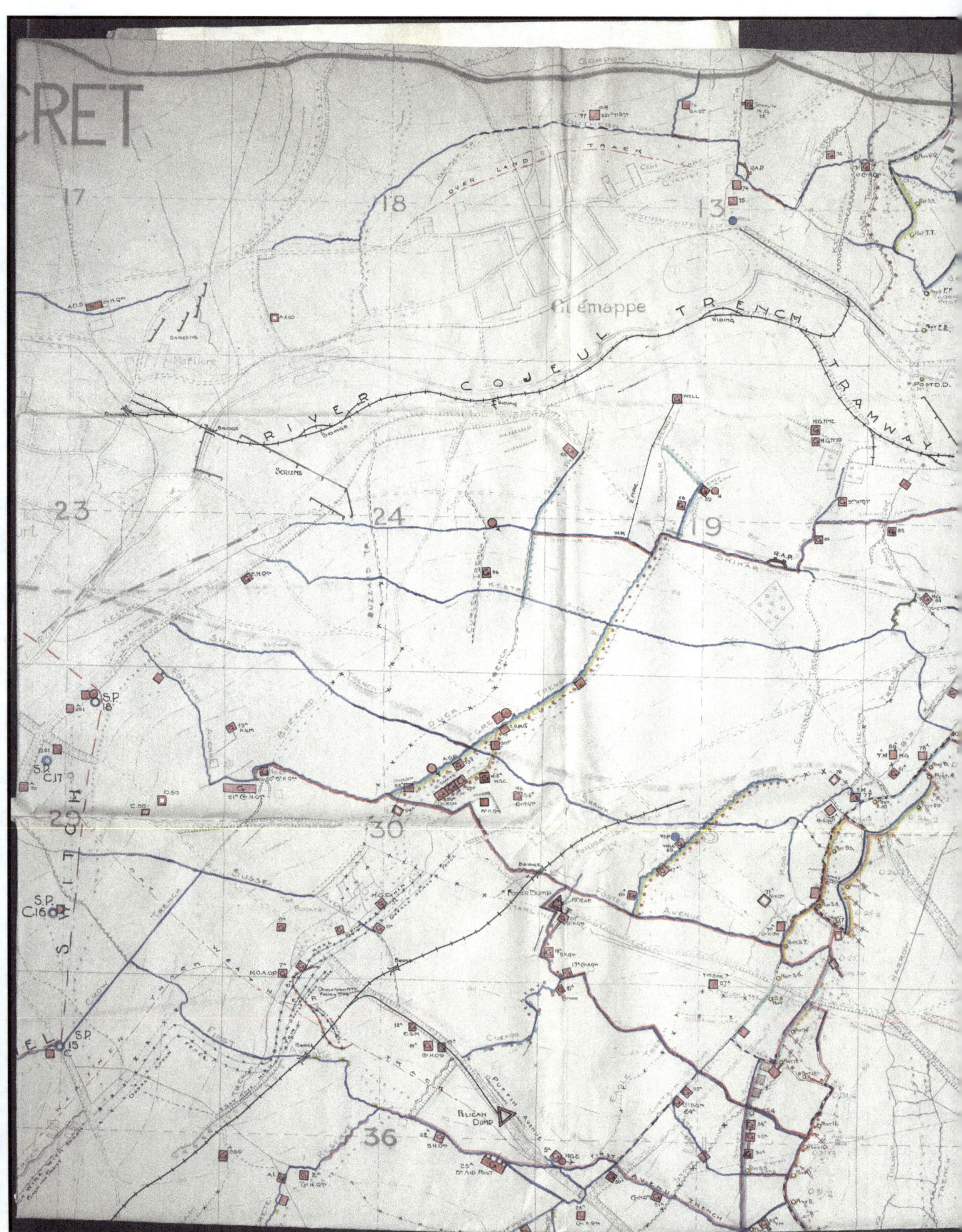

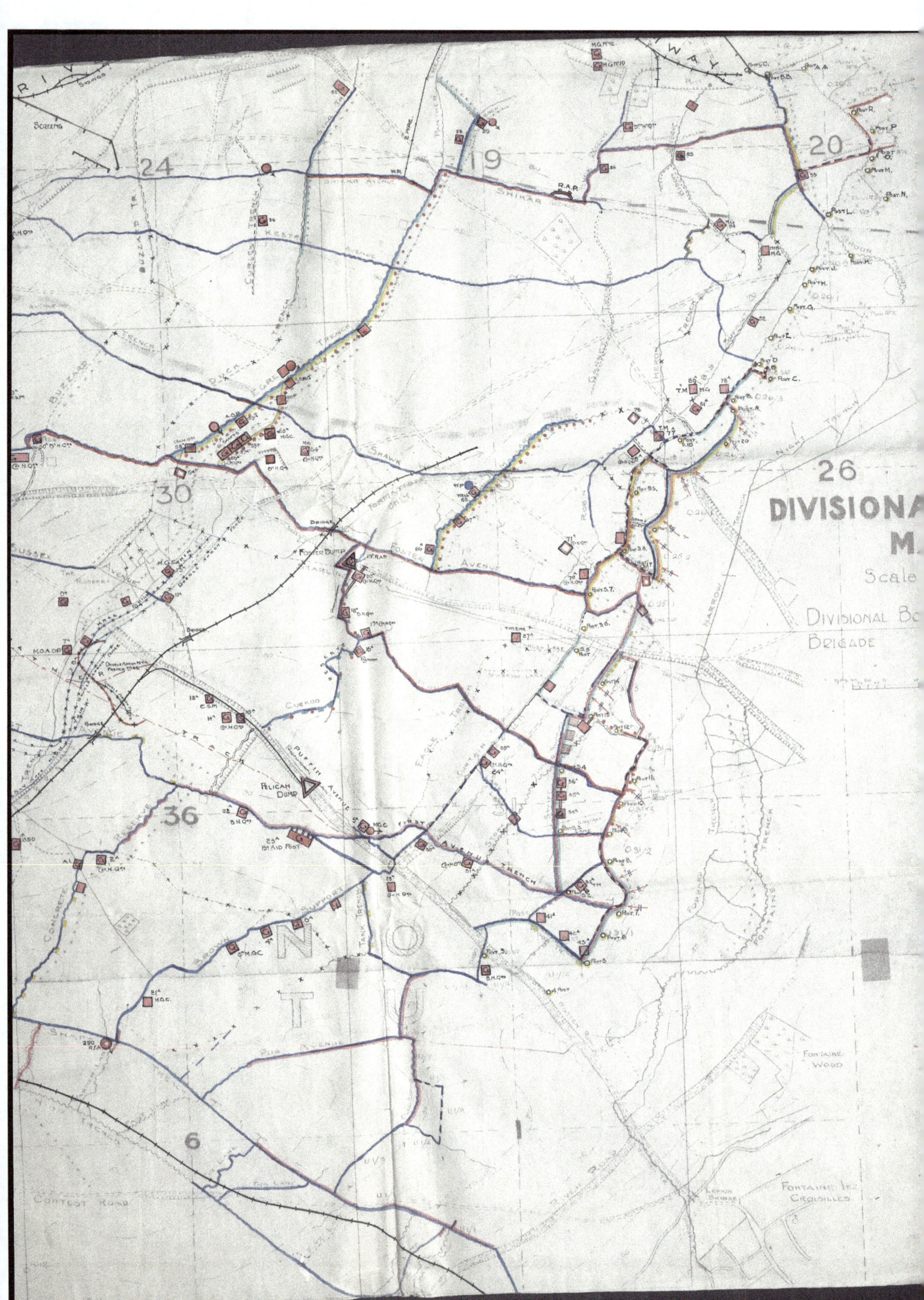

ORIGINAL.

WAR DIARY

of

C. R. E.

50TH DIVISIONAL ROYAL ENGINEERS.

VOLUME XXXII.

NOVEMBER 1917.

WAR DIARY or **INTELLIGENCE SUMMARY.**
Army Form C. 2118.
Vol. XXXII

Place	Date	Hour	Summary of Events and Information	Remarks and references to Appendices
ELVERDINGHE	1-11-17		Visited Camps, west of Canal with O.C. 7th Field Co. R.E. reference improvement of drainage etc.	
	2-11-17		Visited by adjt. 18th Divl R.E. Revised orders re Pinioro & Field Co's. re work in rear of approaching coy of Pinioro & Lansing over part of sector to be taken by 18th Divn. Visited by C.R.E. 18th Divn. & by O.C. 7 Army & Field Companies.	
	3-11-17		To SPRAGOPPE, HULLFARM, MARSOUINE, TOLIE FARM Camps re shelters & protecting tents: back by R's it track & R.E. dump POSINGHE	
	4-11-17		Visited flat coy of work planning on 5th under orders of C.E. XIX Corps with C.R.E. 18th Divn & POSINGHE. Discussed tunnel arrangements	
	5-11-17		To KOEKUIT etc. up Hindenstreel Track by Railway West of NEY Cross Roads	
	6-11-17		BROEMBEEK Road	
	7-11-17		Visited camps & inspected improvement works. Meeting in pm with Field Co. Commanders re training programme etc.	
	8-11-17		Col. Rutter [?] and S.O. proceeded to CAP MARTIN – way Mt. Queen. Journal REPERDU. [?] [?] in 7.F.C.s back [?]. Orders received for Div. to start take over EPERLEQUES – Orders issued [?] 446, 447 Tilbury Operation Order received for move of Divn. to start take over EPERLEQUES. 76 D.L.I. (Pioneers) remain for work on most of divisional pontoons by rate knight? road – 7th & 8th F.C's through with 2 Artillery Home Divisions. J D.L.I. to forward roads – Ix? to take over & under C.E., the 7th F.C. through with C.E. XVIII later to be 20 yds road – be required for various works in new area.	
	9-11-17		Transferred 95, 96, 97 D.B. 446 F.C. 8th of 19 Brand Div. 6 new area. Reported the [?] to G.S.O.1	
EPERLEQUES	10-11-17		D.H.Q. moved to EPERLEQUES. – HQ 446 F.C. & HOUTLE. Visited C.R.E. XVIII Corps tents by detachment & be written to Corps: looking in arrival in this area – find for a clear week for rest & training afterwards to be C.R.E. & the take Tunnels W.E. S.D.O.(C) for reference to XVIII Corps.	

Army Form C. 2118.

WAR DIARY
or
INTELLIGENCE SUMMARY.
(Erase heading not required.)

Vol. No. XXXII.
H.Q. 50th Div R.E. NOVEMBER 1917 — 100

Place	Date	Hour	Summary of Events and Information	Remarks and references to Appendices
EPERLEQUES	11th	—	Visited 446 Co. (HOULLE) re: works & training — also 151 Bde re: materials to apply for timber & training. 447 Co. (disunited parties) arrived WESTREHEM. Received for CE XVIII Corps that sports beyond to be erected, repairing camps & 6 Sec no scattered throughout area — extra 4 FREE. Supposed to last winter (operation from 24/10/17	
	12th	—	Visited 447 Co. re: works & training — Reports & works carried out without interference to 8/11/17) Sent to CE XIX Corps, copy forwarded to 50 Div (9) —	
	13th	—	Visited 447 Co. —	
	14th	—	Inspected site for hut camp in ENEMY NORDAUSQUES, view Tob. Depot & one Coy at THIENBRON — Received orders for camp & site at Camp 20 & Low Standings —	
	15th	—	Orders received to make Low Standings for all horses without cover in Div area — Provided XVIII Corps HQ with Ref CE 22: Work about 6 sites — Visited sites & work at ST MOMELINS MOORBECQUE —	
	16th	—	Visited First (Central) HQ training at PRESS MANSON	
	17th	—	Arranged supply of cubicles, chalk, sand for Horse Standings — Sited Standings in 151, 150 Bde areas — Visited 446 Co. Sent to TOLLERONCAMPS from at Nun Tobe School. Start to Si member of Sch — Ak. Stables & feet. 447 Co. to MOORBECQUE front —	
	18th	—	at XVIII Corps Prisoners Camp — Visited by CE (M&Gen) 7 de la Dominie) —	
			Look arranged on various works for CE XVIII Corps and on horsestandings (or 6 units Orders rec'd by pm for 446 & 447 Coys to move they standing necessary for work Front Tramways under 1st Div — All work for CE XVIII Corps to stop & proceed with	
	19th		446 & 447 F.Coys marched as above (Stables by rail, transport by road) —	
	20th	—	Visited Horsestandings & sites Standings for 150 Bde + Div Troops units —	
	21st	—	", 446, 447 Coys new MASCOT also 7 C MS at ELNEBROUCQUE & 7th DLI (Pioneers) aux BOESMANS.	
	22nd	—	Works horsestandings Continued — works & materials & cubicles —	
	23rd	—	works horsestandings continued & work of Div. — Works, timber & materials subbletts — Tennis	
			Pioneers works carried out at Div. also small detachment of 446, 447 F.Coys returned in case further change of of	

Army Form C. 2118.

WAR DIARY
or
INTELLIGENCE SUMMARY.
(Erase heading not required.)

Place	Date	Hour	Summary of Events and Information	Remarks and references to Appendices
E. PERINNES.	29th		446 +447 F. Coys returned to the STA from work under 12th Bn. Visited various home standings - A Report on the work re done attached - During operations 1/30 Div Inf 3/9/17 - 8/9/17 from henceward R.E. is given in App 5 attached.	
	30th			

C.R.E. 50th Division.

Headquarters, 50th Division.
Chief Engineer, XIXth Corps.

1. The Division took over a Sector astride the YPRES-STADEN RAILWAY on 24/10/17, constituting the Centre Division on XIVth Corps Front, which was a two Division Front prior to the entry of the 50th Division.

2. Consequently no existing R.E. Dumps or stores were taken over, and all R.E. arrangements had to be made "ab initio."

3. R.E. Dump was formed at BOESINGHE at B.12.a.5.5., on what had previously been shell-pocked ground, in very quick time by two Sections 7th Field Company R.E. assisted by Infantry.

4. The main work put in hand was the extension of HUNTER STREET and RAILWAY STREET duckboard tracks towards Front Line, and the insertion of cross connections between them, and during first week's work the number of duckboards used averaged 1100 (=2200 yards) a day.

Unfortunately then and later, casualties caused by shell fire and gas shell were heavy.

5. Considerable trouble was experienced due to removal of duckboards by unauthorised persons.

To reduce this to a minimum Infantry were detailed to patrol the tracks, and sentries were placed over Forward Dumps.

On one occasion, when a patrol was wounded 150 yards of his section of track were removed.

Large quantities of duckboards were used on repairs and replacements.

In all, in 17 days over 7000 duckboards were used.

6.   In order to avoid troubles which had been experienced by other Divisions in getting to forward dumps all the stores that were sent up, it was arranged that:-

(a) Officers should be in charge of transport of each Field Co. RE. and of that of the Pioneers.

(b) Pioneers should patrol the roads used by the transport and make good damage before arrival of the transport.

(c) Pioneer emergency groups should be on hand to get ditched wagons out of difficulties.

This used up a certain number of men, but no transport failed to reach its forward dump, in spite of shelling and bad roads.

7.   The number of Light Railway trucks available to feed the R.E. Dump at BOESINGHE from ONDANK Corps Dump varied from 2 to 3: consequently lorry transport had to be used varying from at first 5 a day (2 trips) to 10 a day (2 trips) later, (excluding some 7 lorries a day drawing fascines from VLAMERTINGHE, one journey, for R.F.A. for 3 days).

All loading at ONDANK had to be done by labour supplied by the Division (40 Infantry).

It is considered:-

(a) That Light Railway truckage ought normally to take up all R.E. material.

(b) All loading at Corps Dump ought to be done by Corps, i.e. by labour personnel supplied by A.D. Labour.

8.   From R.E. Dump at BOESINGHE stores were taken forward by Field Companies and Pioneers transport supplemented by 12 G.S. wagons from D.A.C.

9.   Other work done by the Division included:-

(a) Clearing the channel of the BROEMBEEK to carry off water flooding the road running West from NEY CROSS ROADS, and new bridge over, and repairs to bridges.

(b) Clearing channel of the STEENBEEK and repairs to bridges.

(c) Improvements to Brigade H.Q. at MARTINS MILL.

(d) Road repairs in Forward Area.

(e) Erection of small steel shelters (73) between PASCAL FARM and KOEKUIT for Support Battalion.

(f) Erection of sign and notice-boards (108).

(g) Construction of shelters for troops at JOLIE FARM and MARSOUIN Camps (14 complete and 12 incomplete).

(h) Taping out of assembly lines for Infantry before battle of October 26th.

(i) Getting on to road 2 18 pounder guns and 1 4.5 howitzer, bogged.

(j) Construction of 5 shelters for Signals.

(k) Construction of a Soup Kitchen and a Drying Room on the RUGBY-ROSE CROSS ROADS road.

(l) Construction of shelters at R.E. Dump, BOESINGHE and for 2 R.E. Forward Sections (446th Field Co. RE).

(m) Construction of 3 Drying Rooms.

(n) Completion of an Adrian Hut at DUBLIN CAMP.

(o) Repairs to huts damaged by bombs at CARDOEN CAMP.

(p) Improvements to Camps West of the Canal, and construction of shelters in R.E. and other Camps, and sandbagging tents and huts in other Camps West of the Canal.

(q) Construction of bomb store at GOUVY FARM.

(r) Bedplates for Trench Mortars made (16).

(s) 20 cable drums made.

(t) GOUVY FARM tarpaulin shed erected.

(u) Officers Mess, Sergeants Mess, Ablution Benches and Latrines at 447th Field Co. Camp.

(v) 625 duckboards made.

(w) 900 concertinas made.

(x) Training Ground for 149th Infantry Brigade made.

10. On 5th November the Pioneers passed under control of C.E. XIX Corps for work on roads.

On 8th November 7th Field Co. R.E. passed under control of C.E. XIX Corps for work on Artillery Stables etc.

11. Casualties during the period 24th October to 10th November were as follows:-

	Officers.	Other Ranks.	Total.
Killed.	-	5	5
Wounded.	1	20	21
Gassed.	2	26	28
	3	51	54

Infantry casualties. 96.
Pioneer casualties. 81

12. Appendix "Y" shews the quantity of stores issued at BOESINGHE DUMP for use in Area East of the Canal, and quantity of stores issued from ONDANK DUMP for use in Area West of the Canal.

13. Division went out of the line on 10th November 1917.

Major R.E.
A/C.R.E. 50th Division.

H.Q. 50th D.E.
12th November 1917.

LIST OF STORES ISSUED FROM BOESINGHE R.E. DUMP UP TO 8/11/17
AND ONDANK R.E. DUMP UP TO 7/11/17.

ARTICLES.	BOESINGHE	ONDANK	TOTAL	REMARKS.
Sandbags.	156800	218250	375050	
Trenchboards.	8043	344	8387	
Corrugated Iron, sheets.	1500	1275	2775	
XPM, sheets.	1808	2486	4294	
Wire, barbed, coils.	200		200	
" plain.	16	17	33	
" netting, rolls.		2	2	
" concertinas.	130		130	600 made.
Pickets, screw, long.	1180		1180	
" angle iron, long.	2560	3890	6450	
" " " short.	20		20	
" wood, long, 7'.	200		200	
" " short, 3'.	282		282	
Shelters, French, complete.	5½		5½	
" English, large.	390	126	516	) figures are No.
" " small.	1176	284	1460	) of sheets.
Cable drums.	1	40	41	
Trench pumps, complete with hose.		13	13	
Hose, suction.	1		1	
" delivery.	1		1	
" " canvas.		50	50	
Picks.	62	2	64	
Shovels.	2321	520	2841	
Spades.		4	4	
Sand, cwts.		4	4	
Strainer, hose.		1	1	
Hammers, hand.		1	1	
" sledge.		2	2	
Shelters, English, small, fitted.	83		83	
Saws, hand.		1	1	
Padlocks.		1	1	
Wheelbarrows.		12	12	
Canvas, green, rolls.	4	23	27	
" hessian.	1		1	
Oiled linen, yards.		22	22	
Roofing felt, rolls.		81	81	
Cement, barrels.		42	42	
R.S.Joists.	116	8	124	
Artillery bridges.		10	10	
Tanks, 50 galls.		1	1	
Mine cases, chambers, 6'6" x 2'9", sets.		20	20	
Nails, various.	1929	2561	4490	lbs.
Hinges, "T".		20	20	
Hurdles.		25	25	
Stoves, Canadian.		1	1	
Stove piping, feet.		50	50	
Tar, barrels.		1	1	
Culvert Iron, feet.		12	12	
Split props.	265	3121	3586	
Tracing tape.	162		162	
Fascines.	12	30	42	
Timber, 9 x 3, feet.	280	1018	1298	
" 6 x 2 "		400	400	
" 4 x 3 "	500	3990	4490	
" 3 x 3 "	300	5887	6187	
" 7 x 2 "	500		500	
" 5 x 2 "	520		520	
" 4 x 2 "	1100	3650	4750	
" 3 x 2 "		3940	3940	
" 6 x 1 "	3370		3370	
" 4 x 1 "	30		30	
" 1½ x 1½ "		100	100	

ARTICLES.	BOESINGHE	ONDANK	TOTAL	REMARKS.
T. & G. Boarding, feet.		1270	1270	
Forest boarding, lengths.	100		100	
Pitprops.	400	312	712	
Boarding 1", feet.		15722	15722	
Pickets, all sizes.	987	1126	2113	
Notice boards.	69	41	100	
Sleepers for trenchboards.	2074		2074	

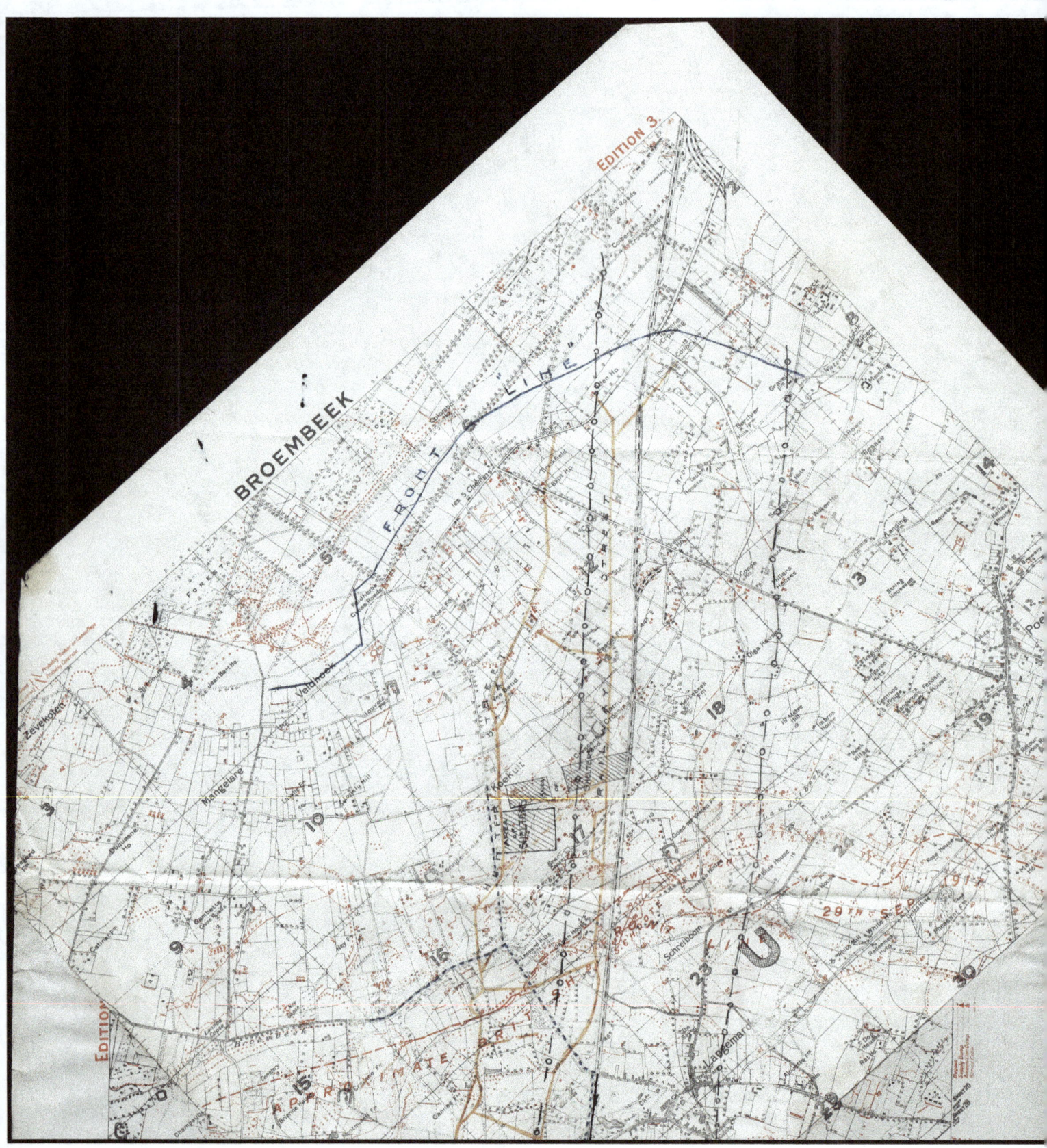

ORIGINAL.

SECRET.

WAR DIARY

of

C.R.E. 50th (Northumbrian) Divisional R.E.

VOLUME No - XXXIII.

DECEMBER 1917.

Army Form C. 2118.

HQRs 50TH DIV RE -
VOL: No XXXIII. - DECEMBER 1917

WAR DIARY
or
INTELLIGENCE SUMMARY.
(Erase heading not required.)

Place	Date	Hour	Summary of Events and Information	Remarks and references to Appendices
EPERLECQUES	1-12-17		Div. in Rest area. Conference held by CE XIII Corps at HQrs of CRE 50th Div.	
	2-12-17		Maj Macpherson on leave to PARIS.	
	3-12-17			
	4-12-17			
	5-12-17		Lieut Rathbone returned from Cap Martin.	
	6-12-17		To YPRES to visit CRE 33rd Div: visited HQ VIII Corps.	
	7-12-17		Visited the 3 Field Companies	
	8-12-17		Left for HQ 33rd Div, Went over ground taken over by 33rd Div.	
			Office: meeting of OC Pioneers & OCs Coys to explain work to be carried out in new sector.	
	9-12-17		Said C's Sheeran & Neon & Penicee Officers Recce to new area by lorry to go over ground & HQ of 33rd Div, in advance of Div HQ.	
YPRES	10-12-17		To Corps HQ & Rec CE. Then to HQ RE 33rd Div, in advance of Div HQ.	
	11-12-17		Inspecting new sector.	
	12-12-17		Relieved 33rd Div in PASSCHENDAELE sector: Adjt & Office Staff assumed YPRES.	
	13-12-17		Called in for Monthly: saw POS & F.POs re arrangements for new SHQ	
	14-12-17		In HQ RE. Movement on morning of 13-12-17. visited others with	
	15-12-17		Adj Wrift for site for new Build dump, as ordered by CE. Corps: visited Hunting for Field Companies & work at SHQ BRANDHOEK to see Div. Commander. h.p.m. b/o SHQ BRANDHOEK to	

Army Form C. 2118.

WAR DIARY
or
INTELLIGENCE SUMMARY
(Erase heading not required.)

202

Place	Date	Hour	Summary of Events and Information	Remarks and references to Appendices
YPRES	16-12-17		To Hq. VIII Corps, BRANDHOEK, Id. Coys. Horse Lines, OAKHANGER Camp dump GOLDFISH Chateau – visited PIONEERS and work on new B.H.Q. noted Col. 8th Divn. re forward Roads.	
	17-12-17		Visited work in front: visited Offr. C.R.E.s, O.C. 171 Tun.g Coy.R.E. Road Above Menin Gate – Raid also B.H.Q. with O.C. 697 2d Coy. R.E. re construction Divl. Comdr. A.A. & Q.M.G. near Menin Gate.	
	18-12-17		Visited No. 3 C.H.Q. & went over old B.H.Q. with O.C. 697 2d Coy. R.E. re rebuilding of OB Visited C.R.E. 8th Divn. Maj. McQueen, Maj. Boast & Capt. Pole mentioned in the Field Marshall's despatch	
	19-12-17		With F.O.I & B.M.G.O. to HAMBURG Shot Bg. re Abraham Heights Huts & Lines Visited by O.C. 171 Tun.g Co. R.E. re noted work at M.G. positions & training – Visited new B.H.Q. recon.n Down to Divl. Comdr. B.H.Q. (Menin Gate): plan of noise Puppet Pole Camps & approved.	
	20-12-17		Visited & took at G.H.Q. Menin Gate: with McQuarie to noted Maj. McQueen to U.K. on 14 days leave.	
	21-12-17		With O.C. 446 Fd. Coy. & Col. R.E. North: then with 7/4th Battalion to PASSCHENDAELE re location of Duck boards: visited other jobs.	
	22-12-17		Conference called by Divl. Commander re system of defence etc.	
	23-12-17		Visited works & C.R.E. 14th Divn.	

Army Form C. 2118.

WAR DIARY
or
INTELLIGENCE SUMMARY.
(Erase heading not required.)

203

Place	Date	Hour	Summary of Events and Information	Remarks and references to Appendices
YPRES	24-12-17		Visited work parties. O.C. 447 Field Coy - CRA: Visited by Corps Water Supply Officer re leaky tank. Offsite Culvert making out dugouts wet.	
	25-12-17		Christmas day. No work except maintenance of ARD track	
	26-12-17		Visited work: prepared report on waterspring supply of RE stores	
	27-12-17		With F.S.O.I + F.S.O.III to Passchendaele. Report (verbally) Visited works of pour Company Comdr. + O.C. Pioneers.	
	28-12-17		Visited Sector of 7th Field Coy at BAVIERE preparing statistics re preparation of works in hand + 33rd Divn I and II and also re proposed work. Visited by Col Clifford with G and 33rd Divn I and II Ire tramline Ostaufer to Passchendaele.	
	29-12-17			
	30-12-17		With N.Z. Army Tramway Co. Ire tramlines in hand. Advance party	
	31-12-17		With F.S.O. to Strand area: Visited works in hand and returned.	
			Belgian "auxiliary" Engineer labour unit reported.	

Matthews
Lt Col
CRE 58th Divn

C. R. E.
149th. Infantry Brigade.
150th. Infantry Brigade.
151st. Infantry Brigade.
7th. D.L.I. (Pioneers).

The Corps Commander wishes his congratulations to be conveyed to all ranks who have organised and are carrying out the work on the duck-board tracks in the 50th. Divisional Area. The progress made since the Division has come into the line is very creditable to those concerned.

C.C.Austey.

Lt.-Col,
General Staff,
50th.Division.

17th. December 1917.

SECRET

WAR DIARY

of

C.R.E. 50TH (NORTHUMBRIAN) DIVISIONAL R.E.

VOLUME XXXIV.

JANUARY, 1918.

January 1918

Army Form C. 2118.

Vol No 34

WAR DIARY
or
INTELLIGENCE SUMMARY

(Erase heading not required.)

Place	Date	Hour	Summary of Events and Information	Remarks and references to Appendices
YPRES				
	1-1-18		Visited in for C.E. VIII Corps who were accompanied by Lieut. Gillam, who received Draft letter "G.S." re Pierochards all teams Mine at SEINE.	
	2-1-18		To G. Office 10-10.15 to meet G.S.O.1. Went above RPP depined at SEINE. To Div. H.Q. 10-2.0 to meet Corps Commander again at 5. to meet Corps Commander talk again to visit works. Preparing statement re difficulties re finding to Div for the Corps. Visited by OC 2nd Field Coy 33rd Div.	
	3-1-18		Handing over notes & reports. Saw Dir. Const. in ques to Corps HQ to see C.E. & dine with Corps Commander.	
	4-1-18		Visited by OC CRE 33rd Div., OC 10th Army Training Co, CRE 29th Div and OC of the new Field Corps. Handing over notes & reports.	
	5-1-18		CRE left on leave. firing to relief of div. moved into 7th M.by Camp.	
	6-1-18		Visited HQ report.	
	7-1-18		Visited 447 MC by.	
	8-1-18		With OC 441 MC by to see works on hypo turned round.	
	9-1-18		Visited 446 MC by.	
	10-1-18		Visited Pioneers.	
	11-1-18		Visited Corps Coy & some works being done by 446 MC by.	
	12-1-18		Visited to report.	
	13- "		Visited 441 field by (446 Pius)	
	14- "		Visited 446 MC by arrived to relieve 446 MC by	
	15-1-18		7th MC by assumed to 7 MC by	
	16-1-18		Visited to report	

WAR DIARY or INTELLIGENCE SUMMARY

Army Form C. 2

Place	Date	Hour	Summary of Events and Information	Remarks
YPRES	17-1-18		446th Fd Coy turned out to assist burial of three killed.	
	18-1-18		(mine) went in late line	
	19-1-18		Nothing to report	
	20-1-18		Nothing to report	
	21-1-18		Moved to WIZERNES. CRE returned from leave.	
WIZERNES	22-1-18		Visited Company Commander & RE School at BLENDECQUES.	
	23-1-18		Saw Field Cos Commanders. Capt Gillespie RAMC joined.	
	24-1-18		Returned to record.	
	25-1-18		Visited CRE 33rd Divn at YPRES with 2nd O.C. & O.C. 2nd Hg Bde.	
	26-1-18		With 9.S.O.II to YPRES to HQ 66th & 33rd Divisions - Pioneers.	
	27-1-18		Proceeded for return to line to "g", & others to Companies & Pioneers.	
	28-1-18		Over to HQ CRE Le CAMBRER 5/S.A.I. joined for temporary duty.	
	29-1-18		To YPRES via VIII Corps HQ. Taking over from CRE 33rd Divn. Visited CRE 66th Divn.	
YPRES	30-1-18		Took over from CRE 33rd Divn. Meeting in a.m. with Field Cos Commanders & Pioneers. 3 American Officers & American NCOs reported for attachment.	
Do-	31-1-18		For 1 day - 6 to forwards area with asst. American Officers guided	

Matthews
Lt Col
CRE 50th Divn

SUMMARY OF WORK DONE BY
Field Companies and Pioneers of 50th Division.
from 13th December 1917, to January 5th 1918.

1. The 50th Division took over the PASSCHENDAELE Sector on 13/12/17 from the 33rd Division, being the right Division of the VIII Corps front.

2. Owing the the Division Headquarters at Menin Gate, in occupation by Headquarters 33rd Division being burnt out on early morning of 13/12/17, accommodation had to be provided for the 50th Division Headquarters elsewhere.

This was done near the Convent and involved erecting 4 Nissen Huts, 2 Cookhouses, and repairs etc. to 6 Dug-outs.

3. The work to be done forward was extension and tripling of Duckboard Tracks, maintenance and extension of ARTILLERY ROADS, North and South, continuation of Tramway alongside Artillery Road, North, and provision of Shelters for Infantry, R.F.A. and R.A.M.C.

4. In addition to the above, Pill-boxes have been reconnoitred and their repair for occupation taken in hand. This work entailed the pumping out of water, clearing debris and bodies, shoring up in some cases, and erection of bunks.

Several Nissen Huts have been erected and supervision given for several more.

5. Re-construction of burnt-out Divisional Headquarters (Menin Gate) YPRES. A large amount of work has been done during the time the Division was in the Line and the job is almost completed; the value of the work done is estimated at £2,000 (Approx). A plan is attached marked "A".

6. Miscellaneous work as shown on the attached Summary of work done.

7. A schedule marked "B" is attached shewing principal items of R.E. Stores issued from the Divisional Dump. This does not include a large quantity of Stores (mostly material for Sleeper Roads and Duck-boards Tracks) sent up by Light Railway direct to works.

Capt, R.E. & Adj.,
for C.R.E. 50th Division.

H.Q. 50th D.E.
January 7th 1918.

GENERAL

1. During the period under review, difficulties have been experienced with the supply and transport of Stores.

2. Frost during the greater part of the period caused difficulty with many works; in some cases hard ground had to be broken up - for excavation - by means of explosives.

   Frost and snow, combined with the lack of white camouflage prevented the excavation of the camouflaged trench at D.12.a.7.4. for R.F.A., O.P.

3. Progress of work on Sleeper roads Artillery North and Artillery South could have been 50% greater, had transport and supply of materials been satisfactory.

4. One Section of 7th. Field Company R.E. was at BAILLEUL on Corps work during the entire period, thus reducing the output of work of that Company on forward work.

5. The frequency of Brigade reliefs militated against large output of work, but the volume of work performed is thought to be quite satisfactory in the circumstances.

6. The health of R.E. has been very good, and the casualties small in number.

7. It is urged that :-

   (a) Fighting troops should not be called on to provide staffs for loading etc. at Corps R.E. Dump and Divisional R.E. Dump (nearly 100 men during this tour). It is considered that for these services, labour should be furnished by the A.D. Labour.

   (b) C.R.E. should have a fixed allotment of lorries: Uncertainty as to the number of lorries that will be forthcoming next day makes the successful organisation and execution of work a difficult matter.

   (c) The Pioneer Battalion should, if possible, be kept up to Establishment.

   (d) The improvement of the KANSAS CROSS - SEINE push tram line, and the provision of a tractor would save much man power, and thereby enable more work to be carried out by the Division.

SHELTERS

1. For Infantry in MARX and SEINE Camps, 50 were completed and Sandbagged.

2. For Machine Gun Company, 1 small shelter was completed.

3. Shelter for Signals Power Buzzer and detachment of Signal Company completed.

4. New Brigade Headquarters, 3 Shelters erected and floored and Gas door made and fixed. Bunking in progress. Camouflage provided.

5.   For R.A.M.C., 5 Shelters completed and sandbagged. Water pumped out of Pill Box and inside revetted. 153 yards of triple duckboard track laid.

        Hamburg R.A.P., 2 Dugouts floored and fitted with Steel Sectors. Partitions and 2 doors made and fixed. 6 Stands for Stretchers fixed. Flooring hut and sheeting back. Sumps made and revetted.

6.   Haalen Switch, 16 Shelters completed, (4 in hand).

7.   For D.R.s, excavated for and fixed 58 Steel Sector Sheets 1 door made and 12 bunks fixed and wired.

8.   Tea Canteen, 5 French steel shelters erected. Hut erected and Soyer's Stove put in. Additional shelves put up, and hut sandbagged against bombs.

9.   For R.F.A., 7 Shelters erected and sandbagged. Old dugout cleared and strengthened for use as Magazine, door made and fixed. Existing Signal Station (English Shelter) enlarged 9 feet, 15 Sectors French Shelter erected. 8 Gas Curtain frames and 2 Gas doors fixed. Clearing debris from side and roof of Pill Box and Sandbag wall built in front. 2 latrines, 2 Cookhouses excavated for and completed.

10.   At 446th. Company's Headquarters, Cellars cleaned and bunks erected.

11.   C.R.E. Headquarters, Cellar whitewashed and stove fitted.

12.   At 447th. Company's Headquarters, 2 Steel Shelters erected and sandbagged. 1 of these to be a guard room.

13.   Crest Farm, 4 Shelters completed.

FASCINE ROAD
for R.F.A. In D.21.c., 120 yards Formation completed. 3 holes filled.

1 Gunpit for D.156 Battery R.F.A. repaired.

TRAMWAY ALONGSIDE ARTILLERY ROAD NORTH

504 yards Tramway formation completed. 7 breaks repaired. 50 sleepers and 56 Slabs salved. Now discontinued.

PILL BOXES

28 Pill Boxes reconnoitred. 4 made fit for occupation. 4 bunks erected in one.

b CONCERTINAS

236 made.

DUCKBOARD TRACKS.

"H" & "K" Tracks were tripled complete, also R.A.M.C. track.

JUDAH Track was constructed as a double width track from Junction with R.A.M.C. track to D.18. Central (near SEINE).

CREST FARM track was constructed as a double width track from Waterfields D.10.d.5.7. to near PASSCHENDAELE D.6.c.8.3., and trestles put in thence to Convent at D.6.d.1.7.

The mesh wiring of above track was proceeded with concurrently over 6000 yards of mesh wire having been used.

Total Duckboard Tracks, New construction work.

TRACK	TRESTLES	DUCKBOARDS	WIRE MESH. YDS.	REMARKS
H,K, & R.A.M.C.	506	2260	2756	Tripling.
JUDAH.	2016	3722	2883	Double width
CREST FARM	1074	2145	1006	" "
	3596	8127	6645	

ROADS

ARTILLERY SLAB ROAD NORTH 692 yards Road done. 12 breaks repaired.

ARTILLERY ROAD SOUTH, Improving Mule Track from DEVIL'S CROSSING FORWARD.
1360 yards done. 1864 Slabs were used of which 110 were Salved. 6562 Sleepers were used, 380 of this Number were Salved. 18 breaks repaired. 5 Turning or passing places made.

HUTTING

C.R.E.'s Office - Office extended, new windows made and stove fixed. Sandbagging round Office.

447th. Field Co. Headquarters. Cycle Shed to hold 30 bicycles erected. Drying Shed erected.

Drying Shed, YPRES for baths completed and concrete slab floor laid. Stove fixed.

Temporary D.H.Q., YPRES. 4 Nissen Huts erected and 4010 Sandbags filled and laid round huts. Stoves were fitted, 2 Cookhouses built, Shelves, 4 Map Boards, 16 Window Blinds, 4 Weather Boards and 4 Footscrapers.

POTIJZE. 2 Nissen Huts erected for prophylactic foot treatment.

BRANDHOEK for Ordnance. 3 Nissen Huts completed.

RECONSTRUCTION OF DIVISIONAL HEADQUARTERS (Menin Gate).

This work was begun on 21.12.17 and handed over to 33rd. Division almost completed on 5.1.18.

The job involved clearing out debris R.S. Joists etc. from 4 Casemates 90 feet X 19 feet and the construction therein of a D.H.Q. vide plan attached.

Effort was made to ensure a nearly fireproof and bomb proof H.Q. by minimising the employment of timber, and using steel, brickwork and concrete as much as possible.

The secondary roofing in the casemates consisted of French steel troughing (curved and straight); Unfortunately there were insufficient curved sheets to admit of these being used throughout, on pitprop stanchions around which C.I. was wrapped.

Partitions are of C.I. on studding. 3 Mess Kitchens were made also.

Interior of rooms and roofing was painted white.

Most of the rooms have brick fireplaces.

The job involved the employment of 2 Sections Field Co. R.E. and an average daily working party of 92 men.

DUGOUTS

PASSCHENDAELE. Reconnaisance of deep dugout, clearing entrance: Work done on O.P. for R.F.A.

Temporary D.H.Q. Improved and drained 6 dugouts, renewal of roof, entrances improved: Dugouts bunked, whitewashed etc.

DEFENCE WORK

ABRAHAM HEIGHTS SWITCH LINE. Position of barbed wire obstacle traced, and wiring well in hand by Infantry.

HAALEN SWITCH. 5 Posts traced, 4 small steel shelters installed in Posts Nos. 2,3,4 & 5.

Work in hand on No. 1.

MISCELLANEOUS

Public Incinerator built for Town Major YPRES.

447th. Field Co. R.E., Camp Improvements, Fixing Stoves, 54 Duckboards laid, 5 loads brick put on Horse Standings. Racks in Harness Shed, Wire buckets made and painted, Ablution benches, Sandbagging Nissen Hut.

Repairs to Baths at BRANDHOEK. Making sumps.

3 Base plates made for Trench Mortars.

Making and painting discs for Infantry.

Stables for C.R.E., accommodation for 10 horses completed, bricking out in progress.

MISCELLANEOUS.

Gas Curtains at Prison, YPRES repaired.

Spray Baths at BRANDHOEK, inspected and tested Hot Water apparatus.

Ridge Camp, 8 Huts protected against bombs from E.A.

Log Shelter at 7th. Co. R.E. Headquarters erected.
Battalion
~~New Brigade~~ Headquarters, Advanced, Sundry Improvements.

Notice Boards, 10 fixed on YPRES - Poperinghe Road as guide for lorries provided in case Reserve Brigade was urgently required forward.

SUMMARY OF WORK DONE BY
Field Companies and Pioneers of 50th Division.
from 23rd December 1917, to January 5th 1918.

1. The 50th Division took over the PASSCHENDAELE Sector on 13/12/17 from the 33rd Division, being the right Division of the VIII Corps front.

2. Owing the the Division Headquarters at Menin Gate, in occupation by Headquarters 33rd Division being burnt out on early morning of 13/12/17 accommodation had to be provided for the 50th Division Headquarters elsewhere.

   This was done near the Convent and involved erecting 4 Nissen Huts, 2 Cookhouses, and repairs etc. to 6 Dug-outs.

3. The work to be done forward was extension and tripling of Duckboard Tracks, maintenance and extension of ARTILLERY ROADS, North and South, continuation of Tramway alongside Artillery Road, North, and provision of Shelters for Infantry, R.F.A. and R.A.M.C. &c.

4. In addition to the above, Pill-boxes have been reconnoitred and their repair for occupation taken in hand. This work entailed the pumping out of water, clearing debris and bodies, shoring up in some cases, and erection of bunks.

   Several Nissen Huts have been erected and supervision given for for several more.

5. Re-construction of burnt-out Divisional Headquarters (Menin Gate) YPRES. A large amount of work has been done during the time the Division was in the Line and the job is almost completed; the value of the work done is estimated at £2,000 (Approx). A plan is attached marked "A".

6. Miscellaneous work as shown on the attached Summary of work done.

7. A schedule marked "B" is attached shewing principal items of R.E. Stores issued from the Divisional Dump. This does not include a large quantity of Stores (mostly material for Sleeper Roads and Duck-boards Tracks) sent up by Light Railway direct to works.

                                             Capt, R.E. & Adj.,
                                          for C.R.E. 50th Division.

H.Q. 50th D.E.
January 7th 1918.

GENERAL

1. During the period under review, difficulties have been experienced with the supply and transport of Stores.

2. Frost during the greater part of the period caused difficulty with many works; in some cases hard ground had to be broken up - for excavation - by means of explosives.

Frost and snow, combined with the lack of white camouflage prevented the excavation of the camouflaged trench at D.12.a.7.4. for R.F.A., O.P.

3. Progress of work on Sleeper roads Artillery North and Artillery South could have been 50% greater, had transport and supply of materials been satisfactory.

4. One Section of 7th. Field Company R.E. was at BAILLEUL on Corps work during the entire period, thus reducing the output of work of that Company on forward work.

5. The frequency of Brigade reliefs militated against large output of work, but the volume of work performed is thought to be quite satisfactory in the circumstances.

6. The health of R.E. has been very good, and the casualties small in number.

7. It is urged that :-

(a) Fighting troops should not be called on to provide staffs for loading etc. at Corps R.E. Dump and Divisional R.E. Dump (nearly 100 men during this tour). It is considered that for these services, labour should be furnished by the A.D. Labour.

(b) C.R.E. should have a fixed allotment of lorries: Uncertainty as to the number of lorries that will be forthcoming next day makes the successful organisation and execution of work a difficult matter.

(c) The Pioneer Battalion should, if possible, be kept up to Establishment.

(d) The improvement of the KANSAS CROSS - SEINE push tram line, and the provision of a tractor would save much man power, and thereby enable more work to be carried out by the Division.

SHELTERS

1. For Infantry in MANX and SEINE Camps, 50 were completed and Sandbagged.

2. For Machine Gun Company, 1 small shelter was completed.

3. Shelters for Signals Power Buzzer and detachment of Signal Company completed.

4. New Brigade Headquarters, 3 Shelters erected and floored and Gas door made and fixed. Bunking in progress. Camouflage provided.

5.   For R.A.M.C., 5 Shelters completed and sandbagged. Water pumped out of Pill Box and inside revetted. 153 yards of triple duckboad track laid.

Hamburg R.A.P., 2 Dugouts floored and fitted with Steel Sectors. Partitions and 2 doors made and fixed. 6 Stands for Stretchers fixed. Flooring hut and sheeting back. Sumps made and revetted.

6.   Haalen Switch, 16 Shelters completed, (4 in hand).

7.   For D.R.s, excavated for and fixed 38 Steel Sector Sheets 1 door made and 12 bunks fixed and wired.

8.   Tea Canteen, 5 French steel shelters erected. Hut erected and Soyer's Stove put in. Additional shelves put up, and hut sandbagged against bombs.

9.   For R.F.A., 7 Shelters erected and sandbagged. Old dugout cleared and strengthened for use as Magazine, door made and fixed. Existing Signal Station (English Shelter) enlarged 9 feet, 15 Sectors French Shelter erected. 8 Gas Curtain frames and 2 Gas doors fixed. Clearing debris from side and roof of Pill Box and Sandbag wall built in front. 2 latrines, 2 Cookhouses excavated for and completed.

10.   At 446th. Company's Headquarters, Cellars cleaned and bunks erected.

11.   C.R.E. Headquarters, Cellar whitewashed and stove fitted.

12.   At 447th. Company's Headquarters, 2 Steel Shelters erected and sandbagged. 1 of these to be a guard room.

13.   Crest Farm, 4 Shelters completed.

FASCINE ROAD
for R.F.A.   In D.21.c., 120 yards Formation completed. 3 holes filled.

1 Gunpit for D.156 Battery R.F.A. repaired.

TRAMWAY ALONGSIDE ARTILLERY ROAD NORTH

504 yards Tramway formation completed. 7 breaks repaired. 50 sleepers and 56 Slabs salved. Now discontinued.

PILL BOXES

28 Pill Boxes reconnoitred. 4 made fit for occupation. 4 bunks erected in one.

b CONCERTINAS

238 made.

DUCKBOARD TRACKS.

"H" & "K" Tracks were tripled complete, also R.A.M.C. track.

JUDAH Track was constructed as a double width track from Junction with R.A.M.C. track to D.16. Central (near SEINE).

CREST FARM track was constructed as a double width track from Waterfields D.10.d.5.7. to near PASSCHENDAELE D.6.c.8.3., and trestles put in thence to Convent at D.6.d.1.7.

The mesh wiring of above track was proceeded with concurrently over 6030 yards of mesh wire having been used.

Total Duckboard Tracks, New construction work.

TRACK	TRESTLES	DUCKBOARDS	WIRE MESH. YDS.	REMARKS
H, K, & R.A.M.C.	506	2260	2756	Tripling.
JUDAH.	2016	3722	2883	Double width
CREST FARM	1074	2145	1006	" "
	3596	8127	6645	

ROADS

ARTILLERY SLAB ROAD NORTH 692 yards Road done. 12 breaks repaired.

ARTILLERY ROAD SOUTH, Improving Mule Track from DEVIL'S CROSSING FORWARD.
1360 yards done. 1864 Slabs were used of which 110 were Salved. 6562 Sleepers were used, 380 of this Number were Salved. 18 breaks repaired. 5 Turning or passing places made.

HUTTING

C.R.E.'s Office - Office extended, new windows made and stove fixed. Sandbagging round Office.

447th. Field Co. Headquarters. Cycle Shed to hold 30 bicycles erected. Drying Shed erected.

Drying Shed, YPRES for baths completed and concrete slab floor laid. Stove fixed.

Temporary D.H.Q., YPRES. 4 Nissen Huts erected and 4010 Sandbags filled and laid round huts. Stoves were fitted, 2 Cookhouses built, Shelves, 4 Map Boards, 16 Window Blinds, 4 Weather Boards and 4 Footscrapers.

POTIJZE. 2 Nissen Huts erected for prophylactic foot treatment.

BRANDHOEK for Ordnance. 3 Nissen Huts completed.

RECONSTRUCTION OF DIVISIONAL HEADQUARTERS (Menin Gate).

This work was begun on 21.12.17 and handed over to 33rd. Division almost completed on 5.1.18.

The job involved clearing out debris R.S. Joists etc. from 4 Casemates 90 feet X 19 feet and the construction therein of a D.H.Q. vide plan attached.

Effort was made to ensure a nearly fireproof and bomb proof H.Q. by minimising the employment of timber, and using steel, brickwork and concrete as much as possible.

The secondary roofing in the casemates consisted of French steel troughing (curved and straight); Unfortunately there were insufficient curved sheets to admit of these being used throughout, on pitprop stanchions around which C.I. was wrapped.

Partitions are of C.I. on studding. 3 Mess Kitchens were made also.

Interior of rooms and roofing was painted white.

Most of the rooms have brick fireplaces.

The job involved the employment of 2 Sections Field Co. R.E. and an average daily working party of 92 men.

DUGOUTS

PASSCHENDAELE. Reconnaisance of deep dugout, clearing entrance: Work done on O.P. for R.F.A.

Temporary D.H.Q. Improved and drained 6 dugouts, renewal of roof, entrances improved: Dugouts bunked, whitewashed etc.

DEFENCE WORK

ABRAHAM HEIGHTS SWITCH LINE. Position of barbed wire obstacle traced, and wiring well in hand by Infantry.

HAALEN SWITCH. 5 Posts traced, 4 small steel shelters installed in Posts Nos. 2,3,4 & 5.

Work in hand on No. 1.

MISCELLANEOUS

Public Incinerator built for Town Major YPRES.

447th. Field Co. R.E., Camp Improvements, Fixing Stoves, 54 Duckboards laid, 5 loads brick put on Horse Standings. Racks in Harness Shed, Fire buckets made and painted, Ablution benches, Sandbagging Nissen Hut.

Repairs to Baths at BRANDHOEK. Making sumps.

3 Base plates made for Trench Mortars.

Making and painting discs for Infantry.

Stables for C.R.E., accommodation for 10 horses completed, bricking out in progress.

MISCELLANEOUS.

Gas Curtains at Prison, YPRES repaired.

Spray Baths at BRANDHOEK, inspected and tested Hot Water apparatus.

Ridge Camp, 8 Huts protected against bombs from E.A.

Log Shelter at 7th. Co. R.E. Headquarters erected.

~~New Brigade~~ Battalion Headquarters, Advanced, Sundry Improvements.

Notice Boards, 10 fixed on YPRES - Poperinghe Road as guide for lorries provided in case Reserve Brigade was urgently required forward.

C.R.E. 50th Division.

SCHEDULE "B"

MATERIAL ISSUED AT TRANSIT DUMP
from
December 13th/17 to January 5th/18.

ARTICLES.

Article	Quantity
Sandbags	243500.
Trenchboards	7882.
Corrugated Iron, sheets	4761.
X.P.M. sheets	2869.
Wire, barbed, coils	1143.
" plain, coils	110.
Wire-netting	129.
Pickets, screw, long	2050.
" " short	3266.
" angle iron, long	3277.
" wood, long	3798.
" " , short	1140.
Shelters, French	83.
" , English, large	1127.
" , " , small	760.
Lift & Force pumps	5.
Canvas, green, rolls	12 & half.
" , hessian, rolls	83 & half.
Oiled Linen	63 yards.
Roofing felt, rolls	205.
Cement, barrels	69 & half.
R.S. Joists	279.
Nails	None.
Nails 1" & 2"	922 lbs.
" 3" & 4"	3353 lbs.
" 5" & 6"	3672 lbs.
" Clout	165 lbs.
Staples 1,1/2 inch	458 lbs.
Spikes	6180 lbs.
Hinges "T"	105.
Wire, weaving, narrow, rolls	335.
" " , large , "	20.
Pickets, park	810.
Lime	14 bags.
Wire, French	60.
Hand-carts	9.
Dogs	1792.
Stoves	105.
Stove-piping, lengths	35.
Sleepers, for trenchboards	220.
Wire-cutters	41.
Tracing-tape, rolls	244.
Notice-boards	156.
Pit-props	1125.
" , split	882.
Camp-boards	130.
Steel troughing, 9'0"	104.
" " , 6'0"	66.
Bridges, artillery	5.
Camouflage, green	28.
" , brown	6.
Stove-piping elbows	10.
Sand	2 trucks.
Doors	50.
Gravel	None.
Ablution benches	2.
Timber 1"	16804 feet.
" 3/4" & 1" boarding	1-853 "
" 4 X 2	8001 "
" 3 X 2	44320 "
Forest boarding	2640 "
Trench Dr.	312

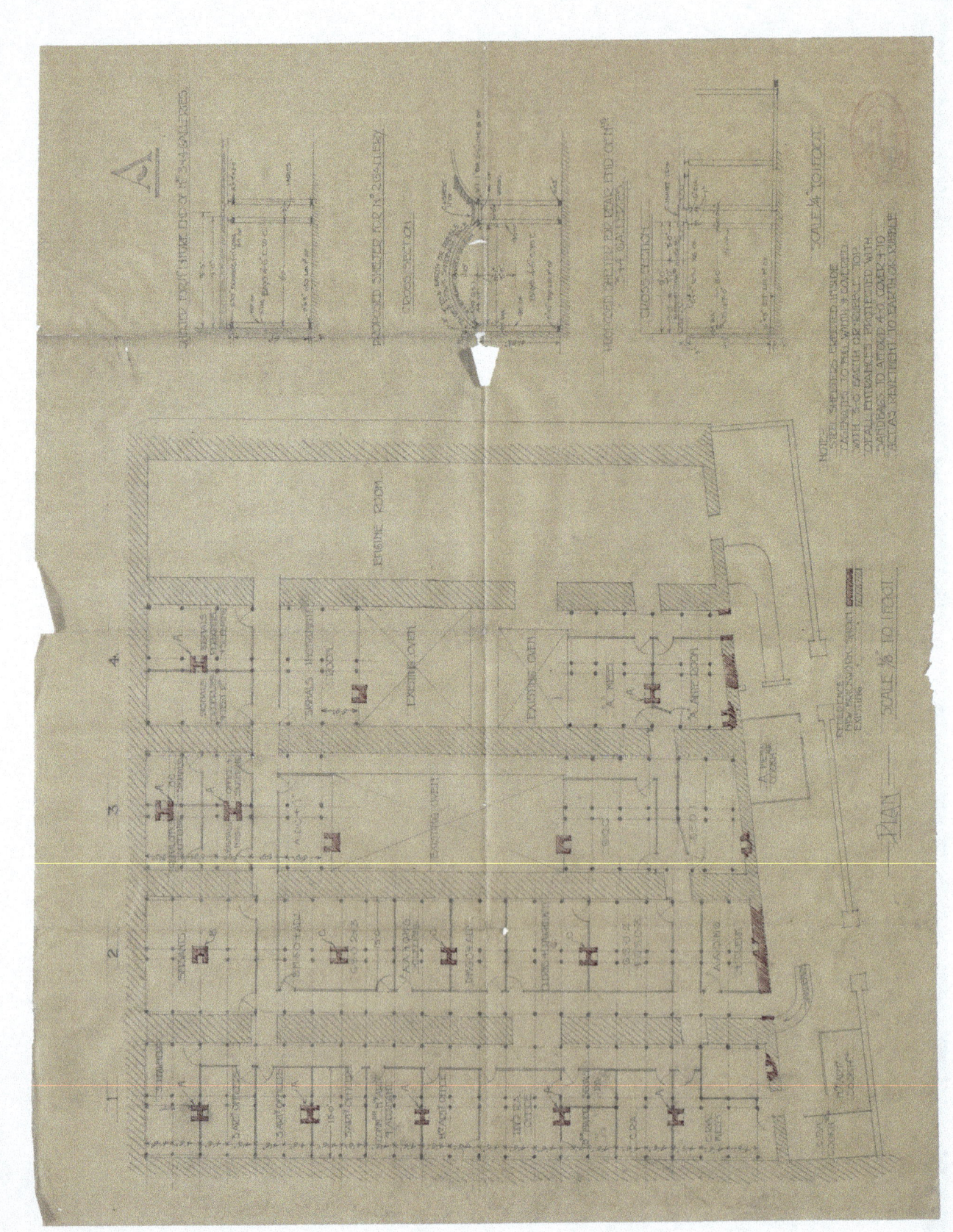

-SECRET-

WAR DIARY

of

C.R.E. 50TH (NORTHUMBRIAN) DIVISIONAL R.E.

VOLUME XXXV.

FEBRUARY, 1918.

Army Form C. 2118.

WAR DIARY or INTELLIGENCE SUMMARY.

(Erase heading not required.)

H.Q. OR's R.E. 50th DIVn
FEBRUARY 1918 — Vol No 35

Instructions regarding War Diaries and Intelligence Summaries are contained in F. S. Regs., Part II. and the Staff Manual respectively. Title pages will be prepared in manuscript.

Place	Date	Hour	Summary of Events and Information	Remarks and references to Appendices
YPRES	1-2-18		With ADMS to Magazine re conversion to use as a detraining Stn in pm to CE YPRES Corps.	
	2-2-18		With OC 446 Fd Co visiting works in hand in forward area.	
	3-2-18		Visited by CRE 66th Divn re transfer of area. Stopped OC 446 Fd Coy R.E.	
	4-2-18		Noted works in hand in YPRES. Noted works in hand was visited by OC Nos Army Tramway Co re transfer to Divn of work on Creat Jam & tramline. Visited Stn 4 re large n° of works ordered & inadequate labour supply. Rec'd telegram ordering Lt Col. Rattray to hand over to Major Kethven & report to War Office on 6-2-18. Attested CRE 50th Divn and	
	5-2-18		During this period the Divn (Passchendaela) front has been by 1 Bde in line (Frequently relieved) — Disposition of RE parties as follows C Major (various) i.e. 3 sections of 7th Co & 1 & 446 Cos working in forward areas — Roster (i.e. 3 sections) of 7th Co & 446 Cos working the alternate area — Remainder in back areas. between these dates in Flanders.	
	6.t.10th		The main works in hand between Passchendaele — Deep dugout works in Passchendaele various locations & Blockhouses (Reinforced), Strong dumps in neighbourhood, Preparation of slotted sidings for forming "Tunnel" dumps in neighbourhood of "SEINE" construction & camouflage by the HARRISON Smith host of maintenance & repair of all existing Plank Roads, Duckboard Tracks.	

Henri Ramuz ?
Major ARE 50 DN

WAR DIARY
INTELLIGENCE SUMMARY

Army Form C. 2118.

HDQRS RE 50TH DIVN

FEBRUARY 1918 — Vol No

Place	Date	Hour	Summary of Events and Information	Remarks and references to Appendices
	10th/11th		for forming shelter takings for forward dumps N.O. SEINE, Construction of Concrete "shelters" for R.A. personnel (18 pr Gun btteries) relief of Cattaui road in YPRES, removal of YPRES magazine into Menin Steenwerck NTE & TTH at Casex. Between these dates Div.st. flank relieved so that 66th on ZONNEBEKE Rd. 1 Brigade frontage being taken over from 66th Divn. The front line was held with 2 Brigades in the line. This entailed an entire readjustment of work & re-allotment of work to Bn. RE. Types. This was effected without hitch in lengthy fatigues & Head'qtrs moving places 448 - 7.6.c.g on Planer in charge of work. Or readjustment through places of "PANORAMA" Park south of CREST Farm. Well onto will left 13 co area East of "PANORAMA" Park South of Cannister Stevenson) & 7 F. Coy. in charge of Cathan Rd. R.d. onwards to ARCY Rd. (north) & 447 Coy. took & took W.R. stone line — During this period work progressed to follow — Roundabout defences (allows be behind) + work which however towards making & keep & Roundabouts method of Construction about CROST Rd. Completion of MAMEEN switch Pills Boy, making new pots forward, but 2 live potted "HILL 60s" defence, clearing flooded pill boxes, completing Cattaui Pots with "inhabitants" Commencement of POS-SITE, starting 5 new Pots in forttant & reserve lines of this front system. Hy. ton to Denullmite (6") emplacement Colony, 2 emplacement for Machine (Cock. on 18 pr Guns), shelter for Gun btteries, & Infantry Cannings Con statices in front of NE Cannings Ho. 6H of Ng(7ch.), ready by 10th. Gunner Com.
	12th & 23rd		

WAR DIARY or INTELLIGENCE SUMMARY

Army Form C. 2118.

HQ ORS RE 50th DIV

FEBRUARY 1918 Vol No.

Place	Date	Hour	Summary of Events and Information	Remarks and references to Appendices
			Civil trial took. Connections & Collieries & CREST FARM Huchin to Japres	
YPRES	23.		HOOGEN CAFE (one 200 * N.H & CREST-FM) Construction & Infantry & Comm[unication] trenches for btty's, revive winning, sitings & housing 2 & 3rd, & new MGs to gallons the Different Reserve lines. Stn Front system, defences & Emblems. Complete the Duckboards links Flank 2nd (then the front being about 13 miles) Dala Board Rounds improvements & labor accompany Spec. Investigations in all Collieries of YPRES improvements in labor accommodation. During this period the Difficulty Batteries in know Spitfiring Reformers. A great deal of work in entraining reviving the front line. 2 forts & had systems. Relief of 50th Div by 33rd Div. Completed by 24th Feb. When Div moved to WIZERNES area. (Training period & G.H.Q reserve.) The FE Cos were located in Brigade front areas. 2 section 446 Co were entrained trucks at Limbres to Coke Bridge School. 7 to Lez Dix to NORTBECQUES to instruct Ring 447 Co. Lizre in orbit to reorg training. D.H.Q. ly – at hp LIZ School. Got restore water training for 10 days. In the army arrangements to supply sanitation were in charge of Divisions are emelle but requirements to Divisions' water & off-plants to retain material available – RARE Health & Esp. reviews good throughout the month.	

Signed Ewen J.H.M.R.
CRE 50-DN

50th (Northumbrian) Divisional Engineers

C.   R.   E.

50th DIVISION.

MARCH 1918

SECRET

WAR DIARY

- of -

C. R. E.
50th. (Northumbrian) Divisional R.E.

Volume No. 36.
March 1918

WAR DIARY

MARCH 1918

HDQRS 50th DIVL: R.E. — Vol No 36

Place	Date	Hour	Summary of Events and Information	Remarks and references to Appendices
INVERNES	1st to 6th		During this period Divl remained in TILLOLOY area & S.H.Q. remained Except A. 2 Sect & 446 F.Co. R.E. 2 Sect. 7th Fd Co. R.E. detached & sent a Camp thrown to send on numbers of N.C.O.s & Sapt. respecting the University of Zoology bone etc to Camp at a limited training — Various Schemes who carried out at the area during this period included: Completion of Delesault Plant at the Divl baths a W36P.N.E.S. return to Inverness (both re information) to Inverness "Pro Training" Accomm of Sect & NCO's (12th Govnt) a Saw Pantry & listing season of other Gas Posts Groud "Nine" TATT'N HEAD. Also a few sentry ways of other Gas Sentry been thrown to L.M. Army (showing the area) for inspection to & Inv Mitry crit'ms of Cttee. – On 2nd inst. C.R.E. visited C.E. 4th Army inspecting lectures in Army R. 3rd inst. C.R.E. visited "N.O.R.S.E.C.N.E.S." to allow of their seeing a "Training". C.E. 4th Army at Inverness & N.O.R.S.E.C.N.E.S. to allow of their seeing a "Training". C.E. 4th Army at L.M.D.R.E.S. + and informed the interviewed in to 446 & 2 Sect 446 F.Co. R.E. visited the Sapt. and found so rest of objections to being at a Sap wake L.M.D.R.E.S. (The Coy. had had no rel of opportunity to carry out all Training training for some 2 Mos: + it is considered most necessary that all Training facilities be secured whenever July in the year before Summer Campaigns). A 4th inst. A.D.M.S. with C.R.E. inspected transport + tech of the Fd Coys R.E. 2 & 6 – Resolution Satisfactory —
INVERNES	7th		C.R.E. lectured "about A. D. to S of India Sapt Battery (1st of min & 3 lectures to be given) – Orders received at 10 P.M. for Divl Group to an area S.W. of AMIENS. Comencing 1 P.M. 8th inst. — Orders due for to hand 2 Coys 7th Coy. for 10 representatives at D.R. Representation A.R.H.

WAR DIARY or INTELLIGENCE SUMMARY

Army Form C. 2118.

MARCH 1918
HQ Rs 50TH DIV: RE. - Vol No 3.

Place	Date	Hour	Summary of Events and Information	Remarks and references to Appendices
MORBECQUE	8th		D.H.Q & R.E. H.Q entered MORBECQUE & took over land in THOUS area billeting no ditto re Curtailed orders to Mobile Eqpts. Returned to HQ Army Div. Scouring - Tchg. Mess before noon Jn -	
MORBECQUE	9th		DHQ & R.E. MDQ obtained MORBECQUE only Jn - Div became 5th Army Reserve	
"	10th		Attended Conference at SDth Div HQ relative protective posts operating and use of 50th Div. Visited METZ & NOYELLES. Things in Total lots NE of PERONNE with Div Staff to preliminary Reconnaissance of ground ✓ check Div's need spots not with Entrusiasts -	
HARBONNIÈRES	11th		DHQ & R.E. MDQ moved from MORBECQUE to HARBONNIÈRES - Set out back with this J Cs 5th Army relative protes of RE Stores Dumps & Only Ystores in front of operations taking place within J Div to open in Michael set on Small J Obstns being made if Fdcy could interfering protecting frontier Dvsn. Many Reports - huge entrance of Fdcy letting Postmen - "Harassing Shells" Returned from 50th Div(J) Infantry protective Postmen. ment to F Corps. Conference Sir J.G.T.D. re railway Train for Postmen - Various Dumps.	
"	12th		"Lateral rodl" in HARBONNIÈRES concerted with tree Postmen - Mines repaired by a futurs round -	
"	13th		Visited Cs 5th Army to obtain Information relating RE dumps & Materials with protects of Patrn - broken out of ebs down by eaun), but that J Div like protective off between. Wrote Cs Nos, 2nd North Mid. Wrote Cs Nos, 5ts Fr. Div lyn. branch entramain. Ltr Lyg 447 C. Lbg 437 forked MorbecQue Calls JW. Putts (20ft) assured for km in relief J St Hodgen - 15 Stop -	

WAR DIARY
or
INTELLIGENCE SUMMARY
(Erase heading not required.)

Army Form C. 2118.

H.Q.RE 50TH DIV.NRE
MARCH 1918 Vol No 9/6

Place	Date	Hour	Summary of Events and Information	Remarks and references to Appendices
MARBEUF	14th		CRE lectured Adv. A.S.C. to Batt.s. Visited OC's 446 & 447 Fd.Coys. about the proposed return of RE employ'd on various projects & reverting to prep'n for their schemes under preparation if brigades of Divisions retention to 1st Army; divisions to 180th Brigade. —	
"	15th		Inspected 446 & 447 F.C's RE on parade v inspected — OC Batt. Lectured Adv NCOs into "field B.rys". — Field recd inst.n for all 3 F.Coys. & 7' D.L.I. (Pioneers) to prepare & two transport by march in ABC. into positions of defence in sector X.IX (A.Corps) — 7 Coy. to MONCHY LACACHE, 446 & 247 Coys & 7' D.L.I. (Pioneers) to TERRY. RE.MR.D.S remain with Div.n	
"	16th		Coy's march as shown above. — CRE & ADC. & HQ off 50 Div. travel as further. Reconnaissance at METZ and NOYELLES instructing Inspection D.C.E. quarters — C.B.E. (Batt. for PUISIEUX PR.) & CRE went into Forward Military who visited C.E. XIX C.M.Bn (Ref'n PUISIEUX PR.) on to be employed in Reserve Defences. — CARBONNEL went when C.R.E. Reserve Battn in the model —	
"	17th		In XIX Corps fr. p.507 & all roads as inspection Reserve Positions onto model — Inspection fr. p.507 of all roads 28:	
"	18th/19th		Visited all Pos.Coys & Pioneer Batts employed under CE, Cav Corps in "Rear Zone" defences in the neighbourhood of TERRY & MONCHY LACACHE. 7th D.L.I. Pioneers Supply'g to reinforced 800 maril labs (1 Employt Coy, 1 Hamilton Coy & 446 & 447 C's making with 50 D.L.I (Pioneers). Heavy bombardment on enemy front commenced about 10.30 p.m. 19th inst. - orders received at 6 a.m. 20th instalants to hold move on further orders) —	
"	20th		Received warning orders duly at 2.pm for RE troops by train & march route to neighbourhood of BEAMETZ —	
BEAMETZ	21st		D.R moved via left = & during night 21/22 marched to occupy the "Green Line". At this time the Field Coys & Pioneer Batt.n hurriedly in GREEN Line further still in neighbourhood of TERRY. —	

Shurmur
Col RE
CRE 50 DN.

WAR DIARY / INTELLIGENCE SUMMARY

Army Form C. 2118.

MARCH 1918

H.Q.R.S. 50TH DIVN R.E. VOL NO 26

Place	Date	Hour	Summary of Events and Information	Remarks and references to Appendices
BEAUMETZ to LE MESNIL	22		By arrangement with 50 Div'l 9" CRE visited Felleys & 7"&SLI (Pioneers) on Rt Rd of PERTEE & arranged for their immediate move. 7/KCoy & Pug Det. front at PERTEE. 446 Coy & 750 Bn at ESTREES & advanced section at FREMICOURT. 447 Coy & 757 Bn H.Q. at CARTIGNY. Bailey at CARTIGNY. Bridge at CARTIGNY - O.C. Fld Coys & C.O.'s Pnrs met into Reflection Bldge & undertook various work to repaired. - 7 Co effort retimating R.E. R. a right 22/23 in Re Sqk'. lack of PERTEE. 1 platoon & Pnrs & 1/449 Btn retaining at T.8 corner line. LAleal repairs of Budges & Pnrs lines (1) BRACO - BOUCHAVESNES - ESTREES & CD. Z in E J CARTIGNY - CRE reconnoitered these lines. - CRE instructed to MONS-EN-CHAUSSEE - DHQ moved back to LE MESNIL in aft. - CRE reconnoitered E J CARTIGNY. front & Peronne & made arrangements for Peronne Bridge win line E J CARTIGNY Bailey & evening made to Peronne bridge & the arrangement Estk in touch with 7th Coy & learned full arrangement & return to repair wh R Somme at St CHRIST Bare & PERONNE by B/y (the air coming returned to the SOMME -	
LE MESNIL to FREMICOURT	23		DHQ moved back to FREMICOURT via CHAULNES - 446 Coy returned to L'ECLUSE as St CHRIST 7 & 447 Coys at BACE 446 & 447 Coys & Pnrs brought into land & evening positive in Re 9.8 - R.O's Kent 447 Gardens held on- Poten W.P.R Somme closed J. Webs developed by Rev Evans the covered before of 9 at Bare bridge evened successfully lean up without assistance being asked bn resistance opposed I fd Nurses CARTIGNT. These ROEWY EN SANTERRE & ENS & resistance repulsed - 446 Co moved to MISSEY & Mons & FOUCAUCOURT - for - 7th & 447 Coys moved to FOUCAUCOURT - Enpn 21. B& 9. Di. b FOUCAUCOURT -	
FOUCAUCOURT	24		DHQ & Felleys remained at FOUCAUCOURT - CRE reconnoitered Bridges Assemblies - ESTREES & DHR - the 9k April 27 Co & 447 Co & subordinate plan of working Knok system & DHR - This. b app R Somme closed. 7 Co & R. Somme when 756 Bde leaving the evening 76 being 2nd & 7ft 0.21 Peronne & 7 0.21 Peronne & Anthony line established & & 2/Sect at front, 447 Co Entering bridge 25th 13N 1st 551 Bde	

Army Form C. 2118.

WAR DIARY or INTELLIGENCE SUMMARY.
(Erase heading not required.)

HDQRS 50TH DIV. RE
MARCH 1918 — 1st No. 36

Place	Date	Hour	Summary of Events and Information	Remarks and references to Appendices
FOUCAUCOURT	25-		76 & 447 Coys with orders to FOUCAUCOURT during morning. Instructions received during evening of 25th of probable further retirement & a 26th CRE with allotted to get position prepared working on the line VAUX & CHUIGNES — ROSIERES —	
FOUCAUCOURT to MARCELCAVE	26th		CRE proceeded at 4 a.m. to above line. Reconnoitred it — 3 FCoys commd MARCELCAVE about 7.30 a.m. & 8 p.m. in two echelons to work on — Lt. Col. F.Coy. given an area B — details & plans of 16 Platoon posts in echelon & depth and pits 32 bays 3½ deep — details of platoon posts to commence about 8 a.m. Posts 36" wide — working parties consisting of 249 & 457 B'de details & 1 infantry Bn to be not at 8 a.m. at VAUX & CHUIGNES & then to battle Stop. Work commenced about 8 a.m. Just as 12 noon commencing D & B Platoon Posts arrangements taken of hostile to be completed by 12 noon. Position received by hostile fire about 5.15 p.m. — MI F.Coy in front position about 2 p.m. trouble MARCELCAVE had a German strafe under the CRE proceeded about 2 p.m. MARCELCAVE a small shelling about 4 p.m. on FOUCAUCOURT for orders. The 3 P.Coys on FOUCAUCOURT a.m. to defensive flank to entrenched line closing by 449 82 on the same night the relieve = chaos. 9 with 446 Coy were left in the VAUX & CHUIGNES Throughout in to MARCELCAVE to positions of 449 Bn that 10 a.m. on 27th 76 & 447 Coys withdrawn — CRE reported BHQR at MARCELCAVE for orders returning to DHQ for orders the night — CRE represented at night.	
	27th		Received instructions & received command of 1 half of 360 details & 151 B/d spare with 7 Coy & a company to support of 13th for action to take positions. This Brigade B.G.'s famed command J.G.O. with an instruction. J. & under verbal instructions 7 Coys & 447 Coys were sent at 7 a.m. a 27th & under verbal instructions J. & under verbal instructions J.G.O. with an instruction J.G.O. military & first days. Got instructions at 7 a.m. to the railway & just under Major Knowles (then took command, unsupported & made into fighting order) Major Baker 447 Coy & self under Major Knowles, 82 on HARBOURSE — about ½ platoon pace had to take left of our right flank of 449 Bn on HANGARDES — about ½ platoon pace Rocks were not to form a defensive flank to our right flank of 449 Bn on HANGARDES expected. An enemy attack had the dawn 2 Ro 215669. to attack developed.	

Army Form C. 2118.

WAR DIARY
or
INTELLIGENCE SUMMARY.
(Erase heading not required.)

HQ RE 50 Div RE
MARCH 1918 Vol No 3/0

Place	Date	Hour	Summary of Events and Information	Remarks and references to Appendices
	27	12 am	Received orders to conform to into MLR from into 2 Bns 7 & 8 Bns to counterattack from MARCHENNEPES on PROYART - These under Major Chorus. 6 & 8 Bns into MARCHENNEPES left arrived at 2 Bns 8 Bns in Trenches. Major Baker & Horse left a cnd abt 1 m NW MARCHENNEPES before the enemy reached it - This ar accompanied by an - 2 Bns 7 & 8 Bns & Force under Major Bilow (who was severely wounded in MARCHENNEPES) covering up the attack of right rear of and of Coys to right Flank - the "confiote artilly" bombarded about 12,000 H.E. PROYARS when existing trial system to eastward. The attack held up for the night 27/28 - L. right to reed for the night.	
	28	Abt 4.20 am	received information that 2 Bns 8 Bns on left was being violently attacked About 4.30 am received orders to withdraw confiote bn. drew out by paths before dawn & about 4.30 am we proceed to Plaquerz & before dawn to HQ MARCHENNEPES & there to CAIX. Took in cmd must be 12 plus Forces 36. & 66 Bn. on our right & the news received & interment confiote bn. without avail but made arrangements storming the late entraining confiote bn. pro res & returning (Major Chorus of 497.G. Sand) forward to the news counter) the Phantom Brigade to inform times - ordered to CAIX when we received notif. about 50 minutes after in reserve through 6 CAIX 65th intention to inform fans or to a cnd at CAIX ready reforming of Bn attached at this purpose. Three 2 Lps to form line CAILLANDS - CAIX but sending upmot of two L Coys on 34 O.R. tomorrow J.I.C.S.) - to Field Lys (7-8447). Cndr to commit S.D. TB W.O. CAIX till returned took thence abt 7.30 pm accepted. Baker I have men S.T. for at last Battalions 5 officers and also counting I evening. Capt. Fally for my Canadian from Battens 3 officers & 24 O.R. having of J.C.S.) - Cherufful officer of the CRE whished 76, 149 & 151SMCowns left. Forte with ARE J A RE WEARS 76 & 149 RE 4 PM by request, we related with the Div. cam I ave. Hew Qpo CRE returning 151 RE at SOISSONS	CRESW

WAR DIARY
or
INTELLIGENCE SUMMARY.
(Erase heading not required.)

Army Form C. 2118.

H.Q's 50TH DIV. R.E.
MARCH. 1918   VOL. No. 36

Place	Date	Hour	Summary of Events and Information	Remarks and references to Appendices
SOURDON to BOVES	29		L't JOHNSON & parties of 446, 447 & 7 Coy & San others of 446 447 & 7 Coy moved to BOVES. 7th to the CASTEL. — C.R.E. proceeded to H'rs 8th Div. at BERTEAUCOURT & in aft's. with O.C. 7 Field reconnoitred roads in neighbourhood of AMIENS at request of S.O.R.A. afterwards proceeding to BOVES. Rear S.H.Q. locate. — 7th Field starting march to BOVES.	
BOVES to SAINS EN AMIENOIS	30		7th & 446 Fld Coys employed in clearing road & reconstructing houseport between BOVES & SAINS EN AMIENS. — Reconnoisance of 2nd RAMSAY — HEBECOURT — VERS & made by 447 Fld. Co. i/c of roads being repaired in area — S.H.Q. moved to SAINS EN AMIENOIS.	
BOVES	31/st		C.R.E. S.H.Q. & Fld Coys moved by road & rail to DRUCAT area —	

John Sim Lt Col
C.R.E. 50 Div

50th Divisional Engineers

C. R. E.

50th (Northumbrian) DIVISION

APRIL 1918.

SECRET.

Original.

WAR DIARY

OF

C. R. E.   50TH (NORTHUMBRIAN) DIVISION

for month of

APRIL 1918.

VOLUME   XXXVII.

WAR DIARY or INTELLIGENCE SUMMARY

HEADQUARTERS 50TH DIVISIONAL R.E.
APRIL 1918. Vol No 34

Place	Date	Hour	Summary of Events and Information	Remarks
DOULIEU	1st		Visited Divisions & Field Coy — Made arrangements with "Q" & relative to Sanitary requirements in two area —	
"	2nd		Visited A.S.O & C.E. 18th. Dn. & arranged for drawing material from Dumps 1 & 2 into Divl. Area — Visited Subs 6 & 7 78 & 82 — Filtop, Transport, & engineer Material — Wrote visiting of Accommodation of Armor —	
"	3rd		Noted R.C. of machines entering R.E. Dumps & of Filtop relative training. L.O.S. of material & Stores Sanitation in area — OE. Merville & arranged for 31 lorries daily two & material & one to take over — Received extra in evening for 2nd Dns & R.O.S. by lorry, & also by lorry to barges & rail & 2	
Ro BECQ	4		Moved to ROBECQ (in the area) — 1 pm — Into POC & 600 R.E. Went over the line. Wire received by Dn is Canal & Lesbois — 2 wires (Rieg E.[?]) BETHUNE) — 2 Rid. supervisions to the line as regards work — Laurieu Siege Ely of BETHUNE	
"	5		Visited 3 Fld.Cos & fire stations, RAOC nigh for making & maintaining Co.	
"	6		Received word of Turks of 2nd Dn to the 1st Dn held for taking over lines or [?]	
MERVILLE	7		to new E.STAMINES — Visited by Mcr GnC.W. SINGR. C.E. XI Corps relative work in & taking over [Received?] wire stating move of Dn — 8th L. to Estaires — Dn of MERVILLE Coys relieved from in telephis to R.L.S. & made preliminary arrangements for R.L.S. & made preliminary arrangements for R.L.S. & made necessary for Estaires to Johnline in Blocks of	
ROBECQ to MERVILLE	8		D.H.Q. moved to MERVILLE — Received wire night relative front in Johnline till Dn F PRONENTIAIGES (4 mile front). Ordered coming as DHQ became reserve till Dn PRONENTIAIGES (4 mile front). Ordered coming as DHQ became reserve till Dn 7 pm — Visited Brots & in the line opposite NEUVE CHAPELLE in evening [?] 2nd Portuguese Dn in the line opposite NEUVE CHAPELLE in evening [?] making arrangements relieving relief with 2nd Portuguese Dn —	

WAR DIARY or INTELLIGENCE SUMMARY

HQ 50th DIV = RE
APRIL 1918   Vol No.

Place	Date	Hour	Summary of Events and Information	Remarks and references to Appendices
MERVILLE	9th		Before dawn enemy shewed keen desire to push on between Estaires & Bataille - hostile patrols being active. Intelligence Brig of 2 Portuguese Div. ?? informed us that [??] he would be forced to act in support of Portuguese troops. This necessity arose through the 02ric. The 3 Field Coys broke up posts in MERVILLE area + proceeded to join the 7 Bn & Forest de Nieppe in accordance with morning order. MERVILLE & Estaires - also Rd 7 Bn & Inner Fort & NE of the LYS can be between these old [demolition] posts - C.R.E. took wa CE 2/Y Tpk - hd by RE infantry troops - & hid & the R LAWE + arrangements for bridges over LYS canal were in hands of RE Tpks - Co?? Troops & to bring the RE hastily. Falling back on the Div very ??? to the ??? LYS canal - Div the any ?? through Estaires ??? seems as to live & the position & road through to ?? intended but here ?? [??] were & me fit to transport & the backs & the LYS that I was to employ to indicate to move ?? bn ??? MERVILLE resumed - (L. 32. a. S.a. St. 36.A). at site of potentially erected ?? blocks between MERVILLE & CONAC DE NIEPPE. This was confided by night.	
		10th	Permission received from Corps to prepare bridge at K 29 a 4.8 [?] near CANAL DE NIEPPE for demolition. [??] hastily laid by 1 Sec 446 & RE (Lts Dr WILLIAMS. M.C) To there was prepared skilled by [?] on time of case with keys red - Div message evacuation & two rafts behind shelter. This duty carried by ??? Reed & 446 & 85 - a tin from bridge to MERVILLE Tpke. This duty completed by ??? transportation & 2 infantry lines + enabled Y Army - About 12 noon Div-alerted the destruction (82 36B) though ???, about 3½ miles in length. The ??? from about 1.30 central & disposal Corps on this work was 3 [?]. BEERWAN b L. 12. 6. 23 - C.R.E. reconnoitered & took platoon at his ??? army & lish platoon where ??? 1 & 8 ? 85 ??? & ?? Tpks & debris blocks to follow up obstacles ?? 1 & 8 ??? on rd in ??? MERVILLE Corp of debris blocks	

Army Form C. 2118.

WAR DIARY
or
INTELLIGENCE SUMMARY.
(Erase heading not required.)

HQ RE 58th DIV. RE
APRIL 1918 — Vol. No.

Place	Date	Hour	Summary of Events and Information	Remarks and references to Appendices

ESTAIRES — MW arrived in aft. of another dangerous & ruinous bridge in LA GORGUE. VEDASTARS had that day fixed at PONT [...] instructed to fix it up [...] & security. EP ESTAIRES had [...] instructed — a case of much time & trouble. EP ESTAIRES had only been slightly [...] attempted to prepare to try & effect complete demolition but may be difficult [...] prevent enemy crossing bridge or seized that bridge in the dark. No one of bombs & primary charges ready & there were out entirely successful in destroying bridge a few holes charges of 24½ —

MERVILLE 11th

LA MOTTE au BOIS

LA MOTTE

WAR DIARY or INTELLIGENCE SUMMARY

Army Form C. 2118.

1st/2nd 50th DIV RE
APRIL 1918   Vol No

Place	Date	Hour	Summary of Events and Information	Remarks and references to Appendices
			The enemy too heavily attacked MERVILLE the time enabling us to get sufficient balance of work of work to extract situation - On S.O. remains with 1st & 2nd 35.a.& 7.52.	(35A)
			his successfully delayed late at night the heavy road bridge (near Lieuware fines at K.29.d.2.5 was hastily destroyed (ought to have been handle to R.E.) and the bridge factory bridge on K.30.6. central was all destroyed being tanks & shell water after dealing off the famous R.9 feer from R.E).	
			After holding up the famous on to LA MOTAUNT, and DEAR & LA MOTTE the S.H.Q. moved during morning to LA MOTAUNT, from MERVILLE, arriving there 12 R. During the night 11/12 the enemy front his way into MERVILLE. At the time our units were holding a line between 9 torts head short of where the bridge had been blown up - about 10 rm times up the river Nth 150g destroyed) force front bridge, & outside of the works until the detachment of R.E party on related survived M.C. has halted command. Still a number of the mens attachment to the bridge - On whichever the ability to present a work.	
LA MOTTE	12th		Owing to I shall have been to this by the enemy was slightly forward. Next message on the heavy front in the country now slightly 902 R.E. out of got as to the 150 R.E. held at about 9 90c and after to between to LA Rue-du-BOIS small-arms 7 R.E bred at reported. On top of a few and we were just into infantry action to and infantry - was now in the infantry action - the 14 G forts were just into infantry action to make hands - were released - per Cop behaving frontforward of 50 G. - has now in and infantry action.	
			During the morning of the 12 h the situation remained sifting E of FORET DE NIEPPE. altering somewhat later on by this time the 01 to will watch of the 7th & 14 G. advancing towards CRICHES by the 8.P. action. 16 G.P. the LAMOTTE - MERVILLE Road of infantry 2nd Cap. was sent forward into the 8.P. action 16 G.P. the 12 to Bn to come. - reinforce in action with four baredaes that made on the coming of the 12 to Bn to come. 25 01 x other reinforcements to had head the situation - 146 G. was also reserved. here to 25 01 x other reinforcements to had head the situation - 146 G. was also reserved. and Cap.	(E. of FORET DE NIEPPE)
	13th		Cop. commented always this night about L.S.PARC. (E of FORET DE NIEPPE)	
			received fat on the 18" 1st 01 and to Ypres + ordered after Ypres.	
			2 men Cap. y defence position in + about the BOIS 201 moved under orders from 82 01 .	

WAR DIARY or INTELLIGENCE SUMMARY

Army Form C. 2118.

WDOC 5DTH DIV. RE

APRIL 1918 — VOL N°

Place	Date	Hour	Summary of Events and Information	Remarks and references to Appendices
THIENNES	14		CRE visited CRE 3rd Div. (Lt. Col. White) with reference to the arrangements & when the relieving troops arriving. Instruction for bridge over canal as 1.8 & 9.7 written to Coys. accordingly. Instructions for bridge over canal as 1.8 & 9.7 arrived by G.O.C. 15th Inf. Bde. (1200) D.H.Q. moved to THIENNES. Option of making a Bat. (Bde.) Contractor. 76, 446 Cos. 7 D.L.I. and all Inf.g of Div. (now making a Bat. Bde.) Contractor 7 units hitherto without pots. Retiring from LAMOTTE through BOIS DES VACHES & about VILLERS with without pots retiring from LAMOTTE through BOIS DES VACHES & about VILLERS not as before 2 extensive belts of ball of Wm fence along 2300 + feet being completed to the main present system of being defence.	
"	15			
" & ROQUETOIRE	16		D.H.Q. moved to ROQUETOIRE, & 446 & 449 Coys (now) to LACOUR + LA JUMEL respectively 76, 7th DLI & 149 Bde being left to construct work in BOIS DES VACHES. CRE visited CRE 50 5 Div & gun pieces instructions re work in BOIS DES VACHES reporting HQ at ROQUETOIRE. & CRE obtained inspection by 149 Bde & 446 C. RE at LACOUR. G.O.C. obtained dispositions of & CRE obtained inspection of 149 Bde & 446 C. RE at LACOUR. CRE attended discussions of 76 (with 149 Bde Group) reported Divl. 76 visited GLOMPENGHEM.	
"	17			
"	18		Bde. Condr. System of told 149 Bde to extend north to Bethune at Bethune at LA JUMELLE - Scheme of CRE into Force of Inspector at Bde. Condr. System of told 149 Bde to extend north of Operations - July last then refusing G.O.C. 50 Div. inspected 447 Co R.E at LA JUMELLE - Scheme of Operations - Midway (Min Ministers of Area points draw as road from Sheet in present use - (Main Ministers – midway ROQUETOIRE, then all points draw as road from Sheet in present use - Sixteenth a	
"	19		Sufficient & teams of Spr. doing any point Sheet in present use - Sixteenth & 8.50 R.E. 15th Bn conducted of 445 on D.A. and of Bn Majr. Offrs. commd - Altersible road. D.H.Q. moved to AIRE - G.O.C. inspected 7th Co. at GLOMPENGHEM - a good view - Bde & Batt. Work the LILLERS (81 Bde) hop	
AIRE	20		8 May 23rd Shanks reported by Rt. Pontalier Bde & Batt. work the LILLERS (81 Bde) hop emphy - Main cycle replaced Manuel by by	
"	21 22		trophy - Main cycle replaced Manuel by by Shadolphi 149 Bde chosen for LA LACOUR. 76 moved to BLESSY - CRE visited all Cos. inspecting training -	

Army Form C. 2118.

WAR DIARY
or
INTELLIGENCE SUMMARY.

(Erase heading not required.)

HDQRS R.E. 50TH DIV
APRIL 1918. Vol No

Place	Date	Hour	Summary of Events and Information	Remarks and references to Appendices
AIRE.	23.		Orders received 2 p.m. for 2 Fd Coys & Divn Pontn Park to work under 5th Divn in FOREST OF NIEPPE Later - CRE proceeded 5th Div. HQ. Interviewed CRE, M.G.O. 5th Div. to arrange re work & rails - & return. Learnt that the others were cancelled & Div was to entrain on the 25th night.	
	24.		Visited all Coys re: coming move.	
	25.		Visited all Brigades re: working of R.E. Lewis Guns officers with Brigades in their schemes. Details Pioneer Battn was attached of Brigadiers & lately 50th Div. - Officer i/c Scheme sent to each F.Coy & each Bn.	
ARCIS LE PONSART	26. 27. 28.		CRE & 2 Fd Coys entrained ARCIS LE PONSART (about 15m NE to SE of SOISSONS) on evening of 27th - Coys & Pontn Park entrained early on 27th arriving and on evening of 28th.	
	29		Visited all Fd Coys (concentrated at COHAN) - Informed them that all & portings such as of training with two men & repairing stream & concentrate in dists, towns etc. Visited Col IX Corps (which takes Divn under command) (Br Genl: CAPPERMANT CRE (R.E.) - 61 Div. Arranged conference at 50 Divn HQ respecting taking over from French Div. in this line. Directing of line - Received notice that the Div. was to be required shortly to relieve the 21st French Div. in the line on Front & AISNE. - Arranged Troat Cond. in our guise of time 8am 1st May - (N.H.Q's at VAULY) Attended conference of B.G.G.S. 50th Div. visited by Gen. Carbeaut CE (Fr.) - Attended conference with F.Coy Comdr. respecting
	30		our front & army - held conference with all trades officers	

Lieut Col. CRE 50 Div.

SECRET.

WAR DIARY

OF

C. R. E. 50TH (NORTHUMBRIAN) DIVISION R.E.

VOLUME XXXVIII.

May, 1918.

WAR DIARY
INTELLIGENCE SUMMARY

HEAD QUARTERS. 50TH DIVISIONAL R.E.
MAY. 1918 - VOL No 38

Place	Date	Hour	Summary of Events and Information	Remarks
ARCIS-EN-PONSART	1st		10th A.F.A visited 21 Div: (French) H.Q at VAULY VAILLY & spent day with front of the 2nd line 21 Div take over later about PT MALMAISON along the N.R RIVETTE. 21 Div test on 5 kilos front, with later about PT MALMAISON along the N.R RIVETTE. 21 Div 2 Sect Reg only. The positions covering the Chemin des Dames. Div hrs 2 kms dy from a Cy: de Ponc. As 21 Div has an alt: Cpl: Cy going at 3 Cpl/Pont looking on the scale used by 1 Regt: the relief will be carried out tonight. The front system as worked out on 6 the line de Rabiks (Ru two) of the front line system (b) the reserve system laying on (9 kms) (c) Road (d) Horse Drawings of lowery (looking further to ensure) for firing Bates in Sufflet or as Reserve upon the Tentorial Battn: attached to Sect Div. Coy Tramway into the Div: on the 4 & Cy of each Battn – The N.M.V are entirely independent of the line the 1st & 2nd kms. Of this Fmk: System (2 Sqdrs de Travailleurs & Pioneers) – the large entirely reformed by Sqdns de Nords & lpt System – a Div: system reforming by the Lope – Unmy the camp of the N.Move is entirely worked by the Lope – Unmy the camp of the N.Move. The Shower a Lighting Scheme, stors of the letterof hutch bridges (in many to count) – was purchased to R. AISETTE (on one Sec) and at site. Note also for N.W. (French) works in the R.M. Ne V (R.E.S) Section. the N.B. forms de Rebits enough in the R. (E.S) also the Cy entering the left (best) System. Reinforces Poré DE MACMAISON to live di Reserves. Interalternate terrain to Relieve PMarines of defence by Brig: trench in return of the resupplying (Candles)
	2nd		Attend a Div: conference – Held meeting P Cy. (Corl's of the area) dining arr: running & of resupplying –
	3rd		Reconn: Div: H.Q. waited over into approximate training Worked Div: during my running Sect to till of Could de Serio 30th that Div in KORO Orders Div: end later to not 51 th Div in LETO CASONETT
	4th		pertaining – Received information that Div: must about front 51 Div in CASONETT Sect L of Could de Serio 30th at Sect to till of Could de Serio 30th that Div in KORO Orders Div: end later to not 51 th Div in LETO CASONETT pertaining – Received information that Div: must about front 51 Div in CASONETT Lt. Col. Ch. Dunderfield R.E. C.R.E 50 Div.

WAR DIARY
or
INTELLIGENCE SUMMARY.

Army Form C. 2118.

HEADQUARTERS 50TH DIV. RE
MAY 1918 — Vol No 38 —

Place	Date	Hour	Summary of Events and Information	Remarks
BOISMONT	5th		Move to BOISMONT. Small HQ Coy on the march. Parties ordered to Genis 51st RE at BOUCHY & arranged lines to Relief between Flops & component French C.Os. Issued orders to Field Coys for relief between the night 7/8/16 — arrive there relieved 447 Fld Coy located at ESPONNE (dugouts in the Bois Platform & S' ENFRONT as 6 Fld Coy & MONACO in relief of Cul de Parc.	
"	6th		During this period Workmen Sources no flank:— Depth of belt about 3 miles — Maced fortress PLATEAU DE SLAMOUNT everywhere on W of Route. Front system well developed on the whole into numerous depts — 2nd Sys where to make the work intercommune. LIGNES DE REDOUTS (or 3 these of these, that being of light) — Behind that many powerful which were all in no well developed trench where possible & mostly formed of which are no in the Road to be interrupt & 2 to the railway systems — Many isolated Posts in rear to miles & inland with large work & green traverses & & little or no trench support would be limited to belong in works on handles & of the French is only in the same being & depending upon the have decided to belong in works on landslide & of the French in the lines out with all 3 Brigades in the line known —at are informing all on the west twenty brown. Sait & Batls in Reserve, 1 in Reserve, 1 in Support — Reports throughout the French GOC during that most support will be in the & of that orders the Generators in proportion division who dispositions arrived as follows:— 447 Fld Re Tried at ESPONNE — 16 Soldiers employed in Gardening — 1 Sect on trans 06 MARAIS Trench look dispositions etc. CANADIAN — 1 Sect on trans 05 MARAIS Trench took dispositions etc. — 14 in trenches to upward of 1 300 B.P.s 1 Sect with Intercommunican to the CANADIEN sending depot to terrain to upward of 1 300 B.P.s — 1 Sect with & the Fenelin, interchanging BORDEAUX SECTOR (what 7 NC depot. Ally held B.P.is & Boris 06 MARAIS — 1 Sect & the the held B.P.is & Boris 06 MARAIS — 1 Sect at late to manner steering the interior of a bout (LA MAITRE & Bois 06 MARAIS — 1 Sect Galilee a/d the steering of Canning by French), Constructing 3 artillery branch on Gr gray Sum. Entrance of (Canning by French), Constructing 3 artillery branch on Gr gray 446 Fld Re Victor between Jerome & Bois to and in Gun pits with proper Va 2 Sector employed extensively on Gun hunting — 1 Sect is & & the church channels — 1 Section on making of strong points & in the Shintan front system of Shintan (waterways) & Bois MARAIS (as MONACO — 1 Section on the me defence (waterways) & Shintan front system of Shintan (waterways) & Bois MARAIS	
"	7th to 27th			

WAR DIARY
or
INTELLIGENCE SUMMARY.

Army Form C. 2118.

HDQRS 50TH DIVISIONAL R.E.

MAY - 1918 -

Vol. No. 38.

Place	Date	Hour	Summary of Events and Information	Remarks and references to Appendices
BEAUREUX	7/6/ 26th (cont)		The FD G.H.E. employed as follows :- 2 sections employing 6 Lieut. Fr. Ing. R.O. (Lieut A. R.A.) 1 Sect. - work on Bgr. dug-outs in HDQS DE REDOUTE (Scene the shining large portions of the bois had been). 1 LIGNE INTERMEDIARE AGREETS, being thinned & required many clearances to be made to enable wire & spit in to be employed. Resistance & trap for ingl. supplied at all strong points - 446 Ly. also of in bdge for RO FD G. Our power employment of Pioneers was 2 Cy with 151 Bde (Centre) Sector, 2 Cy in 2nd & later on in the 1st Bde reserve - MIMERAS Sector 1 Cy with 151 Bde (centre) sector, 2 Cy in 2nd, & later on in the 1st Bde reserve - BEAUREUX (These bde being 3 Cy in reserve of the rapid moving system tried in BEAUREUX PLACES (These bde being 50 in Reserve of reserve. ... & being in bad condition required & renewal of much used by horse transport lorries & being in bad condition required & renewal of deploy -	
	26th		Ahead of 50 Dy. Front on A.F. Front 7/6g. 1 km 100 man used on works, 50 in lodging & one clearing trenches & transport at all dumps - Wholly of 26th informs. Received of probable hostile attack on the front in the vicinity of (26th information reviewed of probable hostile attack on the front of (56) Divisions to the of... this after shelled hours 4 to 8 of 4.46 & 1.15 minutes Morning and fire - A warning went to RAISNE street & instruction for evacuation & collect boats to bridge at RAISNE street & instruction for evacuation be ordered - had previously been told to battle position & energy - BANTOM of CALIFORNIE The F.G. A CENTRE DE TOUZET (Hqrs Lieutenant Davis 446 Cy to be ready immediately instead (yes) come on RAISNE - 447 w. to be up battle station from (3) 150 Bde. Mobile Lietenant (yes) come returned at 1 am (60° minutes) - Shortly afterwards were in andorced by 9 4 & 17 BOARD of the both position. Lt. Thus went on ...... & 2 Sections instructions issued to be Cg to late for the position. Lt. Thus went on ...... & 2 Sections instructions during to take charge of the home trench Head position. This Cy offered excellent covertain during to back charge of the O.c. Bges. BAZOUIN ... & SCM being bided - battle stations procured with known trench to bottle position & Kingdom to live soon engaged with enemy none of his history returning - one man for 447 ly were horizon to live & know & whom 447 ly for history returning - one man for 447 ly were known to live & know & whom 447 ly for example in the effect of his plot. Major ... known of this return. Major Rainford known, D.S.O. being killed, wounded in the effect of his plot.	

Army Form C. 2118.

WAR DIARY
or
INTELLIGENCE SUMMARY.
(Erase heading not required.)

HQRS 50TH DIV RE.
MAY 1918 – VOL NO 38.

Place	Date	Hour	Summary of Events and Information	Remarks and references to Appendices
	27/5/18	4 AM	446 7 Coy received orders to proceed to prepare bridges for demolition about 4 AM. There were two piers already in transit owing to the gas shelling compelling the civilians of the post serving the works & they would call wit. The Canadians somewhat were removed by the bridge guardian piers at Moreno from 7 permanent & holder. The bridges – the parties offered serving a the time available the piers & holder. 15 Pl to 19 bridges. The parties offered serving a the time available line the tributes – 10 bridges were successfully destroyed; 2 failed – a number of small bridges 3 in concrete of nature of plans of concrete of flat iron. All parties stood of their bridges till the last possible moment removed at their work well – CRE traversed bridges & pl 27 to see huge Millikin at Moreno to learn situation as regards the later of his inspection. Whereupon Major Millikin gave orders not to concentrate the being ordered not on the bodies where orders to destroy bridges should react Major Millikin to BC – no thirst to others, this means to destroy bridges should react Major Millikin to BC – now that the others the advance was imperative, the time was essential as ... Route of the railway V with destruction of 3 bridges & statement as concerning – CRE's Route & return by railway V with destruction of 3 bridges & statement as concerning – CRE's Road to be by railway seen Moreno. It was necessary to prepare a foot. CRE visited these & after its being but by shell near Moreno. It was necessary to prepare a foot. CRE visited these & after or concentrate & learned that two bridges tops occupy the demolition – or whatever remainders a fort. It was found that money to in the ground considered E & components in account a fort. It was found that money town in the ground considered E & components in account of when the CRE men made the bridge somewhat & shall not be disturbed by the ten in hands of enemy over the CRE men made the bridge somewhat & shall not be disturbed by the ten in hands of enemy over the CRE men made the bridge somewhat & shall not be disturbed & some times brought and one to CRE hQ. at about time. Some time but without over the bridge from the E & bridge was under M.G. fire – CRE proceeded through where there was one of the bridge from the E & bridge was under M.G. fire – CRE proceeded through where there was one of the bridge from the E & bridge was under M.G. fire – CRE proceeded through where there was one of the bridge from the E & bridge was under M.G. fire – CRE proceeded, interest into DMR & state of demolition orders her of the bridge DMR as his train. Returning & the township 18 the bridge was found to be occupied. The inspector of the bridge E & there gave bear their it stated they were unknown to be occupied. The inspector of the bridge E & there gave bear their it stated they were unknown bearing – Returning to my B Reconnaissance DMR, CRE arrived at 4 panels after a general Journey – Returning to M.B. REconnaissance DMR, CRE arrived at 4 panels after a general finished to a S LEU SJ George & took position, that we considered after & after 1802 am from to a S LEU SJ George & took position, that we considered after & after 1802 am & to L.G. AF Lu Sth... but on covered & Ramm at the command of this party – DMB traded at Ramm at this command of the E to L.G. AF Lu Sth... but on covered without moved under CRE smith to Alivilion or Goubardy. RE knocked in reserved knowing materie moved under CRE smith to Alivilion or Goubardy.	

Army Form C. 2118.

WAR DIARY
or
INTELLIGENCE SUMMARY.
(Erase heading not required.)

H.Q.R.E. 50th Div. R.E.

MAY 1918   Vol No 38

Instructions regarding War Diaries and Intelligence Summaries are contained in F. S. Regs., Part II. and the Staff Manual respectively. Title pages will be prepared in manuscript.

Place	Date	Hour	Summary of Events and Information	Remarks and references to Appendices
	28th		Move to ST GILLES, thence to BRANSLAY — B 446 C.9. W.M. K.T.N. demolition prevented. No proceeded to ROMANY. Here met & C.R.E. & C.O. of 532nd who decided to repair bridge — eventually reporting knocked out 28/29.G.H.Q. & M.P. Col. the a 27.5. 13 officers killed wounded or missing — 28.G.H.Q.	
LUCY	29th		Relay stayed night from BRANSLAY (stand LINDSAY (in Arres PONSONBY) had devoted by tanks to VIELLERS ARSON —	
"	30th		Sgt. went to Cie R.M.&R.E. near CHATILLON — 16 Div. Pontoons found to cover tee — Reminded high lang position. Got C.E. IX Div. run CHATILLON — last =Tournent — Reminded him that amongst .... to abandon No 760 s-a-ft a- 9 more Pontoons. Pont Isigny Futerpuitan ... rowed by TEE Bn? — Reminded marine between CHATILLON & ...... who ...... I return him. Sent word for .... for a rebate to TRALAGE wo w .... which I have him, sent a fair alternating fund & .... to TROISSY remained 44b C.7 I sent 76 return to TROISSY remained Chaplin of all Pontoons at takes ...... — Doing it to shelling being known relatively Pontoon cleared from during the night — Doing it to shelling being known relatively 8 a & 25 s Bri. it in the met the two parties of Pontoon & next the informed — .... cracked out of herself the night of 31s, crust of which 9 faint & fond any after CHATILLON & VERNEYIL until shortly cave under North Breaches ...... — 2nd K'ridge tho hit & taken into two for North hill repaired E.J. CHATILLON — eg. reaching night at TROISSY meaning through IGNY to sees CARRIERES mft .	
LE PORGUEL	31st		D.A.R. ...... LE BREUIL.	

J. Hindere. T. Houls
C.R.E. 50 Div.

SECRET.

WAR DIARY

OF

HEADQUARTERS 50TH (NORTHUMBRIAN) DIVISIONAL

ROYAL ENGINEERS.

VOLUME XXXIX.

June, 1918.

Army Form C. 2118.

WAR DIARY
or
INTELLIGENCE SUMMARY.

H.Q.R.E. 50TH DIV. R.E.
JUNE 1918 — VOL No. 39

Place	Date	Hour	Summary of Events and Information	Remarks and references to Appendices
VERT LA CHAPELLE	1st 2nd		Orders recd to West Locomobile from Le Bosun — Foley to ALLONDRELLE. Reconn. orders to make up 1 Complete Coy. H.Q. from the remains of the 3 F.Coys. These were handed in 3 lists of names & ranks (1 strong) sent J. Ko. R.E. Coy. Running together personnel (6 O + 7 to OR) hand and in ordance to be transport. — The 1 Complete Coy. made cmd. of & Maj. McLennan. It was 70 OR.	
	3rd		2 days of Complete Coy. on 2nd & No. 1 and arrived. Complete Coy. on 2nd. Period of Complete Coy — Saw Chaplaigne in pour l'esprit. Saw E. Le Complete Coy proud to ablaze partially luncheon up — Reconn. cyclists convoys of 1 coy going to and photog. of Maris into the "Buttes Evreupts "Black mets Mtray & Selvenne read".	
	4th		(Coll. Smith R.E.) coys & others arriving into contact by — Saw the Bosh & Bdn. Rear of Sto. Det to Contact officers are to work Coys. Lunched up.	
	5th 6th 7th 8th		Lucked officers + several NCOs J all coys — Called at Go's mess Dropkirks. Whitsun duties K Contr. Cpl — Returned at Go's Mess Dropkirks — Attd. conference at Div. H.Qrs. Visited by Col. Eng. IX Corps (Gen Carlright A.D.C.R.E.) Indent CRE 19 to Div. in lieu now Bosht got Mr. 20. Dr. McIntyre R.E. reported to the line. If its stores + went further in contact D.E. R.E. in reserve to Cmd. agreement to as M. St. notice to part of the Company 9th of scaling one of the Corps. Recd that before leaving H.Q. with to amr — Returned near & band. Suggt. G2.	
	9th		& others went two (6 h. Ed Seconne) D.H.R. & 3 F.Cls. (trains) as movement. Ordered Tres area (6 h. Ed. Selanne) D.H.R. & 3 F.Cls. (trains) as movement. Ordered Grd. recon. disaffine thought in the back of cm 3 F.Coys Enter miles hustwhs i/c transport + pack anml. 20 Ca. hrsts —	
MONSSEMONT G.H.	10th		Lectured Sofh Bah. Comdrs officers + "Div mirtrs — Individual unit convis.	

Army Form C. 2118.

WAR DIARY
or
INTELLIGENCE SUMMARY.
(Erase heading not required.)

HQ RE 50th Divn RE
No. 39
JUNE 1918 — Vol. No. 1

Place	Date	Hour	Summary of Events and Information	Remarks and references to Appendices
MONUMENT	11th		Went for ride with in to Major J. Legg for full "set things" wanted for heads & gun mountings have received most of them equivalents replacement materials. Notices to C.E. for O/Cs for information & for any fittings &c for 22nd armament & for 7th	
"	12th		G.O.C. O.R.E. (Genl J Paxton DSO) inspected all ranks of 7th D.Coy in turn and addressed them extremely mentioning good work done by 446 7 Co in Bridge demolition & RAGNE during the retreat & fighting —	
"	13th		2 Fielding 447, 7 Cos (Colls Bonish & Finney) ride from Monument to Renate stop Vicinity Rouilard Farm — Reviewing 10 days after heavy losses on the 27th May — Reorganising & gaining up in reserve — They were forming & engaged in Equipment and refitting Training tactics. Officers of 447, 446 ... Capt. Sullivan home & written report re movement of Officers of 446 during period incidents of the retreat. 447 [?] Lunch & remaining as S.O.C. refugee arrived accepted — 89 return to rest by Cps. Painting via 8 hidden Path — Other incidents the day of return August by	
"	14th		Various Cos Co take link with view to obtaining extra stores —	
"	15th		Nothing further	
"	16th		Take transport wounded into CPO all news — Poney I had & any Co's now active history, Returned by L'ERMITE (DHQ at JANOUE) & then via C.E. 7th F.C. & have left message & front ward returned after repair ladders, handcarts. Split in native sec depths D Coys who seek repairs. Etc. Birch on material repairs. Lecturer to officers & N.C.Os tonight September & Engineer & Cava stores —	
L'ERMITE	17th		Hand of L'ERMITE (DHQ at JANOUE)	
"	18th		Went Speakin later from Div Hdly — lent 108th Fd by of 25th Div — will be attached to 50th Div.	
"	19th		Nothing further	

Army Form C. 2118.

WAR DIARY
or
INTELLIGENCE SUMMARY.
(Erase heading not required.)

Hqrs. 50th Div. R.E.
June 1918 to No 39

Place	Date	Hour	Summary of Events and Information	Remarks and references to Appendices
L'ERMITE	19th	20"	Inspected 50th Compoid H.Q. by D.R. visited by Lieut G.R. Hodges C.E. 9th Corps	
"	20"	9¼	Nothing to report	
	22"		Visited 100th Fld. Coy R.E. & 25th Div. H.Q. Visited by C.R.E. 25th Div.	
	23		Nothing to report	
	24		C.R.E. 1st Rifle Brig'd – leave – Orders received by Major McClellan 446th Fld Coy R.E.	
	25		Proceeded to Hqrs J 8a 90 100 (Sheet 57C N.W.) to meet preliminary arrangements for taking over work in time by C.R.Es & parties of 50th Div. Received orders for move to Argies. C.Roncourt of 91st Pioneers to 1st Hopes	
	26		Paper at VANVILLERS – Transport to return tomorrow. Subsequent approved conference Captn C.E., 106th Field Coy, a 1/6 Batt. S.N. Borders (Pioneers). Received orders for moving of our back to Argies Zone. Sent out orders for moves to Argies Zone.	
	27			
	28			
	29			
	30			

McClellan Major R.E.
O/C R.E. 50th Div.

SECRET.

Vol 39

WAR DIARY

OF

HEADQUARTERS 50TH (NORTHUMBRIAN) DIVISIONAL
ROYAL ENGINEERS.

VOLUME XL.

****

JULY, 1918.

Army Form C. 2118.

WAR DIARY
or
INTELLIGENCE SUMMARY.
(Erase heading not required.)

Jungis Vol 40

Instructions regarding War Diaries and Intelligence Summaries are contained in F.S. Regs., Part II. and the Staff Manual respectively. Title pages will be prepared in manuscript.

Place	Date	Hour	Summary of Events and Information	Remarks and references to Appendices
L'HERMITE.	1/7/18		Moved to ST LOUP.	
ST.LOUP.	2/7/18		Moved to CONNANTRE.	
CONNANTRAY	3/7/18		Entrained at SOMMESOUS.	
	4/7/18		Detrained at LONGPRE and moved by road to HUPPY.	
HUPPY.	5/7/18		Adjutant visited 447th Company with G.S.O.2. and made arrangements for watering of their horses.	
"	6/7/18		Visited all Field Companies and C.E. XXII Corps.	
"	7/7/18		Received orders from Division for Field Companies to concentrate in MERELESSART Area. Visited 7th Field Company at MERELESSART and 446th and 447th Field Companies at WIRY - AU-MONT.	
	8/7/18		Visited Field Companies daily, and made arrangements for training, construction of 50 yards Rifle Range etc.	
	9/7/18			
	10/7/18		Major-General BUCKLAND, C.E. Fourth Army inspected Field Companies.	
	11/7/18		446th Company started on march to MARTIN EGLISE with Division. Staying during night 12/13th at GAMACHES.	
	12/7/18			
	13/7/18		Visited 7th and 447th Field Companies.	
	14/7/18		Visited 7th and 447th Field Companies at MERELESSART and WIRY -AU-MONT.	
	15/7/18		Proceeded to MARTIN EGLISE and had an interview with Staff Officer of A.D.D.W. (South and Centre) at DIEPPE.	
	16/7/18		Had interview with Base Commandant, and C.R.E. DIEPPE. Went over Camp at MARTIN EGLISE, occupied by 446th Field Company.	
	17/7/18		Was present at Inspection of 5th Bn. Royal Irish Regiment, (Pioneers) by H.O.C. Division. Returned to HUPPY after visiting C.E. 4th Army and endeavouring to get permission for 7th and 447th Companies to join 446th Company at MARTIN EGLISE.	
	18/7/18		Visited 7th and 447th Companies' (Training).	
	19/7/18		Received preliminary notice from 4th Army that 7th and 447th Companies with Headquarters Divisional R.E. would move to MARTIN EGLISE.	
	20/7/18		Visited Companies training at MERELESSART and WIRT-AU-MONT.	
	21/7/18		Transport of 7th and 447th Field Companies started for MARTIN EGLISE staying during 21/22nd at GAMACHES.	
	22/7/18		Headquarters R.E. and personnel of 2 Field Companies proceeded to MARTIN EGLISE. Transport stayed during night 22/23rd at BAILLY en RIVIERE.	
	23/7/18		Transport of 2 Companies arrived at MARTIN EGLISE by lorries.	

Army Form C. 2118.

WAR DIARY
or
INTELLIGENCE SUMMARY.
(Erase heading not required.)

Instructions regarding War Diaries and Intelligence Summaries are contained in F. S. Regs., Part II. and the Staff Manual respectively. Title pages will be prepared in manuscript.

Place	Date	Hour	Summary of Events and Information	Remarks and references to Appendices
MARTIN EGLISE	24/7/18.		Superintended work and training of Field Companies at MARTIN EGLISE.	
	25/7/18.		-do- -do- -do-	
	26/7/18.		Told by G.O.C. Division that Col. McQUEEN had been granted two months' extension of leave by Medical Board.	
	27/7/18.		Superintended work and training of Field Companies.	
	28/7/18.			
	29/7/18.			
	30/7/18.		Major P. de H. HALL, M.C., R.E., newly appointed C.R.E., arrived and assumed duty.	
	31/7/18.		Visited Field Companies and work in progress. Attended Divisional Tactical Scheme in afternoon.	

H.Q. 50th D.E.
1st August, 1918.

[signature]
Lieut-Colonel, R.E.
C.R.E. 50th Division.

SECRET.

WAR DIARY

OF

HEADQUARTERS 50TH DIVISIONAL ROYAL ENGINEERS.

Volume XLI.

AUGUST, 1918.

WAR DIARY
INTELLIGENCE SUMMARY

C.R.E. 50th Div. Army Form C. 2118.
August 1918
Vol 40

Place	Date	Hour	Summary of Events and Information	Remarks and references to Appendices
MARTIN EGLISE	1st Aug to 9th Aug		Field Companies & Pioneer Battalion training, and erecting Cookhouses, water supply & sheds etc in Divl. Camp.	
near DIEPPE	10th Aug		Divisional Tactical Scheme.	
	11th to 26th		As above.	
	27th 28th to 31st		Tactical Scheme for Field Coys & Pioneers.	
			As above.	

Williams
Lieut Colonel
C.R.E. 50th Divn

SECRET.

WAR DIARY

OF

50TH (NORTHUMBRIAN) DIVISIONAL
ROYAL ENGINEERS.

VOLUME XLII.

September, 1918.

Army Form C. 2118.

ORIGINAL

WAR DIARY
or
INTELLIGENCE SUMMARY.
(Erase heading not required.)

Instructions regarding War Diaries and Intelligence Summaries are contained in F. S. Regs., Part II. and the Staff Manual respectively. Title pages will be prepared in manuscript.

Place	Date	Hour	Summary of Events and Information	Remarks and references to Appendices
	1918.			
MARTIN-EGLISE.	1st SEPT:		Supervised Field Companies work and training at Martin-Eglise. Lieut. L. H. Kane. M.R.C. U.S.A. of 1/1st Northumbrian Field Ambulance attached to R.E. Head Quarters.	
"	2-9-18.		Supervised Field Companies work and training.	
"	3rd "		Do.	
"	4th "		Do.	
"	5th "		Taped out jumping off lines for Battalions taking part in Divisional Manoeuvres on 6th inst.	
"	6th "		Inspected Field Companies Musketry exercises on 300 yards range. Captain Potts returned from leave to U.K.	
"	7th "		Supervised Field Companies work and training.	
"	8th "		Do.	
"	9th "		Do.	
"	10th "		T/Lieut: REBBECK left on leave to U.K. Supervised Field Companies work and training.	

Army Form C. 2118.

ORIGINAL

Continued

WAR DIARY
or
INTELLIGENCE SUMMARY.
(Erase heading not required.)

2.

Place	Date	Hour	Summary of Events and Information	Remarks and references to Appendices
MARTIN-ROUSE.	1918. 11th SEPT.		Received orders from G.O.C. regarding role to be played by Field Companies and Pioneers, during Divisional Manoeuvres on 12th inst.	
"	12th "		Took Field Company Commanders over ground stated as timbers for R.E's during Manoeuvres. Field Companies received Warning Order, to be prepared to move by train on the 15th inst.	
"	13th "		Inspected Companies work, training, and preparations for move.	
"	14th "		Received orders from D.H.Q. to move by train on the 15th to BOCQUEMAISON. Entrained at 12.40 p.m. arrived at BOCQUEMAISON. 9.30 p.m. and at LUCHEUX. 12.30 a.m. (15th inst.)	
"	15th "		Entrained at LUCHEUX at 12.40 p.m. arrived at BOCQUEMAISON. 9.30 p.m. and at LUCHEUX at 12.30 a.m. (15th inst.)	
LUCHEUX	16th "		Inspected 446th Field Company at GRINCOURT. 447th Field Company at IVERNAY. and Billets of 7th Field Company at BREVILLERS.	

Continued

Army Form C. 2118.

ORIGINAL

3.

WAR DIARY
or
INTELLIGENCE SUMMARY.
(Erase heading not required.)

Instructions regarding War Diaries and Intelligence Summaries are contained in F. S. Regs., Part II. and the Staff Manual respectively. Title pages will be prepared in manuscript.

Place	Date	Hour	Summary of Events and Information	Remarks and references to Appendices
LUCHEUX.	1918 1st Sept		Lt. R. E. returned from leave.	
	16th	2 p.m.	Went to see C.E. XVII Corps and Field Companies. Divisional Conference.	
	10th to 24th 25th		Companies at Pioneer training. Received orders of move of Division to MONTIGNY Area.	
MONTIGNY.	26th		Division moved to MONTIGNY Area, arrived 12 noon. Personnel by bus. Transport by road. 447th Field Company. R.E. at BAVELINCOURT. 446th (Wilts) Field Company R.E. at AILLONVILLES. 449th (Wilts) Field Company. R.E. at MIRVAUX.	
	27th 28th		Received orders for move of Division to COMBLES Area. Division moved to COMBLES Area. Arrived 1 p.m. Personnel by bus. Transport by road.	
COMBLES.	29th		Division awaiting orders to move.	
	30th		Received orders for move of Division to LIERAMONT Area and to take over the line.	

Sherwood
Lt. Col. R.E.
C.R.E. 50th Division

4 ARMY

CENTRAL REGISTRY.

Army Form A. 2007.

CR5
50 DIV

Central Registry No. and Date.

CHIEF ENGINEER
FOURTH ARMY.
No. E 260/6

Attached Files.

1

SUBJECT, AND OFFICE OF ORIGIN.

Bridging Operations - crossing the River Selle 50" Div 17.10.18

Referred to	Date	Referred to	Date	Referred to	Date
		History 11/19			
				P. A.	Date

Schedule of Correspondence.

C.E. Fourth Army/E.260/6.

Engineer-in-Chief,
G.H.Q.

ENGINEER IN CHIEF,
G.H.Q.
No. RE/11952/36
Date 3-11-18

Forwarded for your information.

Will you please return it in due course.

[signature]
Major General.
C.E., Fourth Army.
****

A.H.Q.
/ :11:18.
****

A.C.

C.E. Fourth Army

Many thanks - a very well organised operation.

[signature]
9/11

7/11/18.

C.E. XIII Corps No.
14/16/344.

**CHIEF ENGINEER,
FOURTH ARMY.**

No. E26016

Date. 30-10-18

Chief Engineer,
Fourth Army.
****

    Herewith an account of the
Bridging of the River SELLE by the
50th Division, in connection with the
operations of 17th October, 1918.

          P.J.Rowes.
         Capt RE
        for Brigadier General,
29/10/18.   Chief Engineer, XIII Corps.

CE IX Corps

**CHIEF ENGINEER,
IX CORPS.**

No. E3043/50

Date. 30-10-18

CE 4th Army
 seen & returned.
    R.H.Cullum
     BS
    CE 9th Corps

BRIDGING OF RIVER SELLE in connection with the OPERATIONS of 17th OCTOBER, 1918.

During the four nights preceding the operations of 17th October, careful reconnaissances of the R.SELLE from LE CATEAU to ST.SOUPLET revealed the fact that the enemy were holding the line of the railway East of the river in considerable strength, with a large number of M.G.Nests in advance of the railway (i.e., between the railway and the river); these reconnaissances also showed that owing to inundations it would be impossible to bridge the river quickly in face of the enemy except just North of ST SOUPLET and also a small front about Q.21.b.8.5 near ST.BENIN.

At the former place the river varied between 12 ft. to 20 ft. in width and from 4½ft. to 5 ft. in depth.

At the latter place it varied from 20 ft. to 26 ft. in width and from 3 ft. to 4 ft. in depth.

At the former place it was therefore possible to make up a portable bridge of the duckboard type which could be very quickly thrown across the stream, while at the latter place owing to the extra width of the stream it was necessary to use a bridge of the floating type, which would take probably about 15 minutes to construct.

As it was necessary to get two Brigades of Infantry over the river under the barrage, it was therefore decided to put 5 Battalions across near ST.SOUPLET, on a front about 500 yards, and 1 Battalion across near ST.BENIN.

Taking the major operation near ST.SOUPLET first -

Before a very careful reconnaissance had been made 12 Bridges (Sketch "A") were made; it was then found that in several places the River was 18 ft. wide and so subsequently 12 bridges (Sketch B) were made, and the stools (coloured in Red on Sketch A) were added to the 12 ft. bridges to make them serviceable for a larger span than 12 ft. if necessary.

All the bridges were made of more or less scrap timber from a German dump near HONNECHY. It took 16 carpenters about 7 hours to make 12 - 18 ft. bridges.

All the bridges were tested at the dump by crowding as many men on to them as possible. The weight of the 18 ft. bridge was 230 lbs.

All the bridges were taken on Field Company Transport to within about 1300 yards of the site by 16.00 hours on the 16th October and were carried forward from there to within about 500 yds. of the stream by 20.30 hours.

The leading Infantry Brigade was to cross on a three battalion front, each battalion on a one company front. The bridging parties were therefore organised in 3 Groups as follows, each group being responsible for the bridges for one battalion.

A group consisted of -

       1 R.E.Officer in command.
       1 Pioneer Officer.
       17 Sappers.
       50 Pioneers.

and was responsible for carrying and placing in position eight bridges (i.e., two for each of the leading Infantry Platoons) 2 sappers ** being allotted to each bridge. These were more than were really necessary but allowance had to be made for possible casualties.

** and 6 Pioneers.

- 2 -

Zero hour was at 05.20 hours on 17th October.

At about 01.00 hours on 17th October the parties were all formed up and gradually worked forward cutting gaps in hedges as they went, being always kept in front of and closely followed by the Infantry. Five bridges were actually placed across the river by 5 minutes before Zero.

The barrage came down about 100 yards East of the river, dwelt for three minutes and then lifted on to the railway. Immediately it lifted on to the railway the bridging parties dashed forward and threw their bridges over the river; all bridges being in position within one minute of arrival at the river bank.

In order that everyone should be fully acquainted with the arrangements 30 copies of the attached sketch C. were forwarded to the leading Infantry Brigade for distribution to the Offices commanding the leading platoons.

As soon as the bridges were in position a large proportion of the R.E. and Pioneers were withdrawn, leaving maintenance parties to repair damage to bridges.

With regard to the bridging neat ST.BENIN, the arrangements were as follows :-

Four bridges (Sketch D.) were issued from Army Park and were carted on Field Company Transport to within about 500 yards of the site, and from there were quietly carried forward and carefully concealed about 50 yards from the sites of the bridges; this was completed by 00.30 hours.

The parties were organised as follows :- One R.E. Officer and one Pioneer Officer to each of the two pairs of bridges. They made two journeys. 8 Sappers were employed constructing each bridge. In this case the barrage passed in enfilade from South to North. As soon as it passed the bridging parties got to work. The time taken to carry the 50 yards, construct and place in position was 10 minutes, the infantry actually commenced crossing after 7 minutes, as the sappers were then merely employed in picketting and lashing down.

The whole of the bridging operations went off without a hitch, the R.E. and Infantry Brigades being in very close liaison throughout the preliminary arrangements and during the actual operations.

The following improvements might be made in the event of such an operation being repeated :-

1. Floats should be attached to the forward end of bridges A. & B. to facilitate launching them across the river. A couple of petrol tins would probably suffice.

2. In both cases, A & B. and D more provision should be made for securely picketting down of bridges, as owing to the number of men crossing and to shell fire, the bridges were frequently displaced and the maintenance parties were barely able to cope with the work.

3. With regard to bridge D.
It was found that the slat at point E. on sketch had to be removed to hook on the decking and also a nail had to be driven through bearers at point D to keep them in place.

4. The Slats need not be more than $\frac{3}{4}$" thick and the hooks on the ends of the bearers should be securely bolted through instead of being only screwed on.

5. In the case of Bridge D. a considerable amount of practice is necessary to ensure rapid construction.

(Sgd.) P.de H. HALL. Lt.Col., R.E.
C.R.E., 50th Division.

26/10/18.

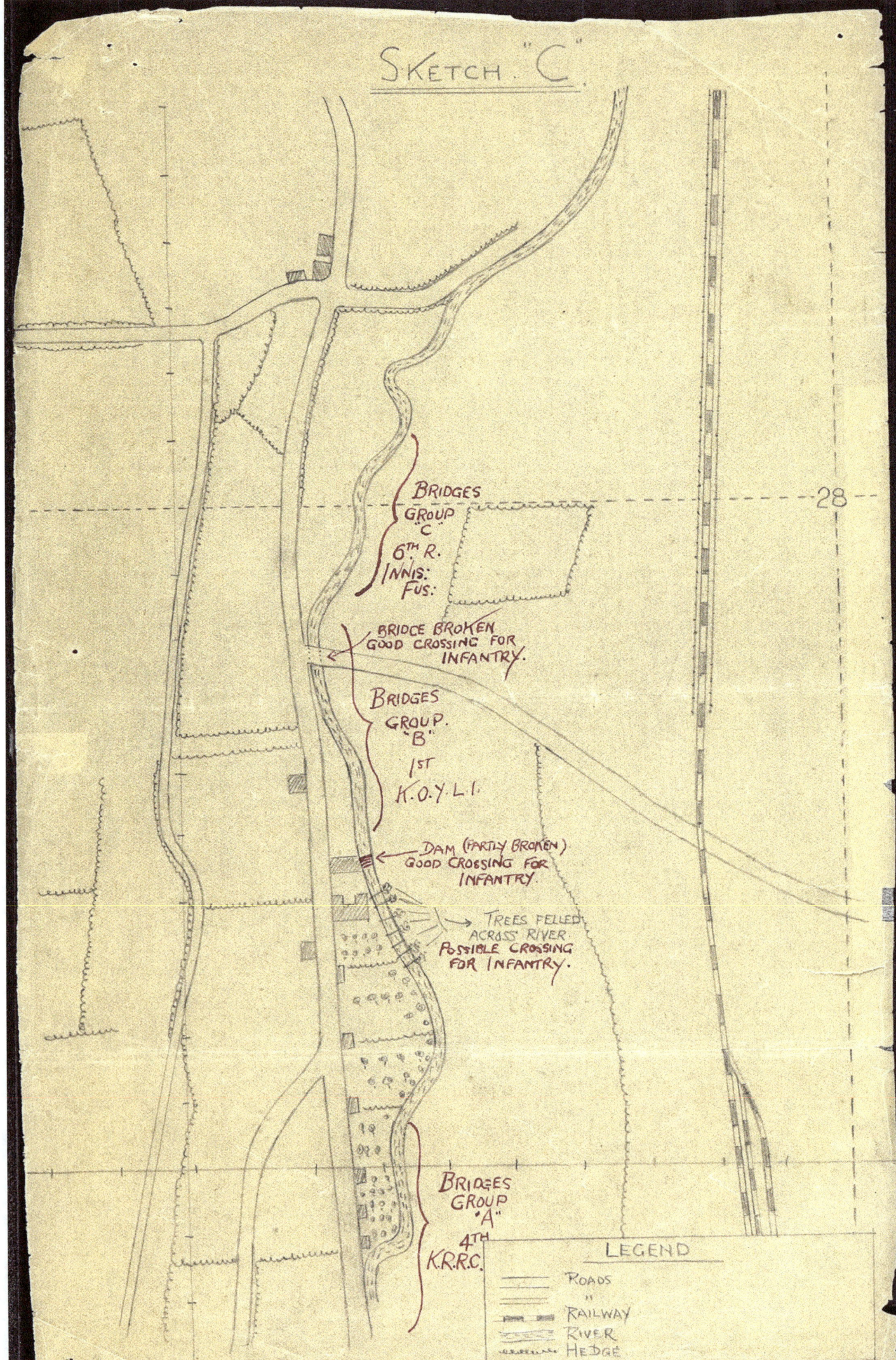

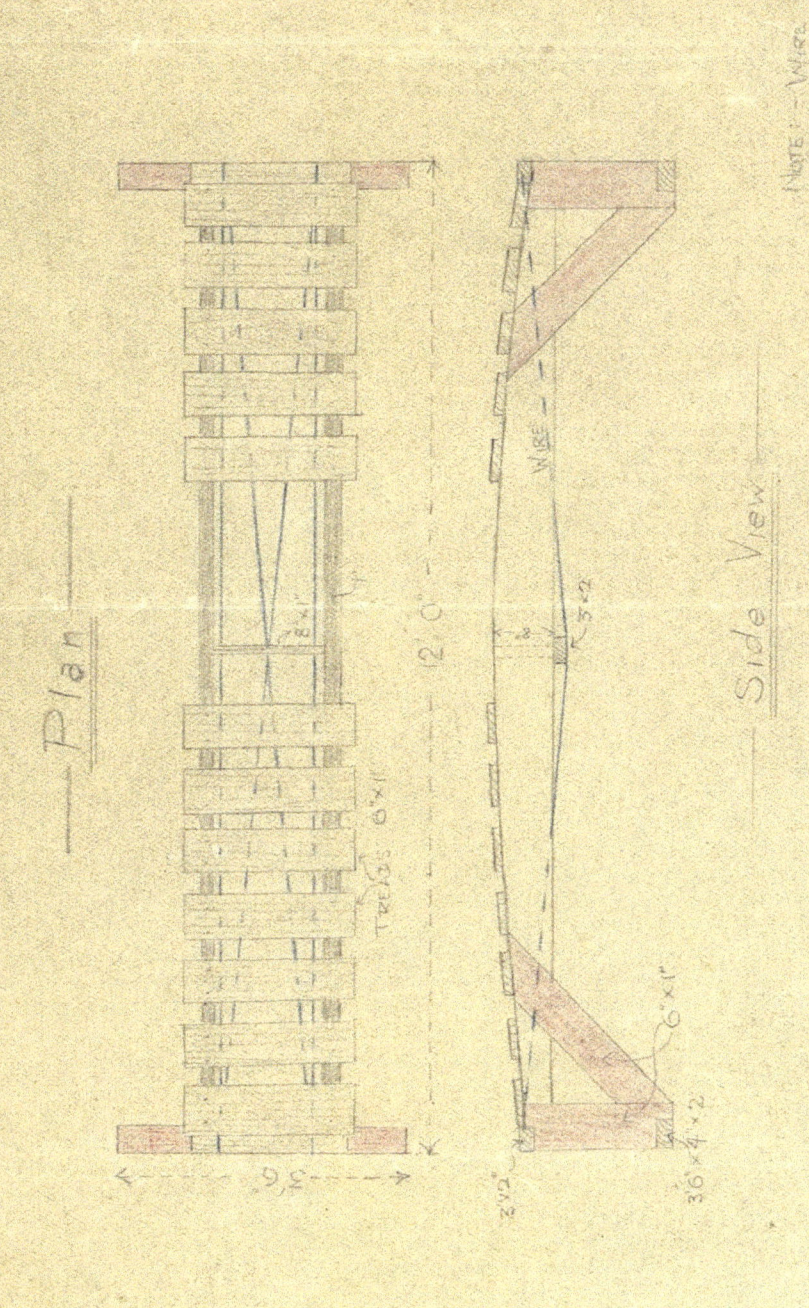

Sketch "B".

Plan.

Pieces 6"×1"–2'0" Spaced 3"

Pieces 3"×2"×1'10".

Wire bracing tightened by Windlass.

13' 0"

Side View.

2 Pieces 9"×1"×1'6"
Piece 4"×2"×1'
6"×1"
Wire bracing
Piece 9"×1"×1'10"
Pieces 3"×2"×1'10".

Scale ½" = 1 foot.

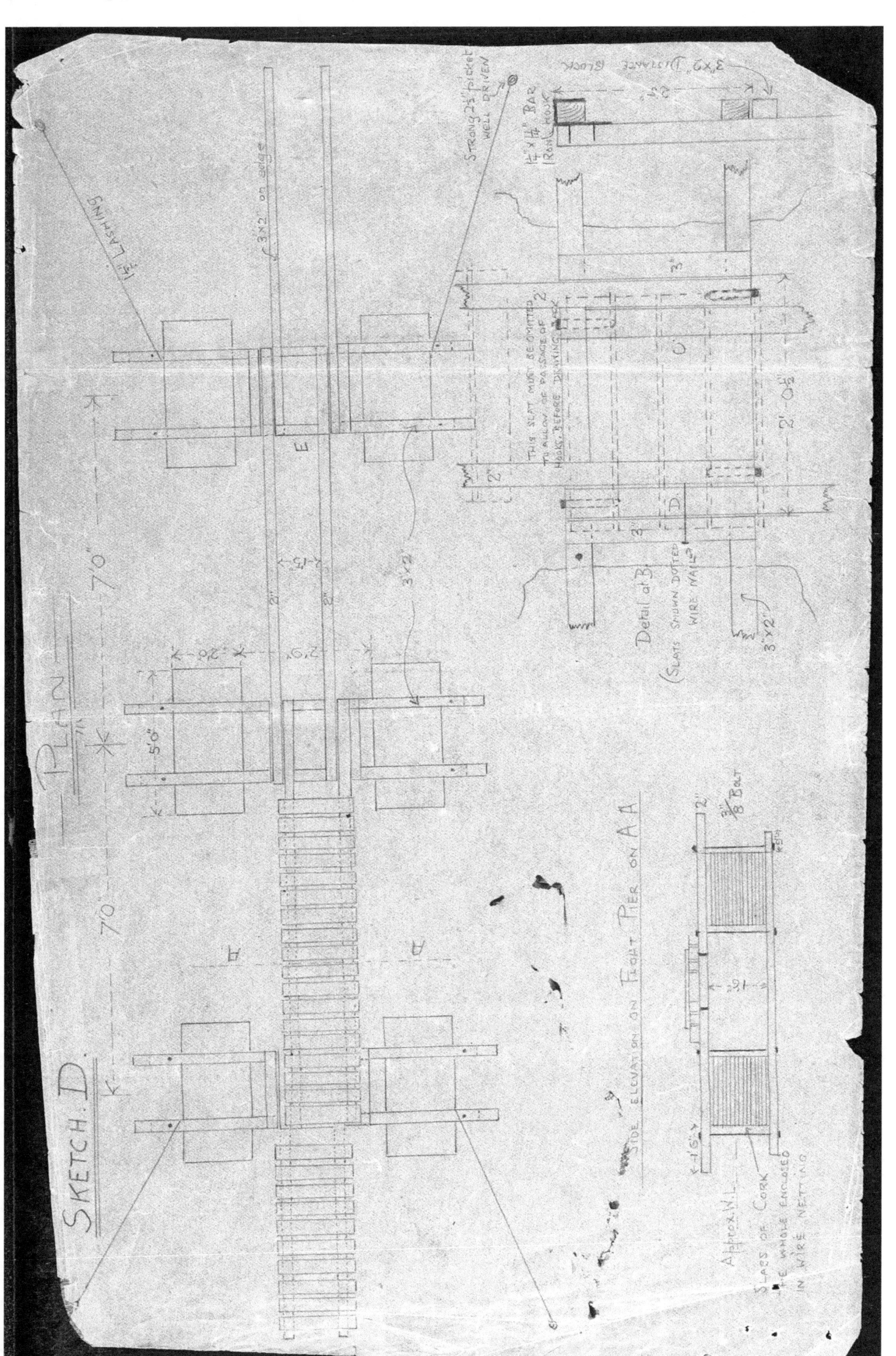

ORIGINAL.   SECRET.
                                                   ****

                        WAR   DIARY

                            of

                         C. R. E.

               50TH (NORTHUMBRIAN) DIVISIONAL R.E.

                       VOLUME   XLIII

OCTOBER, 1918.

Army Form C. 2118.

WAR DIARY
or
INTELLIGENCE SUMMARY. 50" Div"
(Erase heading not required.)

Instructions regarding War Diaries and Intelligence Summaries are contained in F. S. Regs., Part II. and the Staff Manual respectively. Title pages will be prepared in manuscript.

WO No 6 26 Volume No 42

Place	Date 1918	Hour	Summary of Events and Information	Remarks and references to Appendices
COMBLES	Oct 1st		50th Division moved from COMBLES to LIERAMONT and took over line from 25th Division. Field Corps. moved by march route, 446 Field Coy. R.E. & LIERAMONT, 7" & 447 Field Corps. EPEHY.	
LIERAMONT	2		Visited all Companies. Field Companies at work on roads in forward areas and advanced D.H.Q. Field huts at EPEHY by 446 Field Coy. R.E. Water point taken over from the 2nd Australian Division	
do	3		As previous day.	
do	4		As previous day.	
do	5		Advanced D.H.Q. moved to EPEHY. Division commenced an advance from 283 Army Troops Coy. (under C.R.E.) instructed to recce Inglis bridge over ST QUENTIN CANAL at VENDHUILE at 07-40 hours. Bridge erected & completed line was launched by 20-00 hours. 7" Field Coy. erecting medium pontoon bridge over ST QUENTIN CANAL N. of Riqueval bridge to VENDHUILE. Work completed in 6 hours. 446 r 447 Field Coys. heavy bridging on Stone canal at VENDHUILE & Rear D.H.Q. moved EPEHY at 11.00 hours.	

WAR DIARY
or
INTELLIGENCE SUMMARY.

(Erase heading not required.)

Army Form C. 2118.

Instructions regarding War Diaries and Intelligence Summaries are contained in F. S. Regs., Part II. and the Staff Manual respectively. Title pages will be prepared in manuscript.

Place	Date 1918	Hour	Summary of Events and Information	Remarks and references to Appendices
EPEHY.	Oct 6th		Bridging of ST QUENTIN CANAL at VENDHUILE completed. Anglo bridge launched. Ay 283 Army Troops Coy. 446 Field Coy. moved to Nr. LEMPIRE J.1447. Field Corps L. Dt La L'ism. Water supply arrangements taken over from the 2nd Australian division. Handed over to CRE 25th Division.	
do.	7.		Advanced D.H.Q. moved to BONY. CRE visited all Coys. & pioneers who were working on forward roads. Rear D.H.Q. remained at EPEHY.	
do.	8.		Advanced D.H.Q. & CRE returned to rear H.Q. at EPEHY. All Coys. visited.	
do.	9.		Work a previous day. D.H.Q. moved to GUIZANCOURT FARM. Coys. working.	
GUIZANCOURT FARM.	10.		Field Coys. branched to MARETZ.— Boys Bz. GATTIGNY area. CRE visited all Coys.	
do.	11.		D.H.Q. moved to MARETZ. acca. Took on line from 25th Division. & Anicets at LE TROU AUX SOLDATS NR BUSIGNY. Field Coys. realing.	
LETROUAUX SOLDATS	12.		CRE visited all Coys. who were checking by Recce forebridges over RIVER SELLE. Refer of 13/13".	

WAR DIARY or INTELLIGENCE SUMMARY

Army Form C. 2118.

Place	Date 1918 Oct	Hour	Summary of Events and Information	Remarks and references to Appendices
LE TROU AUX SOLDATS	13		RIVER SELLE reconnoitred for bridging facilities & for approaching them. River by enemy, which was causing difficulty owing to area being inundated. Fred Coys. at work on Roads & watch points.	
do	14		Bridg all Coy Parties. Footbridges prepared ready for crossing River SELLE, also material for heavy bridging. Work on forward roads in progress.	
do	15		C.R.E. attended conference at D.H.Q. also conference with G.O.C. 50th Division & Fred Coy Commanders inspecting bridging of the River SELLE. In evening operation orders.	
do	16		Bridge for 60 pounders erected at ST BENOIT by 7 Field Coy. Patrol of Coy Parties standing by ready for work on bridging RIVER SELLE began at 16.117".	
do	17		Attack by XIII Corps on their front. When Infantry bridges were erected over RIVER SELLE 20 footbridges erected.	
do	18		Pontoon Bridge erected by 7 Field Coy at Q.24-B.9.4. (Prov. 57 BHE) over RIVER SELLE. Patrols of Coys standing by for instructions from C.E. XIII Corps. Pioneers at work on forward roads.	

Army Form C. 2118.

WAR DIARY
or
INTELLIGENCE SUMMARY.
(Erase heading not required).

Instructions regarding War Diaries and Intelligence Summaries are contained in F. S. Regs., Part II. and the Staff Manual respectively. Title pages will be prepared in manuscript.

Place	Date	Hour	Summary of Events and Information	Remarks and references to Appendices
LE TROU AUX SOLDATS	Apl. 19		50th Div. relieved by 25th Div. C.R.E. handed over works & C.R.E. 25th Division.	
do.	20th		Corps resting and staffed by: Field Companies at work on cleaning and repairing roads & bridges, and standing by, ready for instructions.	
do.	21st		3rd Army Review. Continued work on cleaning & repairing roads in neighbourhood ST. BENIN and forward from LE CATEAU	
do	22nd		Work continued as before	
do	23rd		Work on ST BENIN – FASSIAUX and continued. Bys standing by for orders.	
do	24th		Clearing debris taking but for road LE CATEAU – BAZUEL.	
do	25th		Work continued on the 24 th. Established Adv D.H.Q. at LE CATEAU	
LE CATEAU	26th		Continued work on a 25th & clearing 1 infantry forward roads.	
do	27th		Continued work on a 26th. Completed temporary crossing for traffic on the SELLE.	
do	28th		Work on clearing 1 infantry forward and LE CATEAU – POMMEREUIL	three forward infantry road crossings on the SELLE.	
do	29th		Work on indians load dump at BUSIGNY. Continued work on road on 28th.	
do	30th		2nd new portion of road 18' – 125' Div. Cleared out LA FAYT FARM ? prepared it for Div R.H.Q.	
do	31st		Completed forward road from BUSIGNY.	

Reference
CRE 50 Div

ORIGINAL
SECRET.

WAR DIARY
of
C. R. E.
50TH (NORTHUMBRIAN) DIVISION.

VOLUME XLIV

NOVEMBER, 1918.

WAR DIARY or INTELLIGENCE SUMMARY

Army Form C. 2118.

50th Division

Volume No. 44

Place	Date	Hour	Summary of Events and Information	Remarks and references to Appendices
LE CATEAU	1/11/18		Moved to LE CATEAU. 61 Coys & Lancers working on roads - maintenance & clearance of obstructions.	Sheet 57A
"	2/11/18		Work continued as above. Also in preparation of roads for Infantry to move up to newly positions.	Sheet 57A
"	3/11/18		Pioneers working on Cross-country track LE FAYT Farm to FONTAINE. Work continued as before, & also in preparation of light footbridges for crossing of SAMBRE Canal (60 ft span) One section of 7" Coy to be detailed in preparation of light footbridges to Divl. Bridging to prepare trestles & setting over ground during the afternoon.	
LE FAYT FARM	4/11/18		Pioneers extended work Cross-country track from FONTAINE & DRILL GROUND CORNER - to be by (?) FONTAINE. 1 Pioneer working on roads through FONTAINE into MORMAL FOREST. 446th & 447th Coys, assisted by Sub 447th Fd Coy engaged on with Bridging material.	
FONTAINE	5/11/18		447th Fd Coy built pontoon bridge over SAMBRE near demolished bridge at B27 Cent - Pioneers 17th Hrs assisted have been working through MORMAL FOREST. 446th (Fd Coy) cleared and filling tracks in western edge of MORMAL FOREST. Much any work of drainage work, & breaches and fallen trees. The track was kept open. Difficult conditions and communication through MORMAL FOREST.	
HACHETTE	6/11/18		Work continued on tracks open the roads through MORMAL FOREST. Forward roads were reconnoitred and a number of Culverts built. Prepared for demolition of 7th Fd Coy small timber trestle bridge over GRAND HELPE River at NOYELLES (3 bays)	

WAR DIARY
INTELLIGENCE SUMMARY
(Erase heading not required.)

Army Form C. 2118.

Place	Date	Hour	Summary of Events and Information.	Remarks and references to Appendices
MONCEAU	7/11/18		Demolished culvert bridged on main road NOYELLES – MARDILLES – MARDILLES and both of GRANDE HELPE River. – & Field Coy.	Maps ref. Sheet 57A
			4th Coy built bridges — 3 Heavy on GRAND HELPE River at NOYELLES. There by 7th Fd Coy. – Num SAMBRE	Sheet 57A
			was bridged by 446th Fd Coy at B.1.8, and C.1.4. (Sheet 67A) for foot transport. LA TARSY River at C.1.8.a was	
			bridged for foot transport by 447th Fd Coy. Seven church roads in area NOYELLES – LEVAL – MONCEAU – ST. AUBIN.	
			filled in craters & actioning mines & contentration on culvert.	
	8/11/18		446th Coy gave half clearing fallen wooden viaducts over two roads from LEVAL to MONCEAU, and in repairing	
			demolished culvert and both of MONCEAU. 4th Coy 7th Fd Coy & part of 1 common. Horse removed from fresh	
			road at PETIT LANDRECIES and other roads in forward areas. 446th Fd Coy built transports bridge on LA TARSY	
			LA TARSY River at LEVAL and made road diversion to same – 447th Fd Coy built flow truck bridge on LA TARSY	
			River at C.18.c and D.13.c. – Seven church roads junction J.7.a.& also worked on roads forward the MONT DOURLERS	
	9/11/18		Continued work on culvert at MONCEAU and began construction of bridge at DOURLERS (447 Fd.Coy.)	
			Horse carried a clearance of obstruction LEVAL – MONCEAU. Rd. & clearing of wood forward to LA SAVATE.	
			7th Coy commenced off to photograph will suitable culvert at LA SAVATE. Work was taken forward.	
DOURLERS	10/11/18		4th Coy & 1 section, working on roads under direction of C.E. 13th Corps.	
do	11/11/18		Received orders that hostilities would cease at 11 am owing to signing of Armistice. Continued work in a 10a.	
do	12/11/18		4th Coy.,1 common (photograph.) on Divisional Parade held by G.O.C. Div. for presentation of medal ribbons. Work for	
			Von Coy cancelled.	

Army Form C. 2118.

WAR DIARY
or
INTELLIGENCE SUMMARY.

(Erase heading not required.)

Instructions regarding War Diaries and Intelligence Summaries are contained in F. S. Regs., Part II. and the Staff Manual respectively. Title pages will be prepared in manuscript.

Place	Date	Hour	Summary of Events and Information	Remarks and references to Appendices
DOURLERS	13/11/18		7th Coy unloading destroyed culvert nr. MAUBEUGE-AVESNES road at E13 b 70 - AA7th Fd Coy completed	Sheet 57A
do	14/11/18		rebuilding of culvert in DOURLERS. AA6th Fd Coy Harvers continued work on road maintenance. Work continued on culvert at E13 b 70. I made no inspection.	
do	15/11/18		On 14th - AA6th Fd Coy also working on bridge at DOURLERS. I men completed filling 4 large craters	
do	16/11/18		at LA SAVATE. Work continued on a 15th	
do	17/11/18		Orders received that work on roads will henceforth be done by Corps troops. Work completed work in hand.	
do	19/11/18 to 29/11/18		Coys engaged in training, general washing, improvement of billets etc. Also in preparing maneuvered for employment of Educational schemes.	

H.W. Green
Lieut Col RE
CRE 55th Div.
1-12-18.

ORIGINAL.   SECRET.

WAR DIARY

of

C. R. E.

50TH (NORTHUMBRIAN) DIVISION.

VOLUME XLV.

DECEMBER, 1918.

WAR DIARY
or
INTELLIGENCE SUMMARY.

Army Form C. 2118.

Place	Date	Hour	Summary of Events and Information	Remarks and references to Appendices
DOURIERS	Dec 1918 1st to 18th		Coy. Ferrinis carrying out return to filled. One man dispatched to England as husband for transfer to Reserve Class W.T. n. 10th inst.	
LE QUESNOY	19th		Moved to LE QUESNOY. Visited Chief Engineer 13th Corps.	
	20th			
	21st to 31st		Coy. training & carrying out general return to filled in Civil area.	

Kennina
Lieut Colonel
C.R.E. 50th Div

ORIGINAL

SECRET

WAR DIARY

of

C. R. E.

50TH (NORTHUMBRIAN) DIVISION.

VOLUME XLVI.

JANUARY, 1919.

618
50th Division
Volume 10 & 6.

Army Form C. 2118.

WAR DIARY
or
INTELLIGENCE SUMMARY.
(Erase heading not required.)

Instructions regarding War Diaries and Intelligence Summaries are contained in F. S. Regs., Part II. and the Staff Manual respectively. Title pages will be prepared in manuscript.

Place	Date	Hour	Summary of Events and Information	Remarks and references to Appendices
	Jan.			
LE QUESNOY	1st		Visited Field Coys. & Pioneers	
	10th		Asst. from I.C.E. 50th Divn	
AUBIGNIES & ST MARAST BY	14th		Visited 447 & 448 Fd Coys & Pioneers	
	15th		Visited 446 Fd Coy 50th Divn R.E.	
			Went to Douay to see about spares to a bridge	
	22nd		Capt. Potts returned from leave G.H.Q.	
	23rd		Capt. Potts proceeded to XIII Corps H.Q. to understudy S.O. to C.E.	
	25th		Attended S.O. at Div R.E. Officers dinner C.E. XIII Corps Present	
LE QUESNOY	26th		Proceeded on 14 days leave to U.K. C.R.E.s duties taken over by Maj. V. McLennon R.E. O.C. 446 Fd Coy	
	"		Lt. Col. Hustled Holds duties as C.R.E.	
HERBIGNIES	29th		Visited 7th Fld Coy R.E. Also inspected water points at Forêt de Mormal & LE QUESNOY with view to taking over Troops	
	30th		Went to ST MARTIN & inspected bridge. Inspected the in charge completion works for tubular hut Camp for Camp (to take 3000 men) outside LE QUESNOY	
	31st			

McLennon, Maj. R.E.
o/c C.R.E.

ORIGINAL
****

SECRET
****

WAR DIARY

of

C.R.E.

50TH (NORTHUMBRIAN) DIVISIONAL ROYAL ENGINEERS

VOLUME XLVII

FEBRUARY, 1919.
****

Feb. 1919.

C.R.E.
50th Division
Volume No 44

WAR DIARY
or
~~INTELLIGENCE SUMMARY.~~
(Erase heading not required.)

Army Form C. 2118.

Instructions regarding War Diaries and Intelligence Summaries are contained in F. S. Regs., Part II. and the Staff Manual respectively. Title pages will be prepared in manuscript.

Place	Date	Hour	Summary of Events and Information	Remarks and references to Appendices
LE QUESNOY	1st Feb		C.R.E. on leave. Major McLellan O.C. 446th Field Coy R.E. actg. C.R.E.	
	2nd Feb		Attended Divl. Advisory Board.	
	3rd & 4th Feb			
	5th		Visited 7th F. Coy.	
	6th to 8th		Inspected works in progress, visited Coys.	
	9th		As above.	
	12th			
	13th		C.R.E. returned from leave. Major McLellan rejoined his Coy.	
	14th to 16th		Inspected works & visited Coys.	
	17th		C.E. XIIIth Corps called.	
	18th to 28th		Inspected works & visited Coys.	

McRae
Lieut. Col. R.E.
C.R.E. 50th Divn.
2-3-19

ORIGINAL.
****

SECRET
****

WAR DIARY
of
C R E
50TH (NORTHUMBRIAN) DIVISIONAL R.E.

VOLUME XLVIII.

MARCH 1919.
****

Army Form C. 2118.

March 1919
50th Division
Volume 46

WAR DIARY

Instructions regarding War Diaries and Intelligence Summaries are contained in F.S. Regs., Part II. and the Staff Manual respectively. Title pages will be prepared in manuscript.

(Erase heading not required.)

Place	Date	Hour	Summary of Events and Information	Remarks and references to Appendices
LE QUESNOY	March 1st to 3rd		Office work, Demobilization and sale of surplus stores to French.	
	4th		Went to HAUTMONT with Adjutant to measure up bridge over R. SAMBRE.	
	5th to 14th		Office work as above.	
	15th		Visit of Field Marshal Commander-in-Chief Sir Douglas Haig. C.R.E., O.C., 447th Field Coy. R.E., O.C. 50th Div. Signal Coy.R.E. and Adjutant present.	
	16th		2/Lieut W.GREEN left 446th Field Coy. R.E. to join 233rd Field Coy, 41st Division, Army of the Rhine.	
	16th to 17th		Office work.	
	18th		Major J.McGILL and Captain W.H.BEASLEY, DSO, left 7th Field Coy. R.E. to join 228th Field Coy. R.E. 41st Division, Army of the Rhine.	
	19th to 20th		Office.	
	21st		Captain G.J.GRIFFIN, Adjutant R.E. left to join 6th Divl. R.E. Army of the Rhine.	
	21st to 27th		Office.	
	28th		Lt.Col., P.de H.HALL, MC, C.R.E., 50th Division left unit to take over C.R.E. Eastern Division (34th Division), Second Army. Major J.McLELLAN, DSO, MC, RE, 446th Field Coy. R.E. took over C.R.E., 50th Division as a temporary measure pending arrival of an Officer for completion of cadre.	
	29th to 31st		Office.	

McLellan, Major. R.E.

CONFIDENTIAL.

Headquarters,
   50th Divisional Packet, "A"

        Attached please find War Diaries for the month of April, 1919, from the undermentioned units:-

Headquarters, R.E.	Vol. XLIX
7th Field Co R.E.	Vol. LVII
446th Field Co R.E.	Vol. LII
447th Field Co R.E.	Vol. XLIX

Please acknowledge.

H.Q. 50th D.E.
2/5/1919.

                                    Major R.E.

C.R.E., 50TH DIVISION.
No. RL631/7
2-5-19

Army Form C. 2118.

C.R.E.
50th Division.
Volume No. 49.

April 1919.

WAR DIARY
or
INTELLIGENCE SUMMARY.

(Erase heading not required.)

Instructions regarding War Diaries and Intelligence Summaries are contained in F. S. Regs., Part II. and the Staff Manual respectively. Title pages will be prepared in manuscript.

Place	Date	Hour	Summary of Events and Information	Remarks and references to Appendices
H.Q. Le Quesnoy	April 1st to April 30th		To Officer in Charge R.E. Hqrs. 50th Div. R.E. C.R.E.'s correspondence & ordinary administrative work dealt with by the undersigned. JM Wollen, Major, R.E. O.C. 446th Field Coy R.E.	W.D. 48

MAY. 1919.

C.R.E.
50TH DIVN VOL 50.

Army Form C. 2118.

WAR DIARY
or
INTELLIGENCE SUMMARY.

(Erase heading not required.)

Place	Date	Hour	Summary of Events and Information	Remarks and references to Appendices
LE QUESNOY	May 1st to May 31st		No Operation — Cadre of Hq R.E. so also the Ordinary administrative work & correspondence attended to by the undersigned.	

McMillan. Major. R.E.
O.C. Cadre H.Q. & Field Coy R.E.

O.C. R.B.B. Records
&
Freetown

[stamp: 7th FIELD COMPANY R.E. No. 958 Date 3/1/19]

Herewith original copy
of War Diary volume 54
for month of January.
Please acknowledge receipt.

J.W. Gill
Major R.E.
O.C. 7th Field Coy. R.E.

Sent

AAG(I)
receipt
5/2/19

Kindly acknowledge
W. Hoyle
Major R.E. for R.R.S

www.ingramcontent.com/pod-product-compliance
Lightning Source LLC
Chambersburg PA
CBHW080906230426

43664CB00016B/2736